A guide to sources for the history of Irish education, 1780–1922

Maynooth Research Guides for Irish Local History

GENERAL EDITOR Mary Ann Lyons

This book is one of the Maynooth Research Guides for Irish Local History series. Written by specialists in the relevant fields, these volumes are designed to provide historians, and especially those interested in local history, with practical advice regarding the consultation of specific collections of historical materials, thereby enabling them to conduct independent research in a competent and thorough manner. In each volume, a brief history of the relevant institutions is provided and the principal primary sources are identified and critically evaluated with specific reference to their usefulness to the local historian. Readers receive step by step guidance as to how to conduct their research and are alerted to some of the problems which they might encounter in working with particular collections. Possible avenues for research are suggested and relevant secondary works are also recommended.

The General Editor acknowledges the assistance of both Professor Raymond Gillespie, NUI Maynooth and Professor James Kelly, St Patrick's College, Drumcondra, in the preparation of this book for publication.

IN THIS SERIES

Maynooth Research Guides for Irish Local History: Number 17

A guide to sources for the history of Irish education, 1780–1922

Susan M. Parkes

FOUR COURTS PRESS

Typeset in 10.5 pt on 12.5 pt Bembo for
FOUR COURTS PRESS LTD
7 Malpas Street, Dublin 8, Ireland
www.fourcourtspress.ie
and in North America for
FOUR COURTS PRESS
c/o ISBS, 920 NE 58th Avenue, Suite 300, Portland, OR 97213.

A catalogue record for this title is available
from the British Library.

ISBN 978–1–84682–127–1 hbk
978–1–84682–128–8 pbk

Printed in England
by MPG Books, Bodmin, Cornwall.

Contents

Illustrations

Abbreviations

ASTI	Association of Secondary Teachers of Ireland
CAISM	Central Association of Irish School Mistresses
CNEI	Commissioners of National Education in Ireland
DATI	Department of Agriculture and Technical Instruction
INTO	Irish National Teachers' Organization
NAI	National Archives of Ireland
NLI	National Library of Ireland
NUI	National University of Ireland
PRONI	Public Record Office of Northern Ireland
RIA	Royal Academy of Ireland
RUI	Royal University of Ireland
TCD	Trinity College, Dublin
TUI	Teachers' Union of Ireland
UCC	University College, Cork
UCD	University College, Dublin

Acknowledgments

I wish to thank Dr Mary Ann Lyons, St Patrick's College, Drumcondra for inviting me to write this guide as one of the Maynooth Research Guides for Irish Local History. My knowledge of Irish education records has come from my experience as a lecturer in the history of education over the past thirty years. Therefore I would like to thank all the research students who have stimulated my interest in the history of education and who often located, and brought to my attention, new, valuable sources. I wish to thank in particular the staff of the National Archives of Ireland for their support and advice to me and to my students, and also to the staff of Trinity College Library who have provided access and constant service, especially in relation to official reports in the British parliamentary papers.

I wish to thank the other archival depositories who have assisted me in the search for sources – these include the National Library of Ireland, the Public Record Office of Northern Ireland, the Representative Church Body Library, the library of Royal Irish Academy, Dublin Diocesan Archives, Dublin City Library, Pearse Street, the library of Agriculture House, Kildare Street, the library of the Religious Society of Friends and the Office of the Commissioners of Donations and Charitable Bequests. In particular I wish to thank Ken Hannigan and Catriona Crowe of the National Archives, Ray Refaussé and Susan Hood of the Representative Church Body Library and Valerie Coghlan, librarian, Church of Ireland College of Education, for their continued expert advice and support. My thanks to Aideen Ireland and to David Craig of the National Archives for granting permission to reproduce files from the ED collection and to the governors of the Church of Ireland College of Education for permission to reproduce the extract from the *Dublin reading book* (1830).

Preface

Research into the history of Irish education has developed greatly in the last twenty-five years. The growth of local history studies has made people more aware of the important role played by schools in social history and the value of examining the implementation of national education policy at local level. Irish educational records may be divided into two major categories – the records of official commissions and of centralized government boards responsible for education in Ireland, and local records belonging to individual schools and educational institutions, including national schools. In the past education records were neglected, but since 1980 much greater care has been taken to conserve and make them more available to researchers. Since the passage of the Archives Act of 1985 records of the government Department of Education and Science have been deposited in the National Archives of Ireland, Bishop Street, Dublin. In addition archivists at the National Archives are collecting the registers of local national schools for safekeeping. Individual school records are valuable documents for social history; especially important are the school registers, which contain data on pupils' ages, parents' addresses and occupations, and also the report books and roll books which record daily school attendance. As many new schools have been built in the last twenty years, it is vitally important that school records are preserved, either in local archives or in the National Archives.

Introduction

Ireland has a long tradition of formal education. From the bardic schools and monastic schools of the Middle Ages to the State-supported system of the twenty-first century, education has been an important part of Irish society and culture. The nineteenth century witnessed the introduction of a National School system of primary education from 1831, an intermediate public examination system from 1878, and State-funded university colleges in 1845. All of these initiatives were administered by central government offices and so are well documented. The other major providers of education – voluntary schools and the Churches – documented their work in parish and diocesan records, in the archives of schools and the annals of the teaching religious orders. The struggle between Church and State for control of Irish education dominated the nineteenth century but by the first decade of the twentieth century a compromise partnership had been reached. The State provided most of the finance for public education including teachers' salaries, while the ownership, management and administration of educational institutions remained in voluntary hands.

The history of education as an academic subject has been formally studied in Irish universities since the beginning of the twentieth century. With the development of university education departments and diplomas in education, the history of education became a core subject in teacher training programmes.[1] The main emphasis was on 'doctrines of the great educators' from Classical times and texts such as Paul Monroe's textbook entitled *Text-book of the history of education* (New York, 1905) and Oscar Browning's *Introduction to the history of educational theories* (London, 1888) were used. However, the history of *Irish* education soon became part of education programmes. The first professor of education at University College, Dublin, the Revd Professor Timothy Corcoran, SJ, strongly advocated that the history of Irish education be studied as part of national history. He published two anthologies of Irish educational documents that he used with his students. *State policy in Irish education* (Dublin, 1916) contained documents from Tudor times to 1816 and *Education systems in Ireland from the close of the Middle Ages* (Dublin, 1928) likewise concentrated on this period. From the 1930s books on the history of Irish education began to appear, including P.J. Dowling's *The hedge schools of Ireland* (Dublin, 1932) and James Auchmuty's *Irish education* (Dublin, 1937). During the 1970s, with the introduction of masters' courses in education in Irish universities, there was renewed interest in education studies. D.H. Akenson's *The Irish education experiment: the National School system in the nineteenth century* (London,

---

1 Chairs of education were founded in Trinity College, Dublin in 1905; in University College, Dublin, in 1909; in University College, Cork, in 1910; in University College, Galway, in 1914.

11

1970) was the most influential study to appear at that time as it was based on detailed research in Irish education primary sources.[2] Norman Atkinson's *Irish education: a history of educational institutions* (Dublin, 1969) was also a pioneer text for third-level education students, while John Coolahan's classic *Irish education: history and structure* (Dublin, 1981, new ed., 2004) became the standard book for education courses. Other significant published studies included Eustas Ó hEideáin's *National school inspection in Ireland: the beginnings* (Dublin, 1967); Eileen Randles's *Post-primary education in Ireland, 1957–70* (Dublin, 1975) and Susan M. Parkes's *Irish education in the British parliamentary papers in the nineteenth century and after, 1801–1920* (Cork, 1978) which lists the official reports on Irish education together with their reference numbers. Ken Hannigan's *The National School system, 1831–1924* (Dublin, 1984), comprising a set of facsimiles documents from the National Archives of Ireland, showed the wealth of official education material available to researchers. Soon after, the series entitled *Irish educational documents* (Dublin, 1987, 1992) edited by Áine Hyland and Kenneth Milne, became a landmark publication. Containing printed extracts from official papers, the series provided easy access to primary sources for education students.[3] The Educational Studies Association of Ireland's first *Register of theses* (Dublin, 1980) testifies to the range of theses completed on the history of Irish education, while the development of local history studies at the National University of Ireland Maynooth resulted in the publication of several valuable education studies in the Maynooth Studies in Irish Local History series edited by Raymond Gillespie. Two of these, Paul Connell's *Parson, priest, and master: national education in Co. Meath, 1824–41* (Dublin, 1995) and Mary Mulryan Moloney's *Nineteenth-century elementary education in the archdiocese of Tuam* (Dublin, 2001) are particularly relevant to those with an interest in Irish education.

This guide aims to assist the researcher in locating and using available records for studying the history of Irish education at national and local levels. There is no single repository of Irish education records; they are held in a wide range of public and private archives. However, the development of State provision of education in the nineteenth century produced a wealth of printed official records that are, in the main, readily available. These include annual reports of government officials such as the Commissioners of National Education in Ireland (CNEI) who were responsible for the administration of the National School system of primary education; reports of royal commissions such as the Irish Education Inquiry of 1825 which surveyed the schools in every parish in the country, and official correspondence files relating to individual schools such as are to be found in the National School files in the National Archives, Bishop Street, Dublin 8.

---

2 See also D.H. Akenson, *A mirror to Kathleen's face – education in Independent Ireland* (Dublin, 1975); idem, *Education and enmity: the control of schooling in Northern Ireland, 1920–50* (Newton Abbot & New York, 1973).   **3** Áine Hyland, Kenneth Milne, Gordon Byrne & John Dallat (eds), *Irish educational documents*; iii, *Documents in the history of education in Northern Ireland from 1922 to 1992* (Dublin, 1995).

This book is comprised of three parts. The first is a broad historical survey of education policy and of the organization and administration of Irish education during the period 1750 to the early 1920s which highlights some of the more significant sources that are available for this era. This section concludes in 1922 when Ireland was partitioned into two jurisdictions, the Irish Free State and Northern Ireland, after which two distinct education systems evolved. The second part surveys the main archival repositories, both public and private, where education records are held and assesses the value and importance of these records for the history of education, and in particular for local studies. The third part offers a sample local study, making use of some of the public records available and showing the value of research into the implementation of education policy at local level.

CHAPTER I

Irish education: history, organization and administration, *c.*1750–*c.*1922

I. EDUCATION POLICY, *c.*1750–*c.*1831

Background

State involvement in Irish education dates from the Tudor era (sixteenth century) and it became a major factor in the religious tensions and conflicts of the seventeenth and eighteenth centuries. In mid-eighteenth-century Ireland, provision of education was the legal privilege of the Established Anglican Church of Ireland. In 1537, as part of the legislation which introduced the Henrician Reformation, the Act for the English order, habit and language (28 Henry VIII, c. 15) was passed which established a system of parochial schools to teach the English language and the reformed Protestant faith. In 1570 the Act for the erection of Free Schools (12 Elizabeth, c. 1) attempted to create a system of diocesan schools that offered a classical grammar school education for sons of the middle ranks in society. This act envisaged that 'that there shall be from henceforth a free school within every diocese of this realm of Ireland, and that the schoolmaster shall be an Englishman, or of English birth of this realm ...'[1] These two early education acts represented 'an operation intended to buttress the position of the Anglo-Irish community of the Pale against Gaelicization' rather than an attempt to establish a countrywide system of education. Reflecting the priorities of successive Tudor monarchs, the emphasis in this legislation was on teaching the English language and on the role of the Established Church in spreading English culture and the reformed Protestant religion.[2]

The humanist classical tradition of the Renaissance had some influence in Ireland, and indeed a number of cities and towns, such as Waterford, Clonmel and Limerick, supported classical schools.[3] One of the best known was in Kilkenny, where a remarkable Catholic schoolmaster, Peter White, opened a school in 1565. White himself had studied at Oxford and he educated his pupils in the classics, preparing them to further their education in continental universities. Among his more eminent pupils was Richard Stanihurst (1547–1618), the Old English

---

1 Act for the erection of Free Schools, 12 Eliz., c. 1 [Ire.] (1570) in S.J. Corcoran (ed.), *State policy in Irish education: selected texts* (Dublin, 1916), pp 47–8. 2 Raymond Gillespie, 'Church, State and education in early modern Ireland' in Maurice O'Connell (ed.), *O'Connell, education, Church and State* (Dublin, 1992), pp 40–59. 3 *Twelfth report of commissioners of the Board of Education in Ireland on classical schools of private foundations*, H.C.

Catholic scholar, tutor, chronicler and one-time speaker of the Irish House of Commons in Dublin who was author of *De rebus in Hibernia gestis libri quattuor* (Antwerp, 1584) among other works. Stanihurst was fulsome in his praise of the enlightened education provided at White's Kilkenny school:

> out of which school have sprouted such proper imps through the painful diligence and laboursome industry of a famous lettered man, Mr Peter White (sometime Fellow of Oriel College in Oxford) and schoolmaster in Kilkenny, as generally the whole weal public of Ireland and especially the southern parts of that island, are greatly hereby furthered ... This gentlemen's (*sic*) method in training up youth was rare and singular, framing the education to the scholar's vein ... he has so good success in schooling his pupils, as in sooth I may boldie bibe [boldly bid] by it that in the realm of Ireland there was no grammar school so good ...[4]

Stanihurst also 'compared the properties of the school to a "Trojan horse", implying that its teaching fashioned the weapons to save Catholicism in Ireland'[5] and a number of Ireland's leading clerics, notably Peter Lombard, archbishop of Armagh (*c.*1601–25), were educated there. As part of the Counter-Reformation, Irish colleges were established across continental Europe for the education of Irish Catholic men, both clerical and lay; two of the earliest were at Salamanca in Spain (1592) and Douai in Flanders (1594).[6]

Within Protestant circles, the best known grammar school in Dublin was founded in 1587 in Great Ship Street by two Scotsmen, James Fullerton and James Hamilton, both of whom were also closely associated with the foundation of the University of Dublin, Trinity College, in 1592. In a manuscript record written by Sir James Hamilton, knight, afterwards created Viscount Claneboye, it is remarked that the co-founder of the first grammar school

> James Hamilton gave very early indications of his great aptitude for, and disposition after, learning and so passed his time in schools until he had received the usual parts of learning taught in that kingdom [Scotland], in so much he was noticed by James I and his grave Council as one fit to

1812 (218), v, 553.   **4** S.J. Corcoran, *Education systems in Ireland from the close of the Middle Ages: selected texts* (Dublin, 1916), pp 14–15.   **5** Helga Hammerstein, 'Aspects of the continental education of Irish students in the reign of Queen Elizabeth I' in *Historical Studies 8* (Dublin, 1971), pp 137–53.   **6** See T.J. Walsh, *The Irish continental college movement* (Cork, 1973); Thomas O'Connor, 'The Irish College, Rome in the age of religious renewal' in Pontifical Irish College Rome (ed.), *Irish College, Rome, 1628–1678* (Rome, 2003), pp 13–32; Patricia O Connell, *The Irish College at Alcalá de Henares, 1649–1785* (Dublin, 1997); idem, *The Irish College at Lisbon, 1590–1834* (Dublin, 2001); idem, *The Irish College at Santiago de Compostela, 1605–1769* (Dublin, 2006); Thomas O'Connor, *Irish Jansenists, 1600–70: religion and politics in Flanders, France, Ireland and Rome* (Dublin, 2008), ch. 3; Mary Ann Lyons & Thomas O'Connor, *Strangers to citizens: the Irish in Europe, 1600–1800* (Dublin, 2008), ch. 3.

negotiate among the gentry and nobility of Ireland for promoting the knowledge and right of King James's interest and title to the crown of England, after Queen Elizabeth's death ... Therefore he was called to keep a public Latin school at Dublin, being instructed in the meanwhile and creditably supplied for conversing with the nobility and gentry of Ireland for the king's service above mentioned, and he was very serviceable and acceptable therein ...[7]

Despite the fact that the two Tudor education acts of 1537 and 1570 constituted an important part of the Anglicization policy, they failed to provide an effective system of education. At the end of the eighteenth century, the report of the Irish education enquiry (1791) recorded that of the Church of Ireland's 838 benefices, only 361 had parochial schools, while there were only eighteen diocesan schools in the country's thirty-four dioceses.[8] By far the most successful of the Tudor initiatives in educational provision in the Irish context was the establishment of the University of Dublin, Trinity College which provided education for the clergy of the Established Church of Ireland as well as for lay Protestant men. In a letter accompanying the foundation charter, the foundress, Queen Elizabeth I (r. 1558–1603) stated that the new college was to be

a college for learning, whereby knowledge and civility might be increased by the instruction of our people there, thereof many have usually heretofore used to travel into France, Italy and Spain, to get learning in such foreign universities, whereby they have been infected with popery and other ill qualities, and so [are] evil subjects.[9]

There had been earlier attempts to found a university in the vicinity of St Patrick's Cathedral in Dublin. In the fourteenth century an initiative failed due to a lack of support and funds. Further attempts were made in 1547 by George Browne, first reformed archbishop of Dublin, and by lord deputies Sir Henry Sidney (1565–7, 1568–71 and 1575–8) and Sir John Perrot (1584–88) to use monies generated by St

---

7 Manuscript record by Sir James Hamilton, quoted in Corcoran, *State policy*, pp 54–5. The two Scots were spies for King James I. One of the first pupils to attend Hamilton's school was James Ussher (1581–1656), who was also among the first students at TCD. Ussher was appointed archbishop of Armagh in 1625. **8** Report of the commissioners of Irish education enquiry (1791) (hereinafter Report of commissioners (1791)) printed in *Report of her majesty's commissioners appointed to enquire into the endowments, funds and actual condition of all schools endowed for the purpose of education*, H.C. 1857–58 (2336–I), xxii, pt iii, 341–79 (hereinafter *Report of her majesty's commissioners appointed to inquire into the endowments* [Kildare commission]) and *Further evidence taken before the commissioners; documents and index*, H.C. 1857–58 (2336–II), xxii, pt iii, 1; *Fourth report of the commissioners of the Board of Education in Ireland on diocesan free schools*, H.C. 1810 (174), x, 209. **9** See Constantia Maxwell, *A history of Trinity College, Dublin, 1592–1892* (Dublin, 1946), pp 5–6; R.B. McDowell & D. Webb, *Trinity College, Dublin, 1592–1952: an academic history* (Cambridge, 1982); W. McNeile Dixon, *Trinity College, Dublin* (London, 1902).

Patrick's to establish a university in Dublin. However, these efforts also ended in failure due to opposition to the proposed use of cathedral funds.[10] Although initially Catholic students were allowed to attend Trinity College, after 1637 they were forbidden, as were dissenters, so Trinity College became an Anglican preserve.[11]

Royal schools, 1608

In the early years of the Stuart period (1603–49) the royal schools, conceived as part of the plantation schemes, were founded to provide classical grammar school education (which included the teaching of the Latin and Greek languages) for the sons of Protestant settlers, and to prepare them to enter Trinity College, Dublin. During the reign of James I (r.1603–25) a Privy Council decree issued in 1608 declared 'that there should be one free school, at least, appointed in every county, for the education of youths in learning and religion'.[12] These schools were subsequently established by royal letter in 1614 and were granted charters in 1627. Five royal schools were established in the towns of Armagh, Cavan, Dungannon, Enniskillen, and Raphoe. Later, under James's successor, Charles I (r.1625–49) two more royal schools were founded in the new corporations of Banagher, Co. Offaly (1632) and Carysfort, Co. Wicklow (1635). Being under royal patronage, the royal schools were well endowed with land and therefore the masterships often became sinecures. In addition, the number of pupils attending remained small. By the end of the eighteenth century, however, these schools were in decline and the 1791 *Report of the commissioners of Irish Education Enquiry* stated that Armagh was the only royal school in a satisfactory condition. There were no pupils at Banagher, the master at Raphoe had not carried out any duties during the previous three years and there was no schoolhouse at Cavan.[13]

Protestant endowed schools

A number of other Protestant endowed schools were established in the course of the seventeenth and eighteenth centuries. The earliest include The King's (Blue Coat) Hospital, founded by Charles II in 1672, twelve years after the restoration of the monarchy; Kilkenny College, set up by James Butler, first duke of Ormond in

10 Colm Lennon, *Sixteenth-century Ireland: the incomplete conquest* (Dublin, 1994), pp 309–10; J.P. Mahaffy, *An epoch in Irish history: Trinity College, Dublin and its foundation and early fortunes, 1591–1660* (London, 1903); J.W. Stubbs, *The history of the University of Dublin, 1591–1800* (Dublin, 1889).　**11** James Lydon, 'The silent sister: Trinity College and Catholic Ireland' in C.H. Holland (ed.), *Trinity College, Dublin and the idea of a university* (Dublin, 1991), pp 29–54.　**12** *Report of her majesty's commissioners appointed to inquire into the endowments* [Kildare commission], iii, *papers accompanying the report (tables of schools and endowments)*, H.C. 1857–8 (2336–IV), xii, pt iv, 1.　**13** *Report of the commissioners of Irish Education Inquiry* (1791). The royal schools were to be reformed in the nineteenth century and under the Educational endowments Act, 48 & 49 Vic., c.78 (1885) the endowments were divided between Catholic and Protestant schools in Ulster. See Raymond Wilkinson, 'The Educational endowments (Ireland) Act and its implications for intermediate schools of public foundation in Ulster, 1885–1900' (MEd thesis, TCD, 1982).

1684; Midleton College, Cork, founded by the countess of Orkney (1696), and the Preston Schools established at Navan and Ballyroan by Alderman John Preston (1686). The early decades of the eighteenth century witnessed further foundations, including Bishop Foy's School in Waterford, under the patronage of the local bishop, Dr Nathaniel Foy (1707) and Wilson's Hospital School at Mullingar, established by Andrew Wilson in 1724. Almost a century later, in 1819, Hannah Villiers opened a school in Limerick. These schools were endowed by prosperous merchants or aristocrats for the education of Protestant children and had a strong religious and charitable ethos.[14]

One of the wealthiest educational Trusts of the seventeenth century was that of Erasmus Smith (1611–91) who founded four grammar schools in Galway, Drogheda, Tipperary and Ennis and set up a network of primary-level English schools that served local Protestant parishes.[15] A Puritan Cromwellian adventurer, Smith acquired a large amount of land in counties Galway, Sligo, Tipperary and Limerick in return for his financial support for Oliver Cromwell's Irish campaign (1649–51). In 1657 he vested a portion of his Irish estates in trustees whom he charged to found and maintain schools 'so that the poor children inhabiting any part of his lands in Ireland should be brought up in the fear of God, and good literature and to speak the English tongue'. In 1669, following the Restoration, his trust was confirmed by charter of Charles II which appointed governors to his schools dedicated to the provision of a Protestant education for the children of tenants living on Smith's estates. The scope of the endowment was broadened in 1723 to allow for the foundation of new 'English schools' and for providing fellowships and professorships in Trinity College, Dublin. The Trust became very wealthy and in the nineteenth century the legality of using the funds for the education of Protestant children only was challenged.[16]

The penal laws, 1695–1782

Following the Williamite Wars (1689–91), the penal laws, which included proscription against education, were enacted against Catholics and dissenters by the Protestant ascendancy in the Irish parliament. The laws were introduced gradually to diminish the Catholic community's religious, political and social power. Historian Dáire Keogh among others has stressed that 'rather than reflecting Protestant triumphalism or a desire for revenge, the penal laws illustrate their [the Protestant ascendancy's] deep insecurity'.[17] The laws were of three kinds. One set intended to sever links between Irish Catholics at home and their continental allies and to

14 *Report of her majesty's commissioners appointed to inquire into the endowments* [Kildare commission], H.C. 1857–8 (2336–I), xxii, pt i, 13–14; Lesley Whiteside, *The King's Hospital* (Dublin, 1975); Trevor West, *Midleton College, 1696–1996: a centenary history* (Cork, 1996). **15** J.W.R. Wallace, *Faithful to our Trust: a history of the Erasmus Smith Trust and the High School, Dublin* (Dublin, 2004); Myles V. Ronan, *The Erasmus Smith endowment: a romance of Irish confiscation* (Dublin, 1937). **16** See Wallace, *Faithful to our Trust*, pp 168–87, 196–205; see also entry on Erasmus Smith in S.J. Connolly (ed.), *The Oxford companion to Irish history* (Oxford, 1998), p. 516. **17** Dáire Keogh, *Edmund Rice, 1762–1844* (Dublin, 1996), p. 1 and idem, *Edmund*

curtail the activities of the Catholic Church by banishing the hierarchy and regular clergy; the secular clergy were allowed to remain but had to registered with the government. The second set aimed to prevent Catholics from holding official and government positions and from entering certain professions by the imposition of a test oath abjuring the authority of the papacy and other Catholic doctrines. The third aimed to deprive Catholics of the right to hold property. The Act to prevent the further growth of popery (1704) (2 Anne, c. 6) prohibited Catholics from buying land, inheriting land from Protestants or taking a lease for more than thirty-one years. Furthermore, Catholic estates were to broken up by the imposition of a gavelling clause by which, on the death of the owner, the estate was to be divided up unless the eldest son conformed to the Protestant faith.[18]

Since education was such an important means of gaining and retaining power in society the penal laws attempted to outlaw the Catholic education system. In 1695 the Act to restrain foreign education (7 William, c. 4) forbade Catholics from sending their children abroad to pursue a Catholic education. It stipulated that

> In case any of his majesty's subjects of Ireland shall go or send any child or other person to be resident or trained up in any priory, abbey, nunnery, popish university, college or school or house of Jesuits or priests in parts beyond the seas in order to be educated in the popish religion in any sort to profess the same … [he] shall forfeit goods and chattels for ever and land for life.[19]

The 1695 act also forbade Catholics to teach or to run a school under pain of fine and imprisonment, declaring 'be it enacted that no person whatsoever of the papist religion shall publicly teach school, or instruct youth in learning … upon pain of £20 and also being committed to prison with bail or main prize for the space of three months for every offence'.[20] The measures against Catholic educators were strengthened by the 1704 Act to prevent the further growth of popery referred to above which gave power to justices of the peace to pursue any person whom they suspected of sending his child abroad to pursue a Catholic education.[21] In 1709 another act (8 Anne, c. 3) 'for explaining and amending an Act to prevent the further growth of popery' declared that 'popish teachers' would be treated in the same manner as priests and would suffer the same penalties. It stipulated that 'whatever person of the popish religion shall publicly teach school, or instruct youth in learning in any private house within this realm, or be entertained to instruct youth as usher, or assistant by a Protestant school master, he shall be esteemed a popish regular clergyman, and treated as such.' Protestant schools were prohibited from employing such individuals.[22]

Rice and the first Christian Brothers (Dublin, 2008).   **18** See T. Bartlett, *The fall of and rise of the Irish nation: the Catholic question, 1690–1830* (Dublin, 1992); S.J. Connolly, *Religion, law and power: the making of Protestant Ireland, 1660–1760* (Oxford, 1992).   **19** Corcoran, *State policy*, pp 91–2. **20** See Akenson, *The Irish education experiment*, pp 40–3.   **21** Corcoran, *State policy*, p. 94. **22** Ibid., pp 95 ff.

The purpose of the penal laws against Catholic education was not so much to leave Irish Catholics in ignorance but to give Protestants control of the education system. The 1695 Act in restraint of foreign education emphasized the need to reorganize and strengthen the original Tudor system of parish and diocesan schools in order to serve the wider public but this did not occur. Instead, Catholics (and indeed Presbyterians in the northern counties) circumvented the penal laws restricting access to education by establishing a network of clandestine hedge schools (later known as pay schools). These hedge schools were little documented, but accounts of them are to be found in nineteenth-century literature and religious records. One of most graphic portrayals of a hedge schoolmaster is in William Carleton's (1794–1869) *Traits and stories of the Irish peasantry* (London, 1854):

> The reader will then be pleased to picture himself a house in a line with the hedge: the eave of the back of the house roof within a foot of the ground behind it; a large hole exactly in the middle of the 'riggin', as a chimney; immediately under which is an excavation in the floor, burned away by a large fire of turf, loosely heaped together. This is surrounded by a circle of urchins, sitting on the bare earth, stones, and hassocks, and exhibiting a series of speckled shins, all radiating towards the fire like sausages in a Poloni dish … In this ring, with his legs stretched in a most lordly manner, sits, upon a deal chair, Mat himself, with his hat on, basking in the enjoyment of unlimited authority. His dress consists of a black coat, considerably in want of repair, transferred to his shoulders through the means of a clothes broker in the country-town … In his hand is a large, broad ruler, the emblem of his power, the woeful instrument of executive justice, and the signal of terror to all within his jurisdiction …[23]

In his diary, Amhlaoibh Uí Shúileabháin, a schoolmaster based in Kilkenny from 1827 to 1836, described the conditions in which he and his father (also a teacher) lived and worked in the late eighteenth and early nineteenth centuries:

> Having spent the summer in Baile Ruairí beside Cill Mogeanna, in the orchard, I came with my father, Donnacha Ó Suilleabháin, schoolmaster, to a sheepfold owned by Seamus Builtéar, between the Crossroads and Baile Uaitéir where he stayed until a school house was built for him at the Crossroads in the summer of 1791. It was certainly a small school cabin, for it wasn't more than ten feet wide and about twenty feet long.
>
> The sod walls were built in one day. The rafters and roof-timbers were put up the next day, and the roof was put on the third day. It was many a long year that myself and my father spent teaching in this cabin …[24]

23 Quoted in A. Norman Jeffares & Antony Kamm, *An Irish childhood* (London, 1987), pp 75–7.   **24** Entry for 14 May 1827 in *The diary of an Irish countryman, 1827–1835: a translation of Cín lae Amhlaoibh*, ed. T. de Bhaldraithe (Cork, 1979), pp 23–4.

Whereas the prohibition against Catholic schools and teachers was stringently enforced at the beginning of the eighteenth century, enforcement of the punitive measures relaxed as time went on. The hedge schools were conducted in secret, in summer on the sunny side of the hedge, and in winter in a house or barn. One pupil was posted as sentry and if a suspicious stranger were seen, the school would break up and reconvene later elsewhere. The hedge schoolmasters, who were usually self-taught or former hedge scholars themselves, were often itinerant, teaching at their own risk, and some had considerable competence in English, modern languages and the classics. The curriculum was generally in English and concentrated on the standard three Rs. Books used included textbooks and chapbooks, comprising 'an eclectic mix of popular literature of the eighteenth century, and … reflect[ing] the diverse literary tastes of the Irish at this time…'[25]

The Catholic relief acts of 1782 and 1793 largely removed the constraints on Catholic education, although the problem of providing appropriate universal education at elementary level remained unsolved. By the end of the eighteenth century hedge schools became known as pay schools because the masters collected fees. Official figures indicate that in the 1820s, between 300,000 and 400,000 children attended (albeit erratically) and the number of schools had risen to 9,000 by 1824.[26] The second report of the 1825 Irish education inquiry contains a detailed survey of these schools in each parish, recording the name of the school master/mistress, the salary earned and the type of school house used, and this survey is an essential source for a local study of education of this period.[27] The 1825 inquiry was greatly concerned about the literature used in the hedge schools and the report printed a long list of titles to show how unsuitable the books were for children.[28] As Antonia McManus has highlighted, the books included criminal biographies such *The life and adventures of James Freney, commonly called Captain Freney* as well as works of entertainment such as *The history of Fair Rosamund, mistress to Henry II and Jane Shore, concubine of Edward IV* and the perennially popular romance *The seven champions of Christendom.*[29]

Irish Catholics continued to travel secretly to Irish colleges in Europe, ordained priests returned home to carry out their ministry and Catholic Church worship and organization survived in spite of the penal laws.[30] The Irish colleges such as St

---

25 Antonia McManus, *The Irish hedge school and its books, 1695–1831* (Dublin, 2002), p. 11; P.J. Dowling, *The hedge schools of Ireland* (Dublin, 1932); Martin Brenan, *The schools of Kildare and Leighlin, 1775–1835* (Dublin, 1935); Philip O'Connell, *Schools and scholars of Breifne* (Dublin, 1942); Kenneth Milne, 'Hedge schools (pay schools)' in Connolly (ed.), *Oxford companion to Irish history*, pp 237–8. **26** Milne, 'Hedge schools', pp 237–8. **27** *Second report of the commissioners of Irish education inquiry (abstract of returns in 1824, from the Protestant and Roman Catholic clergy in Ireland, of the state of education in their respective parishes)*, H.C. 1826–7 (12), xii, 1 (hereinafter *Second report of commissioners of Irish education inquiry*). **28** *First report of the commissioners of Irish education inquiry*, H.C. 1825 (400), xii, app. no. 221, pp 553–9 (hereinafter *First report of commissioners* (1825)). **29** McManus, *Irish hedge schools*, p. 12. For full list of books used in hedge schools see McManus's appendix I, pp 245–54. **30** See Bartlett, *Fall & rise of the Irish nation*; Maureen Wall, *The penal laws, 1691–1760: Church*

Anthony's Franciscan College at Louvain (est. 1607), the Irish Franciscan College in Rome (est. 1625) and Colegio de San Patricio, founded at Santiago de Compostela in 1605, were attended by both lay and clerical Irish students, many of whom later returned to Ireland.[31] Concerned about the failure to suppress popery in Ireland, in 1731 the Irish House of Lords called on the Church of Ireland clergy to make a return on the number of priests, Mass houses, friaries, nunneries and Catholic schools in their respective dioceses. The official *Report on the state of popery* revealed that there were 549 'popish' schools operating in the country, forty-five in Dublin alone.[32]

As one of the main purposes of the penal laws had been to encourage Catholic children to attend Protestant schools, the lack of these schools was a major problem. Therefore the foundation of Protestant charity schools for the poor which taught literacy and useful skills became a feature of the eighteenth century. Dr Henry Maule, later Protestant bishop of Meath, was a leading figure in this movement. He was a founder in Dublin of the Society for Promoting Christian Knowledge, which by 1725 had 163 schools.[33] The Anglican Church's most important educational initiative was the establishment in 1733 of the Incorporated Society for Promoting English Protestant schools in Ireland under the leadership of Hugh Boulter, archbishop of Armagh.[34] This Society was granted a charter to establish and maintain 'charter schools' throughout Ireland. These were to provide free education for children of the poor who would be taught in the English tongue and receive instruction in the Protestant religion. Useful skills and habits of industry were to be an integral part of the curriculum and the Society aspired to 'lifting Catholic children out of their environment of superstition and idleness and turning them into industrious, useful Protestants'.[35] These schools were residential and the children were often 'transplanted' to a school away from their home environment and their neighbourhood in an effort to lessen parental influence. The Society received a large parliamentary grant and by 1748 had a total of thirty schools in operation. However, as the century wore on, the charter schools acquired a reputation for mismanagement and cruel neglect of the children in their care. The lack of central control allowed local masters to abuse their power and to use the children as a source of cheap labour. Catholic parents objected in particular to the proselytism and transplantation of the pupils far from their homes.

---

and State from the Treaty of Limerick to the accession of George III (Dundalk, 1961); see also Corcoran, *State policy*, pp 65, 76 for examples of the enforcement of these laws; P.J. Corish, *The Catholic community in the seventeenth and eighteenth century* (Dublin, 1981); Keogh, *Edmund Rice, 1762–1844* and idem, *Edmund Rice and the first Christian Brothers*. **31** See O'Connor, *Irish Jansenists, 1600–70*, ch. 3; O Connell, *The Irish College at Santiago de Compostela*. **32** 'Report on the state of popery, 1731' in *Archivium Hibernicum*, I (1912), p. 11; Corcoran, *State policy*, pp 103–7. **33** Akenson, *Irish education experiment*, pp 29–36; M.G. Jones, *The charity school movement: a study in eighteenth-century puritanism in action* (London, 1938, 1964 ed.). **34** Kenneth Milne, *The Irish charter schools, 1730–1830* (Dublin, 1997); Connolly, *Religion, law & power*, pp 304–5. **35** Connolly, *Religion, law & power*, p. 305.

In the 1780s a series of reports by eminent visitors drew attention to the deplorable state of the charter schools, the cruel treatment of pupils and the poor education which they offered. In 1782–8 John Howard, the philanthropist and prison reformer, visited many of the schools and was angered by their poor condition: 'The state of most of these schools which I visited was so deplorable as to disgrace Protestantism and encourage popery rather than the contrary.'[36] Howard was a well-known figure and author of *The state of prisons in England and Wales* (London, 1777) and his report drew the attention of the Irish parliament.[37] Jeremiah Fitzpatrick, Ireland's first inspector general of prisons, also reported on these schools in 1786: his evidence and that of John Howard was used in the 1788 parliamentary inquiry into the state of the charter schools.[38] Despite these critical reports these schools continued to receive parliamentary aid and the official report of the commissioners of the Board of Education in 1809 was uncritical. It was not until the report of the 1825 Irish education inquiry, which contained damning evidence of the abuses gathered from the both the staff and pupils of the schools, that public condemnation resulted in a withdrawal of public aid. The Incorporated Society then reformed itself and continued to provide an education for Protestant children during the nineteenth and twentieth centuries. However, the bitter legacy left by the charter schools was fear of proselytism and Protestant State intervention in education. This fear had a marked influence on the Catholic Church's education policy and on its increased demand for the rights of denominational education in the nineteenth century.[39]

II. POLICY, REFORMS AND ADMINISTRATIVE INITIATIVES, *c.*1782–*c.*1830

The 1780s acknowledged the injustice of the penal laws, and the relief acts of 1782 and 1792–3 repealed them.[40] Ireland was influenced significantly by the American War of Independence (1776–83) and there had been strong support for the

---

36 Corcoran, *State policy*, pp 117–19. **37** Milne, *Irish charter schools*, pp 185–9; James Baldwin Brown, *Memoirs of the public and private life of John Howard, the philanthropist* (London, 1823); Robert Steven, *An enquiry into the abuses of the chartered schools in Ireland with remarks upon the education of the lower classes in the country* (2nd ed., London, 1818). **38** Report on the state of the Protestant charter schools of this kingdom, 14 April 1788 in *Journals of the House of Commons of the kingdom of Ireland*, xii, pt ii, p. dccx (14 Apr. 1788) (hereinafter *Commons Jn. Ire.*); Milne, *Irish charter schools*, pp 189–201: Oliver McDonagh, *The inspector-general: Sir Jeremiah Fitzpatrick and social reform, 1783–1802* (London, 1981). **39** *Third report of the commissioners of the Board of Education in Ireland, on the Protestant charter schools*, H.C. 1809 (142), vii, 463, 475, 478 (hereinafter *Third report of the commissioners of the Board of Education, on Protestant charter schools*); *First report of commissioners of Irish education inquiry*, H.C. 1825 (400), xii, 15–30, appendices, 4–172; Milne, *Irish charter schools*, pp 263–300; Akenson, *Irish education experiment*, pp 32–6. **40** An Act to allow persons professing the popish religion to teach school in this kingdom, and for regulating the education of papists, and also to repeal parts of certain laws relative to the guardianship of their children

American cause. Belief in civil rights and in the ideals of justice and equality for all men, which inspired the French Revolution of 1789, became popular. In 1760 a Catholic Committee had been formed by some of the Irish gentry to campaign for the repeal of the penal laws. The formation of the Volunteers in 1778 as an armed force to defend Ireland against invasion increased the demand for reform. Luke Gardiner's Relief Act of 1782 (21 & 22, Geo. III) allowed Catholics to teach and to open schools. A licence from the Church of Ireland bishop was still required and Catholics could not endow an educational institution.[41] However, the relief acts of 1792–3 removed all educational restrictions against non-conformists and allowed Catholic students to attend the University of Dublin.[42]

From the 1780s the Catholic Church had been rebuilding its education system and indigenous Catholic religious education orders were founded. The continental orders like the Jesuits and the Dominicans also returned to re-establish their schools in Ireland. The first Catholic college to be opened was St Kieran's College, Kilkenny in 1783; St Patrick's College, Carlow opened in 1793.[43] The Presentation Sisters, founded by Nano Nagle in 1778, and the Sisters of Mercy, founded by Catherine McAuley in 1820, began to provide education for Catholic girls, while the Irish Christian Brothers, founded by Edmund Rice in 1803, created a network of schools for Catholic boys.[44] The Jesuits established Clongowes Wood College in Clane, Co. Kildare, in 1814 and the Vincentians opened Castleknock College in 1836. In addition, diocesan colleges were founded in each diocese to provide education for future seminarians and lay boys: by 1820 there were seven of these colleges.[45] St Patrick's College, Maynooth was founded in 1795 to provide seminary education for the priesthood. This college received a parliamentary grant as the government was anxious to encourage the education of Catholic priests at home rather than on the Continent, where they could imbibe revolutionary ideas.

(known as Gardiner's Relief Act), 21 & 22 Geo. III, c. 62 [Ire.] (1782) allowed 'persons professing the popish religion to teach school in this kingdom'.   **41** Corcoran, *Education systems*, pp 76–7.   **42** Act to remove certain restraint and disabilities therein mentioned, to which his majesty's subjects professing the popish religion are now subject, 32 Geo. III, c. 21 [Ire.] (1792) and An Act for the relief of his majesty's popish or Roman Catholic subjects of Ireland, 33 Geo. III, c. 21 [Ire.] (1793) printed in Corcoran, *State policy*, pp 124–6.   **43** P. Birch, *St Kieran's College, Kilkenny* (Dublin, 1951); F. Ó Fearghail, *St Kieran's College, Kilkenny, 1782–1982* (Kilkenny, 1982). The motto 'Hiems transit' (Winter is passed) was placed on the college gate to mark the end of the years of persecution.   **44** T.J. Walsh, *Nano Nagle and the Presentation Sisters* (Dublin, 1959); Sr Mary Pius O'Farrell, *Nano Nagle: woman of the Gospel* (Cork, 1991); Keogh, *Edmund Rice, 1762–1844* and idem, *Edmund Rice and the first Christian Brothers.*   **45** The colleges were at Mullingar (St Finian's), Waterford (St John's), Tullow, Ballaghadreen (St Nathy's), Mountrath, Tuam (St Jarlath's) and Wexford (St Peter's). See Seamus V. Ó Súilleabháin, 'Secondary education' in P.J. Corish (ed.), *A history of Irish Catholicism, v: Catholic education* (Dublin, 1971), pp 54–83; *Report of the Council of Education: the curriculum of the secondary school* (Dublin, 1962), pp 38–9; Peter Costello, *Clongowes Wood: a history of Clongowes Wood College, 1814–1989* (Dublin, 1989); Louis McRedmond, *To the greater glory: the Jesuits in Ireland* (Dublin, 1991).

There was also a pressing need for the new seminary as the French Revolution and subsequent wars had resulted in the closure of many Irish colleges in Europe.[46]

A particular feature of education in the late eighteenth century was the foundation of schools by evangelical Protestant education societies that offered literacy and religious instruction to the Catholic poor. The so-called 'Second Reformation' of the 1820s increased tension between the religious denominations, especially in the field of education as the use of schools for proselytism was widespread. Among those Protestant education societies which flourished were the Association for Discountenancing Vice and Promoting Christian Knowledge (APCK) (est. 1792),[47] the London Hibernian Society (LHS) for establishing Schools and circulating Holy Scriptures in Ireland (est. 1806),[48] the Baptist Society (est. 1814) and the Irish Society for Promoting the Education of the Native Irish through the medium of their own Language (est. 1818).[49] These Societies were active in preaching and education work in the country, supporting schools and providing Bibles and religious books. The APCK received a direct grant from the government to promote its work whereas the others received an indirect subsidy through the lord lieutenant's fund. This fund was set up in 1819 nominally to support poor Catholic schools but by 1825 only twelve grants out of a total of 481 had been awarded to Catholic schools.[50] The survey of the 1825 inquiry revealed that both the number of schools in receipt of aid from these education societies and their activities were a cause of much concern for the Catholic Church authorities

---

46 O Connell, *The Irish College at Santiago de Compostela*, pp 25–6.   **47** The aim of the association was 'to promote the knowledge and practice of the Christian religion – the principal means employed have been the dissemination of the Holy Scriptures, of prayer books, and of moral and religious tracts; the extension of catechetical examinations, and the grant of premiums to the best answerers; the establishments of schools, and the grant of salaries and gratuities to schoolmasters'. See *Watson's almanack for 1827* (Dublin, 1827), p. 168.   **48** The LHS was 'instituted for the education of the poor in this kingdom, without interference with their religious opinions, by the establishments of free schools, and the gratuitous circulation of Holy Scriptures without note or comment' (ibid., p. 174). The Society was based in London with an agent in Dublin.   **49** Ibid., p 175. The objectives of the Irish Society were 'to instruct the native Irish, who still use their vernacular language, how to employ it for obtaining a knowledge of English, and also for their moral amelioration, to distribute the Irish version of the scriptures by Archbishop Daniell and Bishop Bedell, the Irish Prayer Book, *where acceptable*, and such other works as may be necessary for school-books.' See Desmond Bowen, *The Protestant crusade: souperism in Ireland, 1800–70* (Dublin, 1978); Akenson, *Irish education experiment*, pp 85–6; idem, *The Church of Ireland: ecclesiastical reform and revolution, 1800–85* (London & New Haven, 1971), pp 139–42. Records of the Irish Society are held in the offices of the Irish Church Missions and those of the APCK in the Representative Church Body Library, Braemor Park, Dublin 14.   **50** The conditions under which applications to the lord lieutenant's fund were considered militated against poor Catholic schools. One condition was that there had to be pledge of local finance, and other was that the site for a school had to be vested in the local Church of Ireland parish.

who became increasingly determined to protect Catholic children from prose-lytism by providing Catholic education.[51]

By the end of the eighteenth century it was clear that Irish education needed major reform if an education system acceptable to both Catholics and Protestants was to be established. With the dismantling of the penal laws and the determi-nation of the Catholic Church to rebuild its education system, it became essential for the government to reform the existing education system if it was to serve children of all religions. This meant that the historic role of the Established Church of Ireland in controlling education had to be weakened. The concept of a non-denominational system of schools, operating under State supervision, gained ground and was seen as one way of increasing religious harmony. In France and Prussia, such State education systems were also developed.[52]

Chief secretary Thomas Orde's plan, 1787

From the 1780s a number of parliamentary education reports advocated the need for a State board to supervise schools in Ireland. In 1787 the then chief secretary, Thomas Orde, presented to the Irish parliament a plan 'for an improved system of education in Ireland'. The plan owed much to the ideas of John Hely Hutchinson, provost of Trinity College, Dublin (1774–94).[53] It suggested that a number of new publicly funded schools should be set up since 'Nothing could be more fruitless or preposterous than the arrangements at present existing in several of the principal features of the scheme of education'.[54] It recommended that the existing parish school system be revived so as to extend the provision of primary education and advised that the diocesan schools be properly funded. The establishment of four new grammar schools, one in every province, each modelled on Christ's Hospital School in London, was proposed. The plan also envisaged the foundation of two new academic preparatory schools for the University in Dublin and a second university in the north-west. This was, therefore, the first major attempt to create a national plan for education ranging from primary to university levels. Although in the immediate term nothing came of Orde's plan – he resigned in October 1787 – its reforming ideas were to influence future plans for Irish education. Whilst the plan intended that the Established Church would retain control of

51 *First report of commissioners of Irish education inquiry 1825*, H.C. 1825 (400), xii, 8–50.
52 David Wardle, *English popular education in the nineteenth century* (London, 1976); idem, *The rise of the schooled society: the history of formal schooling in England* (London, 1974).   **53** *Journal of the House of Commons of the kingdom of Ireland from the nineteenth day of January, 1786 inclusive, to the eighteenth day of April 1788, inclusive, in the reign of his majesty King George the Third*, (Dublin, 1792), p. 138 (12 Apr. 1787); John Giffard, *Mr Orde's plan of improved system of education in Ireland; submitted to the House of Commons, April 12, 1787, with debates which arose thereon* (Dublin, 1787); McDowell & Webb, *Trinity College, Dublin*, pp 53–6.   **54** 'The Orde plan' in Áine Hyland & Kenneth Milne (eds), *Irish educational documents* (4 vols, Dublin, 1987–95), i, 55–8; Akenson, *Irish education experiment*, pp 60–9; see also *The parliamentary register or history of the proceedings and debates of the House of Commons, 1781–99* (17 vols, Dublin, 1782–1801), vii, 486–511 (12 Apr. 1787) (hereinafter *Ir. Parl. Reg.*).

education, it was significant in introducing the notion of an education system that was open to all children, regardless of creed, and also the idea of an annual parliamentary education grant and State supervisory board.[55]

Report of the commissioners of Irish education inquiry, 1791

A year after Orde presented his plan to parliament, the Irish parliament passed a bill to set up an official inquiry into the state of Irish education; it reported in 1791.[56] Seven commissioners, including John Hely Hutchinson, were appointed to undertake the inquiry.[57] This report followed on the work of Orde and surveyed the existing provision of education, including the Tudor system of parish schools, diocesan schools, the royal free schools, the Erasmus Smith schools, charter schools, the King's Hospital school, the Hibernian School for Soldiers' children and the Hibernian Marine School for the children of sailors, two publicly-funded charity schools.[58] The recommendations of the 1791 report were radical: parish schools should be run by a board of governors, who would included two Anglican and two Catholic laymen, thus breaking the monopoly of the Established Church in education. The number of diocesan schools would increase to thirty-two, one in each county and the cost should be shared by the county. In addition, a new collegiate 'great' school offering a classical education to prepare candidates for university should be established along with a professional academy to teach mathematics, science and modern languages. The 1791 report was severely critical of the work of charter schools which, it stated, were in need of complete reform. However, its most radical proposals were that 'there should be no distinction made

55 The Bolton papers, including those of Thomas Orde, Lord Bolton, are held in the National Library of Ireland (NLI), MS 15,885. Orde's autographed notes of the scheme are in the Bodleian Library, Oxford, MSS Top. Ireland d. 2, d. 3.   **56** *Commons Jn. Ire.*, xii, pt i, 402, 411, 413, 419; *Ir. Parl. Reg.*, vii, 395 (18 Apr. 1788). An Act to enable the lord lieutenant, or other chief governor or governors of kingdom, to appoint commissioners for enquiring into the several funds and revenues granted by public or private donations for the purposes of education in this kingdom, 28 Geo. III, c. 15 [Ire.] (1788).   **57** The other six commissioners were: Rt. Hon. Denis Daly, Rt. Hon. Isaac Corry, John Forbes esq., Thomas Burgh esq., Edward Cooke esq., and Rt. Hon. Thomas Hobart.   **58** The Hibernian Military School was founded in 1769 as a school 'for the maintenance, education and apprenticing of orphans and children of soldiers in Ireland'. It was situated in the Phoenix Park. The Hibernian Marine School was founded in 1775 for 'the maintenance, education, and apprenticing of children of decayed seamen in the royal navy and merchant service'. It was situated on Sir John Rogerson's Quay, Dublin. See *Report of her majesty's commissioners appointed to inquire into the endowments* [Kildare commission], iii, *Papers accompanying the report (tables of schools and endowments)*, H.C. 1857–8 (2336–IV), xii, pt iv, 22, 43, 72, 111–12; *Report of the commissioners appointed by the lord lieutenant of Ireland to inquire into the endowment, funds and condition of all schools endowed for the purposes of education in Ireland, with evidence, appendices, and index* [Rosse commission], [C 2831] H.C. 1881, xxxv, 178–84 (hereinafter *Report of the commissioners appointed by the lord lieutenant of Ireland* [Rosse commission]). The Drummond School for the Daughters of Soldiers was founded in 1846 and was located at Inchicore. See *Report of the commissioners appointed by the lord lieutenant of Ireland* [Rosse commission], [C 2831], H.C. 1881, xxxv, 184.

in any of the schools between scholars of different religious persuasions' and that a State board of control should be established to oversee reform and funding of the schools. The report concluded confidently:

> We have now submitted to your excellency, such a plan of education as we have been able to digest from the information that has been laid before us, from which we are able to decide, with perfect certainty, that a plan of national education is not, as has been supposed by many, impracticable in this kingdom.[59]

However, this report may have been considered too radical to be published at a time of increasing political and religious unrest in Ireland. In 1791 the Society of the United Irishmen was founded. In 1793 England went to war with revolutionary France and five years later, rebellion broke out in Ireland.[60] Consequently, the report was not brought before parliament. Indeed, it was not published until 1858 when it appeared in the endowed schools report.[61] While still upholding the historic position of the Established Church, the 1791 report advocated a major reform of the existing system, development of 'mixed education' for Catholic and Protestant children, and the establishment of a central government board to supervise schools. The key ideas contained in this report were known to subsequent education commissions and were to have a marked influence on education policy, particularly regarding the introduction of a State-funded supervisory board and bringing to an end the practice of official proselytism within the education system.

Report of the commissioners of the Board of Education, 1806–12
Following the Act of Union in 1800, the Irish parliament was abolished and one hundred Irish MPs were elected to the Westminster parliament. Thereafter Ireland's education policy was determined by legislation passed at Westminster where it was discussed within the broader framework of British political ideas. The promise of Catholic emancipation to follow the Act of Union made the reform of Irish education even more urgent if a stable and loyal political society was to emerge in Ireland.[62] Therefore in 1806 another education commission was established to take up where the 1791 report had left off. This commission worked for over six years (1806–12) and published fourteen reports, thus moving educational reform policy

---

59 Report of commissioners (1791) printed in Corcoran, *State policy*, pp 149–91. There is a printed copy of the 1791 report in the Trinity College Library (Gall. TT. 15. 10). **60** See Edith M. Johnston, *Ireland in the eighteenth century* (Gill History of Ireland series, no. 8, Dublin, 1974); T.W. Moody & W.E. Vaughan (eds), *A new history of Ireland, iv: eighteenth-century Ireland, 1691–1800* (Oxford, 1986). **61** *Report of her majesty's commissioners appointed to inquire into the endowments* [Kildare commission], ii, *further evidence taken before the commissioners; documents and index*, H.C. 1857–8 (2336–II), xxii, pt iii, 341–79. **62** James Kelly, *Henry Grattan* (Dublin, 1993); G.C. Bolton, *The passing of the Irish Act of Union* (Oxford, 1966).

forward. Only one of the 1806 commissioners, Isaac Corry, MP, had been a member of the 1791 board so a fresh approach was expected.[63] There was a strong Church of Ireland presence on the board of commissioners, including William Stuart, archbishop of Armagh, Charles Agar, archbishop of Dublin, James Verschoyle, dean of St Patrick's Cathedral, J.A. Whitelaw, rector of St Catherine's Church, Dublin and George Hall, provost of Trinity College, Dublin. Another commissioner was Richard Lovell Edgeworth of Longford, author of the influential text *Practical education* (1798) which advocated a liberal and rational approach to child education.[64]

The commissioners presented thirteen detailed, critical reports on the existing system of schools, focusing on parish, diocesan, classical and royal schools. It covered largely the same ground as the 1791 report but in more detail.[65] The third report was on the charter schools where, even in 1806, little had been done to end the abuses alluded to earlier.[66] Although at first published separately, the reports were subsequently bound together with the fourteenth and final report, entitled *View of the chief foundations, with some general remarks*, H.C. 1812–13 (21), vi, 221. This last report was the most important as it contained the key recommendations for developing an education system supported by a State grant and with a supervisory central board to administer the funds. It was envisaged that the new board would have control over teacher training and textbooks used in schools. The report also stated that proselytism, and even fear of it, should end and that the separation of religious instruction from secular instruction was the best solution.[67]

The outcome to this commission's report on Irish education was disappointing for reformers as its more radical proposals such as the establishment of a statuary education board were not implemented. Instead, the government took only limited and cautious measures. A permanent board of commissioners of education was established in 1813 but its powers were restricted to supervising the royal school endowments along with those of older endowed schools such as Preston's Schools at Navan, Co. Meath and Ballyroan, Co. Laois. The annual reports of this

---

63 Harold Hislop, 'The 1806–12 Board of Education and non-denominational education' in *Oideas*, 40 (spring 1993), pp 48–60.   **64** Richard Lovell Edgeworth had presented an unsuccessful education bill to the Irish parliament in 1799. See Akenson, *Irish education experiment*, pp 74–5; Tony Lyons, *The education work of Richard Lovell Edgeworth, Irish educator and inventor, 1744–1817* (New York & Lampeter, 2003). The other 1806 commissioners were Henry Grattan, William Disney, William Parnell, and R.S. Tighe.   **65** The other reports were *Schools of private foundation* (no. 2), *Wilson's Hospital School, Mullingar* (no. 5); *The Blue Coat School (The King's Hospital)* (no. 6), *The Hibernian Military School* (no. 5); *The Foundling Hospital* (no. 8); *Schools of Erasmus Smith* (no. 9); *The Hibernian Marine School* (no. 10); *Parish schools* (no. 11); *Classical schools of private foundation* (no. 12); *English schools of private foundation* (no. 13).   **66** *Third report of the commissioners of the Board of Education, on Protestant charter schools*, H.C. 1809 (142), vii, 463, 475, 478.   **67** The fourteen reports generated by the commissioners of the Board of Education in Ireland, covering the period 1809 to 1812–13, are reprinted in a series with an index – see H.C. 1813–14 (47), v, 1 and also Susan M. Parkes, *Irish education in the British parliamentary papers in the nineteenth century and after, 1801–1920* (Cork, 1978), p. 9, for references to the individual reports.

board (commonly known as the Clare Street commissioners because of the location of its offices) contain accounts of the royal schools' operations throughout the nineteenth and early twentieth centuries.[68] Later, following the report of the Rosse report on educational endowments in 1881 and the establishment of the educational endowments commissioners in 1885,[69] the royal school endowments were divided between Protestant and Catholic schools in Ulster, and these schools remained under the supervision of the Clare Street commissioners.[70]

Kildare Place Society, 1811

Another important outcome of the 1812 report was the granting of a parliamentary annual subvention to the Society for Promoting the Education of the Poor in Ireland (better known as the Kildare Place Society (KPS) from the location of its offices and model schools). The Society had been founded in 1811 by a group of philanthropic Dublin businessmen as a non-denominational and non-proselytizing education body with a strong Quaker influence. Its mission was 'to afford the same advantages of education to all classes of professing Christians, without interfering with the peculiar religious opinions of any'.[71] Religious instruction was not allowed in the schools, except for the reading of the Bible, which was to be undertaken daily 'without note or comment'.[72] Envisaging the

---

68 See the published annual reports of the commissioners of education in Ireland (first report, H.C. 1814–15 (29), vi, 1753, final report of the commissioners of education in Ireland for 1920 [Cmd 1507], H.C. 1921, xi, 381).   **69** The Board also was responsible for the endowments of the Leamy Schools in Limerick, Carysfort School in Arklow, Viscount Limerick Schools in Dundalk, and Bank's endowment in Eyrescourt, Co. Galway. The Board was abolished in the 1920s and its responsibilities transferred to the new endowed schools' branch of the Department of Education.   **70** *Report of the commissioners appointed by the lord lieutenant of Ireland* [Rosse commission] [C 2831], H.C. 1881, xxxv, 1; *Bill, intitled, An Act to reorganize the educational endowments of Ireland*, H.C. 1884–5 (176), i, 445. The educational endowments commissioners, appointed under this act, worked for ten years reorganizing and drawing up new legal endowment schemes for endowed schools. See the published reports of the educational endowments (Ireland) commissioners, with proceedings, evidence and appendices from 1885–6 [C 4903], H.C. 1886, xxvi, 89 down to 1894 [C 7511), H.C. 1894, xxx, pt 1, 501. The Catholic schools in Ulster, which received a share of the royal schools endowments, were St Patrick's College in Armagh, St Patrick's College, Cavan, St Eunan's College in Letterkenny, St Macartan's College, Monaghan, St Michael's College, Enniskillen, and St Patrick's Academy in Dungannon.   **71** *First report of the Society for Promoting the Education of the Poor in Ireland* (Dublin, 1813). Among the founder members were Samuel Bewley, a leading Quaker, Arthur Guinness of Guinness Brewery, members of the La Touche banking family and Joseph Devonshire Jackson, later a judge, who was honorary secretary. The Society had close links with Joseph Lancaster, a London Quaker who was founder of the British and Foreign School Society, which pioneered the monitorial system of school management.   **72** H. Kingsmill Moore, *An unwritten chapter in the history of education, being the history of the Society for Promoting the Education of the Poor in Ireland, 1811–1831, generally known as the Kildare Place Society* (London, 1904); Susan M. Parkes, *Kildare Place: the history of the Church of Ireland training college, 1811–1969* (Dublin, 1984); Harold Hislop, 'The Kildare Place Society: an Irish experiment in popular education' (unpublished PhD thesis, TCD, 1990).

THE

DUBLIN

READING BOOK.

DUBLIN

PRINTED BY P. DIXON HARDY,

CECILIA STREET.

1830.

1 Title page of the *Dublin reading book* (1830) showing a monitorial reading draft
(by kind permission of the governors of the Church of Ireland College of Education).

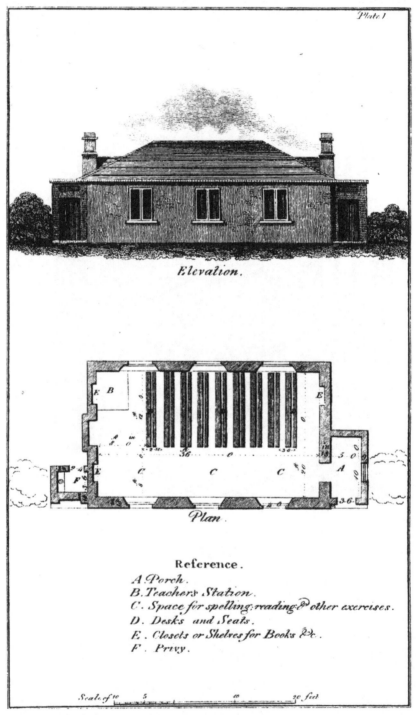

2 Plan of a schoolhouse from *The schoolmaster's manual* (1825), showing bench seats and
desks, spaces for reading and spelling drafts, teacher's station and outside privy
(by kind permission of the governors of the Church of Ireland College of Education).

Kildare Place Society as a possible conduit for education funds, the government chose to support the work of this new voluntary society rather than establish a statutory board of education. The Society used its generous parliamentary grant[73] to support schools throughout the country, to publish schoolbooks, to establish model schools for teacher training and to give gratuities to teachers. Through the years it developed an efficient educational administrative system, keeping records of correspondence with schools, of grants paid out, of teachers trained at the model schools in Dublin and of inspectors' visits to schools. In the long term the Society helped to lay the foundations for a national education system as many aspects of this administrative system were copied by the commissioners of national education from 1831 onwards. The Kildare Place records are very useful to local historians because when the schools applied to the Society for aid, they provided details of their schoolhouse, the number of pupils and teachers, as well as similar details for other schools in the neighbourhood. A summary of the correspondence with each school in receipt of grants was recorded in schools' ledgers for each county. These give details of teachers appointed, gratuities paid, and orders for schools effects such as slates, reading charts and quill pens.[74] In addition to its grants to schools, the Kildare Place Society published a number of 'suitable' and improving books for schools, including library books for general reading. Society members were encouraged in this aspect of their work by the recommendation of the 1812 report that more control was needed over the books used in schools in order to replace some of the 'unsuitable' and immoral books used in the hedge schools.[75] Two of the early KPS textbooks – the *Dublin spelling book* and the *Dublin reading book* – both published in 1819, were among the first Irish graded readers produced for children. The Society adopted the new monitorial system devised by the English educationalist Joseph Lancaster and these methods were taught in the Kildare Place model schools. In 1825 it published the *Schoolmaster's manual*, a work based on the teacher training course taught in the model schools. However, by that time, the Society was losing public support as the insistence on Bible reading 'without note or comment' proved unacceptable to the Catholic Church authorities and Catholic parents began to withdraw children from schools funded by the Society.[76] Furthermore, although the KPS itself was non-denominational, it was paying grants to schools supported by Protestant evangelical education societies and this also impacted negatively on the public's perception of the Society.[77]

---

73 By 1830 the Society was in receipt of an annual parliamentary grant of IR£30,000.
74 The records of the Kildare Place Society are held at the Church of Ireland College of Education, Rathmines, Dublin 6. These include minute books, annual reports, accounts, leases, inspectors' reports, registers of teachers in training and correspondence with schools.
75 Harold Hislop, 'Kildare Place Society chapbooks: curriculum and Irish identity, 1811–13' in Susan M. Parkes (ed.), *Education and national identity: the Irish diaspora* (Hull, 1970), pp 98–117. **76** Kingsmill Moore, *An unwritten chapter*, pp 52–70; Akenson, *Irish education experiment*, pp 80–90. **77** Akenson, *Irish education experiment*, p. 90. In 1824 fifty-seven

By the 1820s the Catholic Church was regaining its power and confidence. St Patrick's College, Maynooth was educating and ordaining priests.[78] In his campaign for Catholic emancipation, Daniel O'Connell made education one of the key issues,[79] withdrawing his support for the Kildare Place Society and demanding parity of financial support for Catholic schooling. An alternative Irish National Society for Promoting the Education of the Poor in Ireland was founded in 1821 and it agitated for a share in the parliamentary education grant for Catholic schools. The lack of State support for Catholic schooling in contrast to that given to the Protestant education societies, in particular the Kildare Place Society, was a major grievance. So was the distribution of education grants from the lord lieutenant's fund, the majority of which (as already noted) were allocated to Protestant schools, even though the fund was created to assist poor Catholic schools.[80] The Catholic hierarchy, in particular Archbishop John MacHale of Tuam and Bishop James Warren Doyle of Kildare and Leighlin, led the campaign for reform and in March 1824 a petition by the hierarchy was presented to parliament requesting a public inquiry into the state of Irish education. The main grievances listed were the lack of grants for Catholic schools, the large grants paid out to the Kildare Place Society, misuse of the lord lieutenant's fund and last, but not least, the proselytising activities of the Protestant education societies. The government, faced with the growing demand for Catholic emancipation, acceded to the request.[81]

Commission of Irish education inquiry, 1825

The report of the commission of Irish education inquiry, established in 1825, built on the foundations laid by earlier reports. In addition, a nation-wide survey of existing educational provision in every parish in Ireland was carried out.[82] This 1825 education census revealed a network of small pay schools in every parish throughout the country and thus represents a major source for the history of education at local level. The survey recorded pupil numbers in each school

schools of the Association for Discountenancing Vice, 340 schools of the London Hibernian Society and thirty schools of the Baptist Society were in receipt of grants from the Kildare Place Society. **78** P.J. Corish, *Maynooth College, 1795–1995* (Dublin, 1995). **79** John Coolahan, 'Primary education as a political issue in O'Connell's time' in Maurice O'Connell (ed.), *O'Connell, education, Church and State* (Dublin, 1992), pp 87–100. For the text of O'Connell's speech at the AGM of the Kildare Place Society on 24 Feb. 1824 see Hyland & Milne (eds), *Irish educational documents*, i, 88–90. **80** Akenson, *Irish education experiment*, pp 83–4. **81** T. McGrath, *Politics, interdenominational relations and education in the public ministry of Bishop James Doyle of Kildare and Leighlin, 1786–1834* (Dublin, 1999), pp 157–245. Two of 'J.K.L.' Doyle's pamphlets, *A vindication of the religious and civil principles of Irish Catholics in a letter addressed to his excellency, the marquis of Wellesey, K.G.* (Dublin, 1823) and *Letters on the state of education in Ireland, and on the Bible societies, addressed to a friend in England* (Dublin, 1824) publicized the grievance of Catholics and the need for reform. **82** The 1825 commissioners were Thomas Frankland Lewis, one of the 1806–12 commissioners, John Leslie Foster, MP for Louth, William Grant from Scotland, a former chief secretary, James Glassford and Anthony Richard Blake. Blake, who was treasury remembrancer, was the first Catholic to be appointed to an education commission.

according to religion and sex, the type and cost of the schoolhouses, the names of teachers' and their salaries, fees charged, the aid received from an education society or patron and whether the scriptures were read and, if so, the version used. The survey shows the extent of voluntary educational provision in Ireland prior to the introduction of the State-aided national school system, and reveals the number of schools attended by both Protestant and Catholic pupils.[83] In order to ensure a fair return, two sets of figures for the attendance at each school, one given by the Protestant clergy and the other by the Catholic clergy, were presented and these differed in terms of the information collected. Pupils' average attendance over the previous three months was used to calculate the overall attendance figures. It is important to examine the two sets of figures as the returns may not be exact or identical. Equally, when interpreting these statistics, researchers need to remember that the Established Church of Ireland wished to show that the existing education system was serving the needs of both Catholic and Protestant children within the same schools, whereas the Catholic Church wanted to show that an alternative system of schools was required to serve the needs of Catholic children. For example, in the parish of Dunganstown, Co. Wicklow there were nine schools listed in 1824, all 'pay' schools, charging fees.[84] Commenting on educational provision in the parish in the mid-1830s, Samuel Lewis, in his *Topographical dictionary of Ireland*, remarked that

> About 190 children are taught in four public schools, one of which is supported by Lieut. Colonel Acton; another, for which a building was erected by subscription amounting to £182, aided by £100 from the parliamentary fund, is supported by subscription. There are three private schools, one of which has about 100 children.[85]

The major landlords in the parish was the Acton family of Kilmacurragh and Hoeys of Dunganstown Castle. Three Protestant schoolmasters, Thomas Sherlock of Dunganstown, George Williams of Kilcandra and Matthew Tindal of Ennisboveen, taught in schools in the district. Sherlock's school was by far the most prosperous – the schoolhouse was built of stone and lime and had been paid for by public subscription and a parliamentary grant of £100. Lewis listed five local parishioners

83 *First report of commissioners of Irish education inquiry*, H.C. 1825 (400), xii; *Second report of commissioners of Irish education inquiry*, H.C. 1826–7 (12), xii. The data for the 1825 survey was collected by both the Catholic and Protestant parochial clergy, each having been requested to make a separate return in order to make the record as accurate and fair as possible. The original manuscript returns were later lost except for those of the diocese of Kildare and Leighlin (Bishop J.K.L. Doyle kept a copy). These returns were published in Brenan, *Schools of Kildare & Leighlin*. See McGrath, *Politics, interdenominational relations & education*, pp 170–211. **84** See Appendix to *Second report of commissioners of Irish education inquiry*, H.C. 1826–7 (12), xii, 838–9. The rural parish of Dunganstown, south west of Wicklow town, was a farming area with some large estates. **85** Samuel Lewis, *A topographical dictionary of Ireland* (2 vols & atlas, London, 1837), i, 577.

and their contributions to the schoolhouse, namely George Putland (£40), Major Warburton (£16), a Mrs Evans, senior (£1 10s.), a Mrs Acton, junior (£5) and the Revd J. Acton (£20). The master's salary was £35 5s. 6d. plus a house and two acres of land. The school was supported by the Protestant Education Society, the Association for Discountenancing Vice, by the rector, Revd J. Acton, who gave £6 per year and by the parishioners who contributed the sum of £2 5s. 6d. Attendance at the school, returned by the Protestant clergyman, was thirty-four children of the Established Church (Church of Ireland), two dissenters and forty-one Catholics. There were forty-three boys and thirty-four girls and the Scriptures were read. No return was made by the Catholic clergy for this school.

The Protestant school at Kilcandra, on the other hand, was a mud and thatched house which had been fitted up by Major Acton at a cost of £20 and the master's salary was £25 with a free house and garden. The school was supported by a grant from the Kildare Place Society and attendance was returned as thirty-five children of the Established Church and twenty-three Catholics (thirty-eight boys and twenty girls in total). The Catholic priest's returns differed a little – his return was for thirty-eight Protestant children and twenty-three Catholics, of whom thirty-eight were boys and twenty-three were girls. The third Protestant schoolmaster in the parish was Matthew Tindal at Ennisboveen, who received a salary of £15. He had built his own school of 'mud and thatch' at a cost of £10. He also received £7 10s. from the chapel collection. This school was largely attended by Catholic children: according to the Protestant clergyman's return they numbered seventy-seven whereas in the Catholic priest's return the figure was higher (eighty-five). The remaining seven pay schools in the parish of Dunganstown were all 'mud and thatched houses' and teachers' salaries were substantially lower.[86] There were two women teachers, Bridget Ford at Ballinabarney who received a salary of £2 only and Ann Terry of Ballymacwade whose salary of £4 15s. was supplement by £1 15s. from the chapel collection. These pay schools were mostly attended by Catholic children. For instance, Thomas Cavanagh at Cornagour was returned as having eighty-five Catholic pupils (thirty-five boys and thirty-five girls), although the Protestant Church's return recorded only forty-six Catholic pupils. These returns are significant as they reveal the extent to which 'mixed education' operated in certain parishes throughout Ireland in the early decades of the nineteenth century and deepen our understanding of the basis on which later education systems were constructed. The levels of female attendance was also noted in the returns and significantly, it was almost on a par with that of boys. However, the poverty of the 'pay' school system stood in stark contrast with the wealth of Protestant schools funded by both the Established Church and the Protestant education societies. In 1835 a local survey undertaken by the commissioners of public instruction in Ireland inquired into the Established Church's

86 The schools were returned for the townlands of Ballymurrain, Balymacwade (two schools), Ennisboveen, Ballynacoe, Cornagour and Ballinabarney. See *Second report of the commissioners of Irish education inquiry*, H.C. 1826–7 (12), xii, 838–9.

participation in education,[87] and it is interesting to compare the returns for a local area with those featured in the 1825 report, thereby tracking the growth in the number of schools throughout Ireland in the intervening ten years.[88]

The report of the Irish education inquiry (1825) recommended a system of national education in which Catholic and Protestant children pupils would be educated together for secular instruction, but separately for religious instruction. It suggested that public funding should be withdrawn from Protestant education societies including the Kildare Place Society and that the funds should instead be used by a government board of education, which had powers to distribute grants and build new 'schools of general instruction' in every benefice. A Catholic and a Protestant teacher should be appointed to each school, and at the specific time set aside, the Protestant clergy man could give religious instruction to the Protestant pupils in the school but a Catholic layman could teach religion to the Catholic children. Thus, a Catholic priest was still not to be allowed to enter the school. The new board would establish an inspectorate to visit schools. In addition, it would have authority to appoint and dismiss teachers and control over the schoolbooks used. One ecumenical recommendation was that a set of scripture lessons that would be acceptable to all Churches for use in the period of combined instruction should be compiled.[89] Thus the 1825 report paved the way for setting up an Irish national school system, based on the principle of combined literary and moral instruction with separate religious instruction (what came to be known as the 'Irish system'). Safeguards such as the setting aside of a separate day or an hour at the beginning or end of the school day for religious instruction were set down in order to protect pupils against proselytism. However, the separation of religious from secular instruction was not acceptable to the Christian Churches. The Catholic Church sought a Catholic education by Catholic teachers for Catholic children and did not approve of a system of 'mixed education' whereby Protestant and Catholics children were educated together. For their part, the Established Church of Ireland and the Presbyterian Church were particularly critical of any system of education which did not have scriptural education as its basis.

In addition to their first two reports of 1825, the commissioners compiled another seven on educational institutions in which they updated data collected for the 1806–12 reports. The third report dealt with the education of the lower

---

87 See *First report of the commissioners of public instruction (Ireland), with an appendix*, H.C. 1835 (45) (46) xxxiii, 1 and *Second report of the commissioners of public instruction (Ireland)*, H.C. 1835 (47), xxxiv, 1. Sr Mary de Lourdes Fahy, *Education in the diocese of Kilmacduagh in the nineteenth century* (Gort, 1972) is an example of a study which compares the returns of the 1825 and 1835 commissions. See also Paul Connell, *Parson, priest and master: national education in Co. Meath, 1824–1841* (Dublin, 1995); Mary E. Daly, 'The development of the national school system, 1831–40' in A. Cosgrove & D. McCartney (eds), *Studies in Irish history presented to R. Dudley Edwards* (Dublin, 1979), pp 150–63.   **88** See below pp 178–92 for sample study of Wicklow parishes.   **89** See recommendations in *First report of the commissioners of Irish education inquiry 1825*, H.C. 1825 (400), xii, 97–101; Akenson, *Irish education experiment*, pp 94–102.

classes[90], the fourth focused on the Belfast Academical Institution, established in 1810 as an academic collegiate college,[91] the fifth reported on the state of diocesan schools;[92] the sixth on the Hibernian Society for Soldiers and Sailors and the Female Orphan House,[93] and the seventh concentrated on the Royal Cork Institution.[94] The eighth report was on St Patrick's College Maynooth's first decade,[95] while the ninth report was *A general view of the proceedings of the commissioners*.[96]

III. ADMINISTRATION OF IRISH EDUCATION, c.1831–c.1900

During the period from the 1830s to the beginning of the twentieth century the history of Irish education was dominated by a protracted struggle between the State and the Churches for control of education. The Catholic Church in particular engaged in a determined campaign to gain authority and control over its own schools while the Established Church of Ireland was loath to lose its historic power. This struggle took place not only in the primary education sector but also in the arena of secondary education (commonly called intermediate level) where voluntary and Church-run schools strove to maintain their independence and resisted State intervention and inspection. In the university sector the conflict was even greater as the Catholic Church sought to establish a Catholic university in Ireland and refused to support the State's new colleges of the Queen's University. However, despite the determination of the State to adopt an apolitical stance regarding personal religion (hence the disestablishment of the Church of Ireland in 1869), the political importance of a policy of appeasement toward the Catholic Church and Irish nationalism became apparent. One result was acceptance of an education system in which religious denominationalism was recognized and enshrined. Education, in particular the 'university question', was to be a major political issue in the second half of the nineteenth century and its final settlement did not come about until the passage of the Universities' Act in 1908.[97]

---

90 *Third report of the commissioners of Irish education inquiry, education of the power classes*, H.C. 1826–7 (13), xiii, 1. **91** *Fourth report of the commissioners of Irish education inquiry, Belfast Academical Institution*, H.C. 1826–7 (89), xiii, 157; see T.W. Moody & J.C. Beckett, *Queen's, Belfast, 1845–49: the history of a university* (2 vols, London, 1959), 1, xliv–li. **92** *Fifth report of the commissioners of Irish education inquiry, state of the diocesan school*, H.C. 1826–7 (441), xiii, 359. **93** *Sixth report of the commissioners of Irish education inquiry, Hibernian Society for Soldiers' and Sailor's Children; Female Orphan House*, H.C. 1826–7 (442), xiii, 385; *Seventh report of the commissioners of Irish education inquiry, Royal Cork Institution*, H.C. 1826–7 (443), xiii, 501; C.T.A. Carter, *Kirwan House (Female Orphan House), the foremost Irish charity, 1790–1995* (Dublin, 1996). **94** *Seventh report of the commissioners of Irish education inquiry, Royal Cork Institution*, H.C. 1826–7 (443), xiii, 501. **95** *Eighth report of the commissioners of Irish education inquiry, Roman Catholic College at Maynooth*, H.C. 1826–7 (509), xiii, 537; Corish, *Maynooth College, 1795–1995*, pp 26–63. **96** *Ninth report of the commissioners of Irish education inquiry, general view of the proceedings of the commissioners*, H.C. 1826–7 (516), xiii, 999. **97** See Akenson, *Irish education experiment*, pp 157–375; David Miller, *Church, State and nation in Ireland, 1898–1921* (Dublin, 1973); O'Connell (ed.), *O'Connell, education, Church & State*;

Introduction of the national school system and the Stanley Letter, 1831

Despite the recommendations of the 1825 commission of Irish education inquiry, it was to take another six years before a system of national education was established. The granting of Catholic emancipation in 1829, whereby Catholics could now be elected to parliament, made it even more urgent to provide education for the lower classes and thus create a literate and loyal electorate. A Whig government was elected in 1830 and the new chief secretary of Ireland, Lord E.G. Stanley,[98] introduced the national school system in October 1831, based on the recommendations of the 1825 commission. The aim of this national school system was to provide a non-denominational 'mixed' education for Catholic and Protestant children together. The rules under which the new Board of National Education was to operate were not laid down in an act of parliament but were contained in the so-called 'Stanley Letter' addressed by the chief secretary to the first chairman of the Board, the duke of Leinster.[99] The scheme was initially regarded as 'an experiment' and this gave the Board a degree of flexibility in interpreting its rules, which in the long run ensured its survival. The fundamental principle of 'separate religious and secular and moral instruction', designed to prevent proselytism, was strictly adhered to. It has been argued that the national school system was 'tried out' in Ireland by the British government as an experiment in social control. In England at the time there was no attempt to establish such a State education system as the government continued the policy of supporting voluntary education societies.[1]

Under the terms of the 1831 Stanley Letter the commissioners of national education in Ireland (commonly known as the National Board) received a grant of £30,000 which had been withdrawn from the Kildare Place Society. The money

D.H. Akenson, 'Pre-university education, 1782–1870' in W.E. Vaughan (ed.), *A new history of Ireland, v: Ireland under the union, part i, 1801–70* (Oxford, 1989), pp 523–37; Susan M. Parkes, 'Higher education, 1793–1908' in W.E. Vaughan (ed.), *A new history of Ireland, v: Ireland under the union, part ii, 1870–1921* (Oxford, 1996), pp 539–70.   **98** Edward George Stanley, later earl of Derby (1799–1869). He was advised by Thomas Wyse, MP for Waterford, who introduced a draft education bill in 1830, which was later withdrawn. See J.J. Auchmuty, *Sir Thomas Wyse, 1791–1862: the life and career of an educator and diplomat* (London, 1939).   **99** *Copy of a letter from the chief secretary for Ireland to the duke of Leinster on the formation of a Board of commissioners for education in Ireland*, H.C. 1831–2 (196), xxix, 757; Akenson, *Irish education experiment*, pp 59–122. The other members of the first National Board were two Anglicans, Richard Whately, archbishop of Dublin and Dr F. Sadleir, provost of Trinity College, Dublin; two Catholics – Daniel Murray, archbishop of Dublin and A.R. Blake, and two Presbyterians, Reverend James Carlile and Robert Holmes (Oct. 1831). See *Hansard's parliamentary debates*, third series, 3, vi, 1249–1305 (9 Sept. 1831).   **1** Oliver McDonagh, 'The age of O'Connell, 1830–45' in Vaughan (ed.), *A new history of Ireland, v: part i, 1801–70*, pp 158–68, 169–92; Martina Relihan, 'The nineteenth-century national school system in Ireland: an egalitarian conception?' in *History of Education Researcher*, 78 (Nov. 2006), pp 84–94. In 1833 the first education grant was given to two major education societies in England, the National Society for Promoting Education of the Poor in the principles of the Established Church, founded in 1811 and to the British and Foreign School Society, established in 1810. See Brian Simon, *Two nations and the educational structure, 1780–1870* (London, 1974); Wardle, *English popular education*.

Copy of a LETTER from the CHIEF SECRETARY for IRELAND, to

His Grace the DUKE of LEINSTER, on the formation of a

Board of Commissioners for Education in Ireland.*

Irish Office, London, October, 1831.

MY LORD,--His Majesty's Government having come to the determination of empowering the Lord Lieutenant to constitute a Board for the superintendence of a system of National Education in Ireland, and Parliament having so far sanctioned the arrangement as to appropriate a sum of money in the present year, as an experiment of the probable success of the proposed system, I am directed by His Excellency to acquaint your Grace, that it is his intention, with your consent, to constitute you the President of the new Board. And I have it further in command to lay before your Grace the motives of the Government in constituting this Board, the powers which it is intended to confer upon it, and the objects which it is expected that it will bear in view, and carry into effect.

The Commissioners, in 1812, recommended the appointment of a Board of this description, to superintend a system of Education, from which should be banished even the suspicion of proselytism; and which, admitting children of all religious persuasions, should not interfere with the peculiar tenets of any. The Government of the day imagined that they had found a superintending body, acting upon a system such as was recommended, and entrusted the distribution of the National Grants to the care of the Kildare-street Society. His Majesty's present Government are of opinion, that no private Society, deriving a part, however small, of their annual income from private sources, and only made the channel of the munificence of the Legislature, without being subject to any direct responsibility, could adequately and satisfactorily accomplish the end proposed; and while they do full justice to the liberal views with which that Society was originally instituted, they cannot but be sensible that one of its leading principles was calculated to defeat its avowed objects, as experience has subsequently proved that it has. The determination to enforce in all their schools the reading of the Holy Scriptures without note or comment, was undoubtedly taken with the purest motives; with the wish at once to connect religious with moral and literary education, and,

*This is a copy of the letter from Mr. Stanley as finally settled. The points of difference between it and the draft letter originally received by the Commissioners of National Education are indicated in the Report of the Royal Commission of Inquiry into Primary Education (Ireland), Vol. I., pp. 22–26.

3 Extract from the 'Stanley Letter' of 1831 setting up the national school system. This letter from the Irish chief secretary, Lord Stanley, was addressed to the duke of Leinster, chairman of the new Board of Commissioners of National Education in Ireland, laying down the principles and rules under which the Board was to operate (H.C. 1831–2 (196), xxix, 75).

was to be spent on building schools, training teachers, inspecting schools and publishing schoolbooks. Responsibility for running the schools was divided between the central Board and local school management and the system was built on the foundations of the existing network of voluntary pay schools. In the first instance, the schools had to apply to the National Board for aid. They had to be able to provide a suitable local site, one third of the building costs and the teacher's salary. In return the Board paid two thirds of the building costs, gratuities for teachers, and funding for schools fittings and effects. In an effort to encourage co-operation between the local Catholic and Protestant communities the Board looked with 'peculiar favour' on joint applications for aid from the two religious groups.[2] In national schools which were in receipt of aid from the Board, no religious emblems were allowed, religious instruction had to take place at a fixed hour or on a separate day and children could be exempt from religious instruction if their parents so wished. In addition, the Board had control over the books used in the schools and published its own a series of lesson-books, which were given as free stock to every new national school. This pioneer set of graded school readers was used widely both in Ireland and abroad. The content of the five books, comprising English poetry and prose, general knowledge and moral education formed the curriculum of the national schools until the 1870s.[3] English was the language of instruction and Irish was neither taught nor used in the schools. An inspectorate was established to ensure that the rules of the Board were adhered to and each national school was required to keep a register of the pupils as well as a roll book of attendance and a daily report book.

Although criticized by the Churches for its policy on the strict separation of religious from secular education, the national system proved a successful compromise. By 1833 there were 789 schools in operation under the National Board and by 1840 the number had risen to 1,978.[4] Through the years the Board established an effective nation-wide administrative bureaucracy, which was based

---

2 See, for example, the application for aid in building school house at Rathmines, Dublin, Jan. 1832 (National Archives of Ireland (hereinafter NAI), ED (education files) 1/28/3, published in Kenneth Hannigan (ed.), *The national school system, 1831–1924, facsimile documents* (Dublin, 1984), pp 22–4. This application for constructing a school at the rear of the chapel in Rathmines was signed by ten Protestants who were evidently in support of the school and also by fourteen Catholics. There were said to be two other schools for boys and two for girls in the area. **3** R. Goldstrom, *The social content of education: a study of Irish school textbooks* (Shannon, 1972); Eileen T. Whelan, 'Primary school readers in Ireland, 1800–1870 (social and pedagogical aspects)' (MEd thesis, UCC, 1976). **4** By 1846 the total number of national schools had risen to 3,637 of which 1,528 were in Ulster, 779 in Munster, 891 in Leinster and 439 in Connacht. (*Thirteenth report of the commissioners of national education in Ireland for the year 1846*, H.C. 1847 (832), xvii, 187–90.) On entering the system, each national school was allotted a roll number, which was used for correspondence and record keeping by the National Board. These roll numbers, after the first initial numbering in the 1830s, were allocated sequentially and thus are useful for ascertaining the date of the opening of a school.

in Tyrone House, Marlborough Street, in Dublin. The commissioners of national education in Ireland published annual reports from 1833 and these provide a detailed record of the growth and development of the system. The reports, which increased in size as the years went on, contain lists of schools in the system, attendance figures, numbers of teachers trained, lists of books published by the Board as well as its rules. From the 1850s the reports also include inspectors reports, reports of the Board's model schools and teachers' examination papers.[5]

However, opposition from the Churches caused the National Board over the years to adapt its rules to allow more denominational control. Local school patrons had to apply to the Board for aid and both the site for a new school and one third of the building costs had to be provided locally. Initially application forms had to be signed by both Protestant and Catholic members of the community but by the 1840s this requirement had been dropped, due largely to opposition from Presbyterian communities. Thereafter, applications from one denomination were accepted and this eventually led to a proliferation of small denominational national schools.[6] By 1900 there were over 8,000 national schools throughout Ireland and the illiteracy rate decreased dramatically from 53 per cent in 1841 to 14 per cent by the end of the century.[7]

The National Board attempted to uphold the non-denominational principle and established its own teacher training college and model schools in Marlborough Street in Dublin, as well as a network of twenty-six district model schools. In the first half of the century teacher training was based on the monitorial apprenticeship model whereby older pupils of around twelve to fourteen years of age stayed on at national schools as monitors, assisting the master/ mistress and learning to teach.[8] According to the commissioners of national education in Ireland, the teacher

> should be a person of Christian sentiment, of calm temper and discretion; he should be imbued with the spirit of peace, of obedience to the law; and loyalty to his sovereign; he should not only possess the art of communicating knowledge, but be capable of moulding the mind of youth, and of giving the power which education confers a useful direction …[9]

---

5 The annual reports of the commissioners of national education in Ireland are published as British parliamentary papers from 1833 to 1921. See below pp 147–53.   **6** Akenson, *Irish education experiment*, pp 157–87.   **7** Ibid., p. 376; *Census of Ireland, 1901, pt ii, General report, with illustrative maps, diagrams, tables, and appendix* [Cd 1190], H.C. 1902, cxxix, 1. **8** Monitors were paid a small annual salary, £4 for the first year, £5 for the second, £6 for the third and £7 for the fourth year. See *Fourteenth report of the commissioners of national education in Ireland for the year 1847*, H.C. 1847–8 (981), xxix, 245. Much emphasis was placed on the character and general qualification of the teacher as he or she was expected to set an example in the community. The majority of teachers trained as monitors and then were classified into five categories, first class (1st, 2nd and 3rd divisions), second class (1st, 2nd and 3rd divisions), third class (1st and & 2nd divisions), probationary teachers (in their first year), assistant teachers, and mistresses of needlework.   **9** Ibid., 244.

National teachers were classified in grades and were encouraged to improve their classification and hence their salary by progressing through a system of annual National Board examinations. Examinations for teachers were organized by the inspector in each district. There were three sets of exam papers for each grade as examinations had to take place at different times. The programme for teachers and copies of examinations papers were printed in the commissioners' annual reports. Up to the 1860s the majority of teachers were trained in this way.[10]

Marlborough Street Training College and the district model schools
The Marlborough Street Training College, which opened in 1838, offered a short, six-month training course for teachers, most of whom were already in teaching positions. Two professors, Robert Sullivan and Revd J.W. McGauley, were appointed – Sullivan to teach arts and McGauley, mathematics and natural philosophy. Both male and female students were residents of the college: the men occupied a house in Glasnevin while the women stayed in Talbot Street. All undertook their practical training in the Board's model schools, which were attached to the institution in Marlborough Street.[11] In 1855 the Revd McGauley wrote an extensive report on the work of the college and outlined what needed to be done in order to improve teacher training. He suggested that the course be extended to one year in order to facilitate a broadening of the curriculum. At that time, the training institution was only providing students with what was in reality a six-month in-service training course. McGauley stated that the numbers trained at the college were insufficient and that upgrading of the college's facilities, such as a library and science laboratory, was required.[12] However, McGauley's report fell on deaf ears: no steps were taken to improve the training institution and it failed to develop in the next decades.

The Board's district model schools offered pupil teacher apprenticeships, which were paid more than ordinary monitors. These model schools were viewed as the 'show pieces' of the national school system as they propagated 'mixed education' of Catholics and Protestants as well as a high standard of teaching methods. Model school consisted of three separate schools, each devoted to boys or girls or infants.

10 By 1855, of the 5,042 teachers employed by the National Board, only 2,006 were trained. *Twenty-second report of the commissioners of national education in Ireland for the year 1855*, I, H.C. 1856 (2142–I), xxvii, pt i, 7.   11 Synopses of Sullivan and McGauley's lectures, plus an account of the teaching methods used in the Marlborough Street model schools, are in the *Seventh report of the commissioners of national education in Ireland for the year 1840*, H.C. 1842 (353), xxviii, 320–35. The curriculum was closely based on the content of the Board's five lesson-books. Heavy emphasis was placed on character and general qualifications.   12 See *Appendix to the twenty-second report of the commissioners of national education in Ireland for the year 1855*, H.C. 1856 (2142–I) (2142–II), xxvii, pt i, 1, pt ii, 1. McGauley, who was an ordained Catholic priest, was forced to resign the next year, following an indiscretion involving a former female student with whom he was residing. See *Copy of minutes of the proceedings of the Board of National Education, Ireland with reference to the resignation of the Reverend J.W. McGauley and of correspondence connected therewith*, H.C. 1857 (297–II), xlii, 433.

It was originally planned to establish thirty-two model schools, one for each county, but because of the Catholic Church's opposition to these non-denominational schools, their construction was curtailed in the 1860s and in all only twenty-six were built.[13] From 1849 inspectors' reports on the work of the district model schools were included in the Board's annual reports. These record details concerning the organization, staffing, pupil teachers, attendance and progress of the schools. The early reports indicated the initial confidence which the National Board had in these fine architecturally designed schools as centres of good educational practice. However, as the years passed, Catholic Church opposition to the schools reduced the number of Catholic children attending and the purpose of the schools as local training centres for teachers failed.[14] A local study of the history of an individual model school can be undertaken using these annual reports. For example, the *Sixteenth report of the commissioners of national education in Ireland* (1849) features reports on the opening of the first four district model schools at Newry, Ballymena, Clonmel and Dunmanway.[15] Each had an official public opening, attended by local dignitaries and clergy and the end of year examination of the pupils was another public occasion. A significant number of middle-class children attended these model schools and their parents' occupations were noted in the commissioners' report. For example, in Clonmel the children of farmers and mechanics formed the largest group, followed by children of shopkeepers and 'holders of inferior public offices'. Male pupil teachers, who resided in the schoolmaster's house, were also key figures in these schools. Their routine included teaching in the school by day and study at night, as well as cleaning and maintaining the schoolrooms. Female pupil teachers were called monitresses and were non-residential.[16] The country's largest model school, located on the Falls Road in Belfast, opened in 1857. Patrick Keenan, head inspector, wrote a detailed account of the opening of that school. He described the extensive lavish building,[17] recorded the names and salaries of the teachers, and outlined the

---

13 *Thirteenth report of the commissioners of national education in Ireland for the year 1846*, H.C. 1847 (832), xvii, 194–6. The first four district model schools were opened in 1849, two in Ulster (at Ballymena and Newry) and two in Munster (at Clonmel and Dunmanway). Three more opened in 1850 in Trim, Coleraine and Bailieborough. Others were opened in 1852 in Athy and Galway, in 1854 in Kilkenny, in 1855 in Limerick and Waterford, in 1856 at Ballymoney, in 1857 in Belfast, in 1862 at Enniscorthy, in 1863 in Sligo, in 1865 in Cork and in 1867 in Enniskillen. In addition, the Board introduced a group of minor model schools which were smaller and non-residential. These were built at Omagh and Parsonstown in 1860, at Carrickfergus, Monaghan and Newtownstewart in 1861, at Newtownards in 1862 and at Lurgan in 1863. The model schools enjoyed considerably more support in Ulster among the Protestant population – hence a larger number were built there. There were also two model schools in Dublin, the West Dublin Model School on School Street and the Inchicore Railway Model School, which catered for the children of men employed on the railway works there. **14** Robin Wylie, *Ulster model schools* (Belfast, 1997). **15** *Appendix to the sixteenth report of the commissioners of national education in Ireland for the year 1849*, H.C. 1850 (1231, 1231–II), xxv, 367–421. **16** Ibid., i, 407, 415–17. **17** The 1857 report included a set of drawings of the school and of its schoolrooms, which portray 'an

curriculum, timetable and routines of its pupil teachers and monitresses. He also presented the commissioners of national education in Ireland with a copy of the public address which he delivered at the opening ceremony. In it, he discussed the aims and purposes of model schools and their importance in the national school system.[18]

The inspectors also wrote lengthy reports on their specific districts in the annual reports. These contain accounts of individual schools which they visited, as well as attendance figures, classification of pupils according to the national lesson-books, and results of the teachers' examinations for the whole of their district. These reports provide the historian with a substantial body of data from which to construct a local study as they offer valuable insights into the workings of the national system at grassroots level. For example, Patrick Keenan visited fifty-three schools in Donegal in 1857 and wrote individual notes on each. Some schools were excellent, other were not. In relation to Muckress National School, for instance, he wrote:

> This is one of the best country school I have ever been in. The children come immense distances to it – passing other schools on their way. No less than fifty come from Kilcar and the neighbourhood, upwards of two Irish miles, along an exceedingly wild and dangerous road. The results produced by the master are perfectly marvellous. Better answering I have never heard, a more business-like school I have never visited, and a sharper intelligence I have never seen amongst children.[19]

ideal school' of the 1850s: see *Twenty-fourth report of the commissioners of national education in Ireland for the year 1857*, 1, H.C. 1859 (2456–I), vii, 1; 2, 1859 (2456–II), vii, 363; Belfast Model School, 1, H.C. 1859 (2456–I), vii, 104–52, plans of Belfast Model School, 1, H.C. 1859 (2456–I), vii, 153–75. Keenan became resident commissioner of national education in 1872 and was sent to both Trinidad and Malta to report on the education systems there. Fiachra Ó Dubhthaigh, 'A review of the contribution of Sir Patrick Keenan (1826–94) to the development of Irish and British colonial education' (MEd thesis, TCD, 1974). For Keenan's report on the state of education in Trinidad see H.C. 1870 (450), l, 655 and for his report on the education system in Malta see [C 2685], H.C. 1880, xlix, 225. **18** See *Appendix to the twenty-fourth report of the commissioners of national education in Ireland for the year 1857*, 1, H.C. 1859 (2456–I), vii, 305–61; Sean Farren, 'Irish model schools – models of what?' in *History of Education*, 14:1 (1995), pp 40–60. There were also eighteen model agricultural schools built by the National Board where the skills of farming husbandry were taught. These were in Ballymoney, Bailieborough, Templedouglas, Bath, Dunmanway, Glandore, Farrahy, Tervoe, Mount Trenchard, Kyle Park, Derrycastle, Gormanstown, Athy and Woodstock. The twenty-fourth report (1857) included a full report by Dr T. Kirkpatrick, inspector of agricultural schools, on the agricultural schools and on the Albert College, Glasnevin, which was the National Board's own agricultural institution. **19** *Appendix to the twenty-fourth report of the commissioners of national education in Ireland for the year 1857*, 1, H.C. 1859 (2456–I), vii, 228. Keenan argued a case for the use of Irish in schools serving Irish-speaking districts, see *Appendix to the twenty-second report of the commissioners of national education in Ireland for the year 1855*, H.C. 1856 (2142–II), xxvii, pt ii, 1; *Twenty-fourth report of the commissioners of national education in Ireland for the year 1857*, H.C.

His impression of Crove National School was altogether different:

> A stone building; in fair repair; ventilation bad. Only three forms in the
> school; no desks; teacher states he has received timber from the manager to
> have desks made; there were desks in the school but they have worn out;
> clay floor; no tablets; two large maps and a blackboard. Time-tabling only
> middling; no simultaneous instruction; supply of books bad; order and
> cleanliness satisfactory. Teacher not trained; class third, second division; manner
> and tone of voice very good; teaches very sensibly, and with a good deal of
> professional skill; examines tolerably well in Irish. Proficiency of the few
> children present satisfactory. The school is situated in an awfully wild,
> mountainous place – nothing but dreariness and wretchedness on all sides. It
> ought to be treated exceptionally, and paid by capitation allowance.[20]

Powis report on primary education, 1870

Although the national school system began as 'an experiment' in non-denominational education aimed at educating Catholic and Protestant children together,
during its first forty years it became increasingly denominational. Applications for
national schools were received from local parishes, both Catholic and Protestant,
but despite the statement in the Stanley Letter that the commissioners of national
education would look with 'peculiar favour' on joint applications from parishes,
the Board began to accept applications from parishes of one denomination. The
flexibility of the wording of the Stanley Letter and the fact that the rules of the
national system were not enshrined in an act of parliament allowed commissioners
to adapt these rules to suit the reality of the situation and thus ensure that the
national school system would survive. The rule regarding separation of religious
and secular education was strongly contested by the Presbyterian Church in the
north and so by the 1840s the National Board applied a set of separate rules
in relation to so-called 'non-vested' national schools. These regulations empowered
the manager to prohibit religious instruction of another denomination in his
school while accepting the right of pupils to opt out of religious instruction.
Furthermore, whereas previously religious instruction had to be provided on a
separate day of the week or at the beginning or end of the school day, now it
could take place at any time during the school day. All of the Churches adhered to
these rules and so by 1870 seventy per cent of Ireland's national schools were non-
vested.[21] The Church of Ireland, which also opposed separation of religious and

---

1859 (2456–I), vii, 1: *Twenty-fifth report of the commissioners of national education in Ireland for
the year 1858*, H.C. 1860 (2593), xxv, 1; Adrian Kelly, *Compulsory Irish: language and education
in Ireland, 1870s–1972* (Dublin, 2002). **20** *Appendix to the twenty-fourth report of the
commissioners of national education in Ireland for the year 1857*, 1, H.C. 1859 (2456–I), vii, 228–9.
21 A 'non-vested' national school received aid only for salary and school effects, but the
school building was paid for by local sources. See John A. McIvor, *Popular education in the
Irish Presbyterian Church* (Dublin, 1969); Akenson, *Irish education experiment*, pp 161–87.

secular education, established the Church Education Society (CES) in 1839 to defend 'scriptural education' and sustain its own parochial schools. The Society was supported by both Protestant clergy and laity and collected substantial revenues to fund their activities. As a result, the number of Protestant children attending national schools in the 1840s and 50s was further reduced, making the practice of 'mixed education' very limited indeed. However, by the 1860s the CES was unable to finance its schools and Anglican parish schools gradually entered the national school system. Whereas in 1860 Anglicans represented 5.63 per cent of pupils attending national schools, by 1890 this figure had risen to 11.2 per cent.[22]

One of the key issues on which the Catholic Church and the National Board clashed was teacher training. In the 1860s the Catholic hierarchy was strongly opposed to the Board's teacher training institutions (the district model school and the Marlborough Street Institution) on the grounds that both were non-denominational and State managed.[23] The bishops constantly maintained a campaign for recognition of denominational training colleges and in 1863, having failed to secure this recognition, the hierarchy led by Paul Cullen, archbishop of Dublin, effectively banned Catholics from attending district model schools or the Central Training Institution. It was against this backdrop that in 1868 the government eventually agreed to establish a royal commission on primary education, chaired by Lord Powis, to review the workings of the national school system.[24]

Report of the Powis commission, 1870

The report of the Powis commission is regarded as a 'watershed' in the history of Irish primary education as it gave official recognition to the denominational management structure of the national system. It examined all aspects of the national school system's work during its first forty years, including management of schools, the curriculum and books, the inspectorate, teacher training and remuneration. The commissioners also instituted a nation-wide educational census (conducted by the Royal Irish Constabulary) of the children present in every primary school on 1 June 1868.[25] Ten sample area studies were also carried out by assistant

---

22 The income of the CES rose from stg£1,839 in 1839 to £5,979 in 1849: see Akenson, *Irish education experiment*, pp 187–202 and the Annual report of the Church Education Society for 1840. **23** E.R. Norman, *The Catholic Church and Ireland in the age of rebellion, 1859–1873* (London, 1965); Emmet Larkin, *The Roman Catholic Church and the creation of the modern Irish State, 1878–1886* (Dublin, 1975); idem, *The making of the Catholic Church in Ireland, 1850–1860* (Chapel Hill, NC, 1980), idem, *The consolidation of the Roman Catholic Church in Ireland, 1860–70* (Dublin, 1987). **24** The Powis commission was part of Gladstone's Liberal government's policy, which aimed to appease Catholic opinion. The main reforming legislation was the 1870 Irish Land Act, 33 & 34 Vict. c. 46, and the 1869 Irish Church Act, 32 & 33 Vict. c. 42, which disestablished the Church of Ireland. There were fourteen members of the Powis commission, seven Protestants and seven Catholics. Three members of the commission refused to sign the report on the grounds that it was destroying the system of united education, which had been the fundamental tenet of the national system. **25** *Royal commission of inquiry into primary education (Ireland)* [Powis

commissioners.[26] As a whole the Powis commission report is an essential bench-mark source for historians assessing the progress of the national system in a local area since its inception in 1831.[27] For example, one finds that in 1868 the parish of Dunganstown, Co. Wicklow had four national schools, two (one male and one female) at Barrendarrig, one at Ballincarrig and another at Newbawn while the parish of Rosenallis in Queen's County had five national schools, three in Mountmellick and one each at Derlamogue and Rosenallis.[28] Overall the Powis commission report favoured recognition of denominational rights in the manage-ment of schools and teacher training colleges, and it officially accepted that the national system had become *de facto* if not de jure denominational. Evidence was taken from a wide range of witnesses including Paul Cardinal Cullen, Catholic archbishop of Dublin, Alexander Mc Donnell, the resident commissioner, and Patrick Keenan, chief of inspection. As the report covered primary education in general and not just the national system, evidence was taken from other educational bodies such as the Christian Brothers and the Church Education Society.[29]

A special report on the Board's training institutions was highly critical of model schools on the grounds that they were too expensive to maintain and too large to be 'models' of ordinary rural national schools. Consequently the report stated that these schools should be closed. The Central Training Institution was criticized for under-performing and its non-denominational character made it unacceptable as a training college for Catholic teachers in the eyes of the Catholic Church authorities.[30]

commission], vi, *Educational census: returns showing number of children actually present in each primary school, 25 June 1868, with introductory observations and analytical index* [C 6–V], H.C. 1870, xxviii, pt v, 1. **26** *Royal commission of inquiry into primary education (Ireland)* [Powis commission], ii, *Reports of assistant commissioners* [C 6–I], H.C. 1870, xxviii, pt 2, 381. **27** *Royal commission of inquiry into primary education (Ireland)* [Powis commission] [C 6–VII], H.C. 1870, xxviii. The 1870 Powis commission report is contemporary with the 1861 Newcastle commission on the state of popular education in England and also the Argyll commission on schools in Scotland (1864–7) which is indicative of a government policy of reforming educational provision. The 1870 Forster Education Act established local school boards in England, while in Scotland the Education Act of 1872 laid the foundations of a national education system. **28** *Royal commission of inquiry into primary education (Ireland)* [Powis commission], vi, *Educational census: returns showing number of children actually present in each primary school, 25 June 1868, with introductory observations and analytical index* [C 6–V], H.C. 1870, xxviii, pt v, 1. **29** *Royal commission of inquiry into primary education (Ireland)* [Powis commission], iii, *Minutes of evidence taken before the commissioners, from March 12th to October 30th, 1868* [C 6–II], H.C. 1870, xxviii, pt iii, 1; iv, *Minutes of evidence taken before the commissioners, from November 24th, 1868 to May 29th, 1869* [C 6–III], H.C. 1870, xxviii, pt iv, 1; v, *Analysis of evidence; and index to the minutes of evidence, and appendices* [C 6–IV], H.C. 1870, xxviii, pt iv, 547. **30** *Royal commission of inquiry into primary education (Ireland)* [Powis commission], i, pt ii, *Appendix to the report and also special report by royal commissioners on model schools (district and minor), the Central Training Institution, etc., Dublin, and on agricultural schools* [C 6–A], H.C. 1870, xxviii, pt ii, 1. This report was carried out by two of her majesty's inspectors who were members of the commission, Nasmyth Stokes, a Catholic, and Rev Benjamin Cowie, a Protestant, both of whom were sympathetic towards denominational

Payment by results, 1872

One of the main outcomes to the Powis report was the introduction in 1872 of a system of payment by results in order to supplement teachers' salaries. This policy which had been introduced in England in 1867 following publication of the Newcastle commission report (1861), was an attempt to tackle three major problems in primary education, namely, poor attendance, low teachers' salaries and a lack of a standard core curriculum. Under the payment by results scheme, teachers were paid an annual bonus, in addition to their salary, which was based on the performance of their pupils in an annual examination conducted by the inspector. A core examination curriculum was laid down for each class and no pupil could be entered for the annual examinations unless he or she had attended the school for a minimum of ninety days each year. The onus was placed on teachers to encourage regular attendance and to advance the progress of their pupils since higher fees were paid for more senior classes. However, the detrimental effect was that the curriculum became standardized and was narrowed down to the examination syllabus. Pressure was put on teachers and pupils alike, and the inspector's role became that of the dreaded examiner.[31]

The pupils' annual exam results were recorded in the school register so one can follow a pupil's progress through his or her years in the system. It is also possible to establish which extra subjects were on offer at a particular school. For example, the register of St Luke's school in Douglas, Co. Cork shows that a pupil, Robert, whose father was a spinner, entered the school in 1895 when he was aged six, and he stayed for seven years until 1901. In the first class results examination he passed all four exams in reading, spelling, writing and arithmetic. The following year, when in second class, he passed in spelling and reading, but failed his writing and arithmetic examinations. In third class he again failed writing and also geography

education. The minutes of the Powis commission are held in the National Archives, Bishop Street, Dublin (3 vols, 1a–50–36). The other commissioners were Edward James, earl of Powis (chairman), E.R. Windham, earl of Dunraven and Mount Earl, Samuel Singer, bishop of Meath, Robert Clonbrock, Justice Michael Morris, Sir Robert Kane, William Brooke, David Wilson D.D., James Dease esq., James Gibson, W.K. Sullivan esq., Lawrence Waldron esq. Three of the commissioners, Kane, Wilson, and Gibson did not sign the final report as they considered the fundamental non-denominational principles of the national system were being undermined.   **31** *Report of the commissioners appointed to inquire into the state of popular education in England etc.* ... [Newcastle commission], H.C. 1861 (2794), xxi, pt 1, 1; H.C. 1861 (2794–II–IV), xxi, pts ii–iv; H.C. 1861 (2794–V), xxi, pt v, I; H.C. 1861 (2794–VI), pt vi, 1; *Appendix to the fortieth report of the commissioners of national education in Ireland for the year 1873* [C 965], H.C. 1874, xix, 114–27. The core subjects for the results examination, for example, in third class were reading, spelling, writing, arithmetic, grammar, geography and needlework. There were also a number of extra subjects which could be taught for extra results fees including vocal music, drawing, the classics, French, geometry, algebra and science. The Irish language was introduced as an extra subject in 1879, following a request from the Society for the Preservation of the Irish Language: see *Memorial of the Council of the Society for the Preservation of the Irish Language and others, in favour of placing the teaching of the Irish language on the results programme of national schools*, H.C. 1878 (324), lx, 495.

(a new subject) and music (an extra subject). We also learn from the register that St Luke's offered agriculture as another extra subject. In fourth class Robert failed his spelling exam, but in fifth class he passed all examinations. He repeated fifth class before progressing into sixth class for his final year (1900–1).[32] Unfortunately no results were recorded for his last two years as the system of payment by results was abolished in 1900. In the female students' register one finds a student named Hester whose father was a teacher. She entered school in 1895 when she was aged six. She passed all of her first and second class examinations in 1896 and 1897 respectively, having taken music as an extra subject in second class. In fourth class Hester was less successful, failing in writing, arithmetic, grammar and agriculture as an extra subject. However, she continued her schooling until 1904, repeating both fifth class and sixth class, by which time she would have reached fifteen years of age.[33]

Compulsory school attendance: the Irish Education Act, 1892
The payment by results system helped raise the attendance level at national schools. In 1892 the Irish Education Act for the first time made attendance at school compulsory for children aged between six and fourteen years and stipulated that those under eleven years were not to be employed, except in periods of seasonal labour such as planting potatoes, hay-making and harvest.[34] School fees were abolished in national schools and a school grant was instead provided by the Board. The 1892 act did not apply to rural areas until the establishment of county councils in 1898, and even then the right of compulsion remained a local option. There was considerable opposition to the notion of compulsory education enunciated in the bill as it prevented younger children from working on the farm or in the family business. Among those who opposed the idea were members of the Catholic hierarchy who argued that the measure constituted an infringement of parents' rights. In spite of their protestations the 1892 act was passed.[35] This legislation was also significant as while the act was still at bill stage, the issue of whether the Christian Brothers schools could be allowed to enter the national school system and thus receive grants from the government was debated. Previously the Brothers' schools had remained outside of the system owing to the National Board's ruling on the separation of religious and secular instruction and its prohibition on

32 Alicia St Leger (ed.), *St Luke's School, Douglas, Cork* (Cork, 2002), p. 19. **33** Ibid., p. 20. **34** Irish Education Act, 55 & 56 Vict., c. 42 (1892). Compulsory education was introduced in England in 1880. **35** Akenson, *Irish education experiment*, pp 344–9; see *Copy of correspondence in the year 1895 between the Irish government and the commissioners of national education for Ireland, with extracts from minutes of the proceedings of the commissioners, in relation to certain proposed changes in the rules under which grants are made by parliament for elementary education in Ireland*, H.C. 1893–4 (55), lxxvii, 657; for further correspondence and proceedings see H.C. 1895 (324), lxxvii, 527, H.C. 1896 (89), lxxi, 1; *Correspondence between the national education commissioners (Ireland) and the Irish government, on the difficulties experienced by them in bringing into operation the Irish Education Act, 1892 (as regards compulsory education)*, H.C. 1893–4 (508), lxviii, 641.

devotional exercises and the display of religious emblems in schools. Despite a long debate between the commissioners of national education and the chief secretary, John Morley, no compromise solution was found. As a consequence, the Christian Brothers schools remained outside the national system until 1924.[36]

Denominational training colleges, 1883

Another eventual outcome of the Powis report was official recognition from 1883 of denominational national teacher training colleges, which received funding from the National Board and offered a two-year, full-time initial training course.[37] These denominational training colleges were to play an important role in the development of the national teaching profession. The new colleges were residential, with a strict regime and an emphasis on religious and moral values, and the students carried out their teacher practice at model schools attached to each training college.[38] Entry to the colleges was by way of the competitive queen's or king's scholarship examination and students were known as queen's or king's scholars. The examination covered a wide range of subjects, including English, geography, mathematics (algebra and geometry for men), book keeping, agriculture (again, for men), drawing, needlework for women, and theory of method and practical teaching. Optional subjects included vocal music, Latin, French, Irish and domestic economy and hygiene for women.[39] To gain admittance to one of the colleges was considered a privilege and students who received 'the call' to training were admired by their community.

36 Daniel Kelleher, *James Dominic Burke – a pioneer of Irish education* (Dublin, 1988), pp 171–88. Brother Burke was a leading figure in the negotiations between the Irish government, the CNEI and the Christian Brothers: see Áine Hyland, 'The recognition of the Christian Brothers' schools as national schools, 1924–5' in *Proceedings of the Educational Studies Association of Ireland* (1980), pp 254–75; Keogh, *Edmund Rice* (2008), pp 211–24. **37** *Correspondence between the Irish government and the commissioners on the subject of training schools in Ireland*, H.C. 1883 (144), liii, 471. The Catholic teacher training colleges in Dublin were St Patrick's College, Drumcondra for men and Our Lady of Mercy College, Baggot Street (later Carysfort College, Blackrock) for women (both recognized by the National Board in 1883). Beyond Dublin, Mary Immaculate College, Limerick, for women was recognized in 1898 and De La Salle College, Waterford was recognized in 1888. The Church of Ireland Training College, Kildare Place, for Anglican men and women was recognized in 1884. St Mary's College, Belfast, for women was recognized in 1898. The National Board's own teacher training college in Marlborough Street, which had previously offered only a six-month, short term in-service courses, also introduced the two-year initial training: see John Coolahan, 'Education in the training colleges, 1877–1977' in *Two centenary lectures: Our Lady of Mercy College, Blackrock* (Dublin, 1981), pp 20–52. **38** James Kelly (ed.), *St Patrick's College, Drumcondra, 1875–2000: a history* (Dublin, 2006); Angela Bolster, 'Catherine McAuley, her educational thought and its influence on the origin and development of an Irish training college' in *Two centenary lectures*, pp 1–19; Parkes, *Kildare Place*.   **39** Male candidates had to select one option, female candidates had to select two, one of which had to be vocal music or domestic economy. After 1900 the course was expanded to include history, manual instruction, elementary science and object lessons and physical drill which were new subjects on the 1900 revised programme of

These denominational training colleges transformed national school teaching into a fully-fledged profession: by 1895, out of a total of 11,850 national teachers employed, 56.2 per cent were trained. The annual reports of the National Board featured reports on the training colleges which list their staff and record details of subjects taught and examinations. For example, in 1906–7, the general report on the training colleges showed that there were 187 second year, male king's scholars in residence in the six colleges as compared with 326 second year female scholars. The largest institution for men, St Patrick's College, Drumcondra, had 165 students in residence whereas the largest for women, Carysfort College, had 100 in total. The inspectors reported that there was already a shortage of male recruits. In relation to Marlborough Street College they remarked that

> Though the full number of well-qualified women (165) for which the college is licensed can easily be obtained, the number of male candidates still falls below the college requirements. To fill the 130 places, only 95 men were to be had in 1905–6, but the last session showed some improvement in this respect, as 105 men candidates qualified for admission.

Similarly, at Kildare Place, 'it had been found difficult or, rather impossible, to keep up the fill supply of men students for which the college is licensed, and though this year shows some improvement in that respect, the deficiency is far from being made up.'[40]

IV. EDUCATION REFORMS, *c.*1900–*c.*1922

During the period 1900–20 key issues in primary education were reform of the curriculum, increased salaries for teachers and the establishment of local education authorities which would have responsibility for management of primary schools. The three were closely inter-linked as teachers' salaries and resources and the successful implementation of the new curriculum was dependent on the government increasing its financial provision. However, the government's policy of attempting to decentralize education funding to local education authorities, as happened in England under the Balfour Education Act (1902), was strongly resisted by the Catholic Church which fought successfully to retain clerical management of national schools. Therefore the structure and public financing of education became a major political issue between Church and State during the first two decades of the twentieth century.

instruction for national schools: see *Appendix to the rules and regulations of the commissioners of national education in Ireland for the year 1898* (Dublin, 1898), pp 132–40 and *Appendix to the rules and regulations of the commissioners of national education in Ireland for the year 1902* (Dublin, 1903), pp 74–5. The rules of the CNEI were published separately and appeared in the annual reports.   **40** *Seventy-fourth report of the commissioners of national education in Ireland for the year 1907* [Cd 4291], H.C. 1908, xxvii, 841.

Belmore commission, 1898 and the Dale report, 1904

Following the report of the *Belmore commission on manual and practical instruction* (1898) the payment by results system in national schools was terminated and a revised programme of instruction introduced in 1900. This programme encouraged a heuristic methodology and was influenced by the kindergarten ideas of German child educator, Friedrich Froebel (1782–1852). Practical subjects such as drawing, woodwork, elementary science and cookery for girls became part of the curriculum.[41] However, the implementation of this ambitious programme caused difficulties for teachers and inspectors alike due to a lack of preparation and resources. In 1904 F.H. Dale, an inspector from the Board of Education in England, was invited by the Irish chief secretary, George Wyndham, 'to inquire and report how typical Irish elementary schools compare with similarly circumstanced public elementary schools in England'.[42] The Dale report criticized the lack of resources and clerical management, and recommended the introduction of local education authorities to improve funding for national schools. The report provoked a serious political clash between the government and the Catholic hierarchy on the matter of clerical management and consequently no action was taken.[43] However, the report itself provided a valuable external assessment of the state of Irish education three years after the introduction of the revised programme.

Teachers' salaries

The campaign for increased salaries for national teachers was led by the strong teachers' union, the Irish National Teachers' Organization (INTO), founded in 1868. In an attempt to resolve the issue the Dill vice-regal committee of inquiry into primary education (Ireland) was set in 1913.[44] It critically examined the National

41 Akenson, *Irish education experiment*, pp 372–3; see reports of the *Royal commission on manual and practical instruction in primary schools under the Board of National Education in Ireland* [Belmore commission] [C 8383, 8531, 8532, 8618, 8619, 8923, 8924, 8925], H.C. 1898, xliii–xliv. For details of the payment by results curriculum, see *Appendix the thirty-ninth report of the commissioners of national education in Ireland for the year 1872* [C 805], H.C. 1873, xxv; for the 1900 revised programme of instruction see *Appendix to the sixty-ninth report of the commissioners of national education in Ireland for the year 1902* [Cd 1679], H.C. 1903, xxi; Thomas Walsh, 'The revised programme of instruction, 1900' in *Irish Educational Studies*, 26:2 (June 2007), pp 127–44; A. Hyland, 'Educational innovation – a case study. An analysis of the revised programme of 1900 for national schools' (MEd thesis, TCD, 1975). **42** *Report of Mr F.H. Dale, his majesty's inspector of schools, Board of Education, on primary education in Ireland* [Cd 1981], H.C. 1904, xx, 947. **43** Miller, *Church, State & nation*; Brian Titley, *Church, State and the control of schooling in Ireland, 1900–44* (Dublin, 1983). **44** *Vice-regal committee of inquiry into primary education (Ireland)*, 1913 [Dill report], *First report of the committee* [Cd 6828], H.C. 1913, xxii, 231 and *Appendix to the first report of the committee, minutes of evidence 13th February–12th March, 1913* [Cd 6829], H.C. 1913, xxii, 235; *Second report of the committee* [Cd 7228], H.C. 1914, xxviii, 1914; *Appendix to the second report of the committee, minutes of evidence 13th March–25th June, 1913* [Cd 7229], H.C. 1914, xxviii, 5; *Third report of the committee* [Cd 7479], H.C. 1914, xxviii, 583; *Appendix to the third report of the committee, minutes of evidence 26th June–17th September, 1913* [Cd 7480], H.C. 1914, xxviii, 587;

Board's inspectorate along with the system of assessment and promotion of teachers. Following the abolition of payment by results, the issue of promotion was proving problematic and especially so from 1900 when a system of graded salaries, with triennial increments dependent on inspectors' reports, was introduced. Dissatisfaction with the new system caused a serious deterioration in the relationship between the inspectorate and teachers. Much of the blame for the situation was directed at the then resident commissioner, W.J. Starkie. In his defence, in 1913 Starkie presented to the Dill committee a detailed account of his stewardship of National Board since 1900.[45] The committee failed to achieve a satisfactory outcome to the dispute and the INTO continued their campaign. In 1917 the government proposed 'the Duke scheme', which would have increased the graded salaries and introduce annual rather than triennial increments but the scheme was rejected by the INTO, which threatened strike action.

Killanin vice-regal committee of inquiry, 1918
The matter of teachers' salaries continued to cause friction and so a further inquiry was set up in 1918, the Killanin vice-regal committee on teachers' salaries, which eventually did lead to improved pay and conditions for teachers. The committee recommended abolition of the system of graded salaries and the introduction of a basic salary scheme for all teachers, featuring a set of increments and super-normal payments dependent on status and size of the school.[46] In order to find increased funding for such a scheme, the Killanin committee recommended the establishment of local education authorities, which would shoulder part of the financial burden. Once again, therefore, the need for radical reform of the structure of the Irish education system in order to make it more efficient and cost-effective was raised.

MacPherson education bill, 1919
A year after the Killanin vice-regal committee of inquiry report, the government attempted to bring in legislation aimed at reforming the existing system and rationalizing the provision of education for primary, secondary and technical

---

Final report of the committee [Cd 7235], H.C. 1914, xxviii, 1; T.J. O'Connell, *A hundred years of progress: a history of the Irish National Teachers' Organization, 1868–1968* (Dublin, 1968); Síle Chuinneagáin, 'The politics of equality: Catherine Mahon and the Irish National Teachers' Organization, 1905–1916' in *Women's History Review*, 6:4 (Dec. 1997), pp 527–49; Mahon was president of the INTO and was one of the chief witnesses at the Dill Committee. **45** W.J. Starkie, *Copy of evidence presented to the Dill committee of inquiry, 1913* (Dublin, 1913); C.T. O'Doherty, 'William Joseph Miles Starkie (1860–1920), the last resident commissioner of national education' (PhD thesis, University of Limerick, 1997). Starkie had already antagonized the Catholic Church by his pamphlet *Recent reforms in Irish education, primary and secondary, with a view to their co-ordination* (Dublin, 1902) which also criticized clerical management. **46** *Vice-regal committee of inquiry into primary education (Ireland) 1918. Final report of the committee*, i, *Report* [Cmd 60], H.C. 1919, xxi, 741; *Report of the committee*, ii, *summaries of evidence, memoranda, and returns* [Cmd 178], H.C. 1919, xxi; O'Connell, *A hundred*

education on a county basis. The MacPherson education bill (1919) proposed to establish local education authorities along with a new central department of education in order to administer and co-ordinate education at national level. The 1919 bill was strongly opposed by the Catholic hierarchy as it was feared that it would undermine the Church's control of primary and secondary education. The INTO, on the other hand, supported the bill as the union hoped it would provide better pay and conditions for teachers. Thus the union found itself in opposition to the powerful lobby of clerical school managers.[47] The Irish parliamentary party, under the leadership of Joe Devlin, also opposed the bill on nationalist grounds and the four remaining Irish MPs at Westminster successfully 'talked out' the bill in November 1919.[48] Faced with such strong opposition, the education bill was dropped and an opportunity to restructure and co-ordinate Irish education was lost.[49] Therefore the local denominational managerial structure, dating from the Stanley Letter of 1831, continued into the Irish Free State from 1922, while in Northern Ireland local education authorities were introduced by the London-derry Education Act (1923).[50]

V. EDUCATIONAL PROVISION FOR POOR AND DELINQUENT CHILDREN

Another important area where the National Board extended its role was in the provision of education of pauper children within the workhouse system. Under the 1838 Poor Law, workhouses became refuges for pauper and destitute families. The children were housed separately from their parents and other adults, and workhouse schools were connected to the National Board, which paid gratuities to the teachers. Basic literacy and an industrial education were offered in these schools, but the children received little preparatory training for life outside. By 1848 there were 109 workhouse schools in operation in the country and the

years of progress, pp 176–82.   **47** O'Connell, ibid., pp 288–331.   **48** The four remaining Irish MPs at Westminster were Devlin, Redmond, Kelly and Harbison. Following the 1918 election, the Sinn Féin MPs had refused to sit at Westminster and had established the Dáil as the independent Irish parliament.   **49** *Bill to make further provision with respect to education in Ireland and for other purposes connected therewith* [MacPherson bill], H.C. 1919 (214), i, 407; *Bill to make further provision with respect to education in Ireland and for other purposes connected therewith*, H.C. 1920 (35), i, 563; John Coolahan, 'The education bill of 1919 – problems of educational reform' in *Proceedings of the Educational Studies Association of Ireland Conference, 1979* (Galway, 1980), pp 11–31; Séamus Ó Buachalla, *Education policy in twentieth-century Ireland* (Dublin, 1988).   **50** The Education Act (Northern Ireland), 13 & 14 Geo. V, c. 21 [N.I.] (1923); see Sean Farren, *The politics of Irish education, 1920–65* (Belfast, 1995), pp 59–85; D.H. Akenson, *Education and enmity: the control of schooling in Northern Ireland, 1920–1950* (Newton Abbot, 1973). Local education authorities were established in England in 1902 and in Scotland in 1918. See John McCaffrey, 'Education and national identity: the Scoto-Irish experience and aspirations' in Parkes (ed.), *Education & national identity*, pp 55–71.

National Board presented annual reports on these.[51] In addition, the Board supported a number of industrial schools where part of the day was devoted to learning a trade such as tailoring or shoemaking for boys and needlework for girls. By 1848 there were nine such schools in operation, catering for orphans and pauper children, some of whom were lodged in the school. The four most important industrial schools were in Belfast, Ballymena, Limerick and the Claddagh Piscatory School in Galway.[52] Annual reports on these schools, featuring accounts of the work done by pupils, were presented by inspectors of the National Board. For instance, St Mary's Industrial School in Limerick, which was run by the Sisters of Mercy, consisted of two departments – one for orphan girls and the other as a refuge for 'servants out of place'. St Mary's was praised by the inspector who remarked 'I know no other institution of greater practical utility, effecting more positive good, and preserving from more positive evil'.[53]

However, the poor condition of workhouse schools caused concern for the Board. In 1853 James Kavanagh, one of its head inspectors, wrote a very critical account entitled 'Discipline and management of workhouses schools' in which he highlighted poor quality teachers, large classes, harsh punishment and use of children to turn the capstan wheel. He remarked

> There are capstan mills in the unions of Cork, Midleton (girls and boys), Killarney, Athlone (worked by the girls), Dublin South. In South Dublin union the master brought me into the capstan room, and working the mill were some fifty women, many of whom, he stated were *girls of the town*, and these mixed up between spokes for hours with doubtless, many virtuous females.[54]

---

51 *Fifteenth report of the commissioners of national education in Ireland for the year 1848*, H.C. 1849 (1066), xxiii, 91. There were 28 schools in Ulster, 35 in Munster, 28 in Leinster and 18 in Connacht. By 1895 there were 155 workhouse schools with a total of 5,617 pupils: see *Appendix to the sixty-second report of the commissioners of national education in Ireland for the year 1895* [C 8185], H.C. 1896, xxviii, 463–4; Helen Burke, *The people and the Poor Law in 19th-century Ireland* (Dublin, 1987); Joseph Robins, *The lost children: a study of charity children in Ireland, 1799–1900* (Dublin, 1980). **52** Alf MacLochlainn, 'The Claddagh Piscatory School' in idem (ed.), *Two Galway schools* (Galway, 1930), pp 5–20. **53** *Appendix to the fifteenth report of the commissioners of national education in Ireland for the year 1848*, pp 42, 184–94, H.C. 1849 (1066), xxiii, 91. By 1895 31 schools had industrial departments, most of which were in large convent national schools: see *Appendix to the sixty-second report of the commissioners of national education in Ireland for the year 1895* [C 8185], H.C. 1896, xxviii, 1. **54** See Kavanagh's report quoted in Burke, *People & the Poor Law*, p. 205. Kavanagh was also involved in a conflict with the CNEI concerning the rights and duties of the inspectors. His case became a major public issue and Kavanagh emerged as a strong critic of the national school system itself: see *Copies of report of the committee of the National Board of Education in Ireland, appointed … to inquire into the conduct of J. W. Kavanagh, Esq., head inspector of national schools …*, H.C. 1857–8 (386), xlvi, 461; *A copy of all correspondence … between the commissioners and Mr James Kavanagh … and return of names of members appointed on the special committee … in reference to Mr Kavanagh …*, H.C. 1859 (254– I), xxi, pt ii, 131. Kavanagh's book, *Mixed education: the Catholic case stated* (Dublin, 1859), was strongly critical of what he

Kavanagh's 1853 report on workhouse schools enraged the Poor Law commissioners who replied to it in their eighth annual for 1855 report, repudiating the charges.[55] He was not allowed to visit any more workhouse schools and although he protested, the commissioners of national education were not prepared to fight his cause as they had no direct control over workhouse schools. Kavanagh eventually resigned.[56] However, in 1861 a select committee of the House of Commons was set up to examine conditions in workhouses. One outcome of committee's report was the passage of the Industrial schools (Ireland) Act in 1869, which provided for separate custodian institutions for pauper children.[57]

By the middle of the nineteenth century education was seen to have an important role to play in the reform of criminal behaviour and increasingly it was thought that destitute and criminal children should be placed in dedicated institutions away from prisons. Reformers such Mary Carpenter influenced public policy and custodial industrial and reformatory schools were established.[58] In 1858 the Reformatory Schools Act for Ireland, modelled on the 1854 Reformatory Schools Act in England, provided custodial institutions for juvenile offenders, thus separating them from adult criminals in prisons.[59] Under the terms of the act, voluntary organizations could receive government grants, which enabled them to provide residential care and a literary and industrial education. The schools were subject to inspection by a government inspector, who presented official annual reports to parliament.

The main Catholic reformatory schools for boys were at Glencree, Co. Wicklow and Daingean, Co. Offaly while the schools for Catholic girls were High Park, Co. Dublin and St Joseph's in Limerick. The reformatory for Protestant boys was at Belfast, Malone (Road). Under the terms of the 1869 Industrial Schools Act,[60] voluntary organizations, mostly religious orders, were given authority to provide for children at risk under fourteen in institutions outside of the workhouse and to receive maintenance grants from the government. The children were committed directly to industrial schools if found begging, destitute or homeless. The Sisters of Mercy were to the fore among the religious orders in running schools for Catholic girls: by 1873 they had twenty-five industrial schools. Other orders

viewed as the anti-Catholic policy of the National Board.   **55** *Appendix to the eighth annual report of the Irish Poor Law commissioners for 1854*, quoted in Robins, *Lost children*, pp 229–30. **56** Burke, *People & the Poor Law*, pp 202–11; Robins, *Lost children*, pp 222–43. **57** Industrial Schools (Ireland) Act, 31 & 32 Vict., c. 25 (1869).   **58** Jane Barnes, *Industrial schools of Ireland, 1868–1908* (Dublin, 1989); Mary Carpenter, *Reformatory schools for the children of the perishing and dangerous classes and for juvenile offenders* (London, 1851); idem, 'Reformatory schools for girls' in *Reformatory and Refuge Journal*, nos xxxiv–xlv (1867–70); R.J.W. Selleck, 'Mary Carpenter, a confident and contradictory reformer' in *History of Education*, 14:2 (June 1985), pp 101–15.   **59** *Bill to promote and regulate reformatory schools for juvenile offenders*, H.C. 1857–8 (224), iv, 25.   **60** The annual reports of the inspector appointed to visit reformatory and industrial schools date from 1862 to 1919, after which responsibility for the schools passed to the new Department of Education: see H.C. 1862 (2949), xxvi, 651 to [Cmd 1128], H.C. 1921, xxvii, 405.

involved were the Sisters of Charity who had five schools, the Sisters of the Good Shepherd who ran three schools and the Sisters of St Louis, the Presentation Sisters, Poor Clares and the French order Daughters of Charity, who each had one school. The Christian Brothers became the main founders of industrial schools for Catholic boys, establishing schools at Artane in Dublin, Salthill in Galway, Tralee, Co. Kerry and Letterfrack, Co. Galway.[61]

For Protestant boys the Balmoral Industrial School was in Belfast, as was the Hampton House Industrial School and the Shamrock Lodge for girls. In Dublin, the Meath Industrial School, Blackrock was for Protestant boys and the Meath Industrial School, Wicklow was for Protestant girls. There were also Protestant industrial schools for boys and girls in Cork. The denominational nature of the industrial schools and their strong religious ethos were interpreted as victory for advocates of Catholic denominational schooling. In the same year as the Industrial Schools (Ireland) Act was passed, the Church of Ireland was disestablished. The following year the Powis report on primary education recommended recognition of denominational rights in education. These developments were regarded as further victories for the Catholic Church in Ireland.[62]

Though established with high motives of caring for and educating destitute children, both reformatory and industrial schools earned a bad reputation for their harsh discipline and frequent punishment. The first inspector, Sir John Lentaigne, who held office from 1869 until 1886, had a major influence on the growth of industrial schools. However, the voluntary nature of the reformatory and industrial schools system afforded limited power to the inspector, and the day-to-day running of the schools remained in the hands of managers.[63] Nevertheless, the Aberdare report (1884) on reformatories and industrial schools in Britain and Ireland expressed support for the schools and recommended that the system be expanded. No attempt was made to question their existence or to consider an alternative system.[64]

61 Barnes, *Industrial schools of Ireland*, pp 45–6; Older charity schools among the Protestant community were the Female Orphan House in Dublin, founded in 1790, and the Pleasants Asylum for Female Orphans, founded in 1818. The largest Society, the Protestant Orphan Society, which was organized on a county basis, was established in 1809. The records of the Pleasants Asylum are in the NLI (MSS 1555–1561, 12096–12098, 12101–12204) and those of the Protestant Orphan Society are held in the National Archives, Bishop Street, Dublin. **62** Barnes, *Industrial schools of Ireland*, p. 41 and pp 153–60 for list of 69 industrial schools operating by 1902; orphans of soldiers and sailors were cared for in special institutions. **63** Ibid., pp 51–7.   **64** *Report of the reformatories and industrial schools commissioners; with evidence, appendix and index* [C 3876], H.C. 1884, xlv, 1. Reformatory schools were intended to cater for children convicted of crime whereas industrial schools were for children 'at risk' who were neglected or destitute: see Barnes, *Industrial schools of Ireland*, pp 71–3.

VI. AGRICULTURAL EDUCATION

The National Board also attempted to establish special schools providing education in farming and husbandry with a view to improving the standard of Irish agriculture. In 1838 the Board founded its own agricultural school at Glasnevin, Co. Dublin (later the Albert College, 1853) where teachers were trained. A special inspector, Dr Thomas Kirkpatrick, was appointed to supervise the agricultural schools[65] and his annual reports were printed in the appendix to reports of the commissioners of national education. Among the best known of these model agricultural schools were Kyle Park, Co. Tipperary, Munster Model Agricultural School, Co. Cork, Ulster Model School Farm in Belfast and Limerick Agricultural School. The enterprise was very successful for the first ten years and the Board had high hopes of what could be done to improve the standard of agriculture though education. However, the schools proved expensive to maintain and results were limited. In the 1870s the government decided, due to the rising costs and low numbers attending, to close down and sell off all the model school farms with the exceptions of the Albert College in Glasnevin and the Munster Institute in Cork. In 1883 Sir Patrick Keenan, the resident commissioner, in a letter to the lord lieutenant, outlined the history of agricultural education under the National Board and expressed his deep regret at its demise. At that point, the best option seemed to be support for the teaching of agriculture in ordinary national schools.[66] Under the

---

65 *Fifteenth report of the commissioners of national education in Ireland for the year 1848*, pp 57, 182–8, H.C. 1849 (1066), xxiii, 351–62. By 1848 there were eight model agricultural schools in operation with another twenty-one 'in the course of building'. There were also twenty-one ordinary agricultural schools (attached to local national schools) in operation. By 1859 there were thirty-eight agricultural schools, of which twenty were under the exclusive management of the commissioners and eighteen were under the management of local patrons. In addition there were forty-five agricultural schools attached to ordinary national schools and fifty workhouse agricultural schools. This 1849 report includes the names of the students attending the Albert College with their subsequent destinations as well as a list of pupils at Loughash Agricultural School, Co. Tyrone. See *Appendix to the sixteenth report of the commissioners of national education in Ireland for the year 1849*, H.C. 1850 (1231–II), xxv, 434057 and *Appendix to the twenty-sixth report of the commissioners of national education in Ireland for the year 1859*, H.C. 1860 (2706), xxvi, 634–54.   **66** Keenan's letter was subsequently printed in the *Second report of the royal commission on technical instruction* [Samuelson commission] [C 3981–I], H.C. 1884, ii, 271–81, and later printed in W.P. Coyne (ed.), *Ireland; industrial and agricultural* (Dublin, 1902), pp 137–45. In 1862 funding provided by the National Board for agricultural education in workhouse schools was withdrawn: see R. Jarrell & A. O'Sullivan, 'Agricultural education in Ireland' in N. McMillan (ed.), *Prometheus's fire: a history of scientific and technological education in Ireland* (Carlow, 2000), pp 376–404.

system of payment by results teachers taught 'extra' subjects including agriculture for an extra fee and were paid a bonus based on pupils' examination results. Agriculture was taught to boys from fourth class for a result fee of 2s., rising to 3s. in sixth class. The Board published *The agricultural class book* as a textbook. This scheme was more successful and by 1895 there were forty-six agricultural schools under local management. Pupils were assured of a balance between basic literacy and numeracy in the ordinary school and instruction in the theory of farming. The Board also encouraged the creation of school gardens for practical horticultural education and by 1895 forty-three of these were in existence.[67]

VII. SECONDARY AND INTERMEDIATE EDUCATION

The Intermediate Education Act, 1878 and the Board of Intermediate Education, 1878
At secondary level in the nineteenth century the government did not provide grants until the Intermediate Education Act of 1878.[68] Hitherto secondary education, which included the teaching of classics, was largely in the hands of voluntary schools, both Catholic and Protestant. Catholic religious orders such as the Jesuits, Carmelites and Vincentians established schools and colleges and a network of Catholic diocesan colleges were developed from the 1820s.[69] Among Catholic religious teaching orders which established convents for girls were French orders including the Ursulines, the Sisters of St Louis and the Sisters of the Sacred Heart as well as Irish orders such as the Loreto Sisters and the Dominicans.[70] The older Protestant endowed schools, notably the royal schools (est. 1610), the King's Hospital (est. 1670), Midleton College, Cork (est. 1668), Villiers School in Limerick, and the schools of the Erasmus Smith Trust (est. 1669), served the Protestant population. However, by the mid-nineteenth century, with the convenience of the railway, many well-to-do families began sending their sons to public schools in England, notably Rugby, Haileybury, and Marlborough. Secondary schools for girls developed from the mid-century, the most important being Victoria College, Belfast (est. 1859) and Alexandra College, Dublin (est. 1866). Co-educational Protestant schools such as Methodist College in Belfast (est. 1869),

---

67 *Appendix to the sixty-second report of the commissioners of national education in Ireland for the year 1895*, 387–8 [C 8185], H.C. 1896, xxviii, 467–8.   **68** Intermediate Education (Ireland) Act, 41 & 42 Vict. c. 66.   **69** Clongowes Wood College, Co. Kildare was founded by Jesuits in 1814; Castleknock College, Co. Dublin, was founded by the Vincentians in 1835, and the Carmelites established a school at Clondalkin in 1830.   **70** See Costello, *Clongowes Wood College*; Walsh, *Nano Nagle & the Presentation Sisters*; Ursula Clark, *The Ursulines in Cork, 1771–1996* (Cork, 1996); Corish (ed.), *A history of Irish Catholicism*, v *Catholic education*; J.H. Murphy (ed.), *Nos autem: Castleknock College and its contribution* (Dublin, n.d.).

Newtown School in Waterford (est. 1798) and Wesley College, Dublin (est. 1845) provided boarding education.[71] Both Catholic and Protestant voluntary schools strongly resisted any attempt by the State to impose inspection or accountability.

The struggle between Church and State that took place in the context of the national school system and later in the university sector following the founding of the State-funded Queen's colleges in 1845[72] made the State reluctant to intervene in the secondary sector. Therefore, the Intermediate education Act (1878) was a compromise measure which allowed the voluntary secondary schools to receive State grants through a system of payment by results based on public examinations. One million pounds from the assets of the Church of Ireland set aside for educational and social purposes under the terms of the Irish Church Act (1869) was made available to support the new examination system. This allocation could be seen as a fair redistribution of public funds.[73] The introduction of the Intermediate examination system was largely the work of the conservative chief secretary, Sir Michael Hicks-Beach, and the resident commissioner of national education, Sir Patrick Keenan.[74] (The latter had seen a similar system working in Trinidad where he had been sent by the British government to advise on education.)[75] The Intermediate Education Board consisted of seven members, appointed by the lord lieutenant, and two permanent assistant commissioners. The Board was 'to promote secular education in Ireland' by means of a system of public examinations, payment of prizes and exhibition, awarding of certificates to students, and providing 'payment to managers of schools complying with the proscribed conditions of fees dependent on the results of public examinations of students'. No fees were to be paid for examinations in religious instruction and a conscience clause was included, giving a pupil the right to opt out of the school's religious instruction. The examination system was made open to girls' schools by a last minute amendment to the Intermediate education bill[76] which provided 'for applying, as far as conveniently may be, the benefits of this Act to the education of girls'.[77] Thus, girls' schools were allowed to enter for public examinations from 1878 onwards, and their success in the Intermediate Education Board examinations

---

71 See school histories, for example, Anne O'Connor & Susan M. Parkes, *Gladly learn and gladly teach: the history of Alexandra College and School, 1866–1966* (Dublin, 1984); Trevor West, *Midleton College: a tercentenary history* (Cork, 1996); Maurice Wigham, *Newtown School, Waterford: a history, 1798–1998* (Waterford, 1998); Alison Jordan, *Margaret Byers and Victoria College* (Belfast, n.d.); Ernest Armitage, *Wesley College, Dublin, 1845–1995* (Dublin, 1995); Wallace, *Faithful to our Trust*; Lesley Whiteside with Andrew Whiteside, *Where Swift and Berkeley learnt: a history of Kilkenny College* (Dublin, 2009). **72** See T.W. Moody & J.C. Beckett, *Queen's, Belfast, 1845–1949* (2 vols, London, 1959). **73** T.J. McElligott, *Secondary education in Ireland, 1870–1921* (Dublin, 1981). **74** Ibid., pp 16–29. **75** Keenan compiled reports on the state of education in Trinidad (see H.C. 1870 (450), i, 655) and in Malta ([C 2685], H.C. 1880, xlix, 225). **76** *Bill, intituled, An Act to promote Intermediate Education in Ireland*, H.C. 1878 (249), iii, 533; amended in the House of Commons, H.C. 1878 (275), iii, 543. **77** Deirdre Raftery & Susan M. Parkes, *Female education in Ireland: minerva or madonna, 1700–1900* (Dublin, 2007), pp 76–9; another late amendment was the addition of Celtic language and literature as an examination subject.

proved important in showing that females were capable of both serious academic study and the same standards of academic attainment as males. By 1900, out of a total of 8,287 pupils entering for the examinations, 2,194 were female. Ten years later 4,381 of the total 13,092 entering were female.

The Intermediate programme of examinations was contained in the 1878 act and the content showed a dominance of the classics in the school curriculum. The programme included

> the ancient language and literature and history of Greece; the ancient language, literature and history of Rome; the language, literature and history of France, Germany, and Italy, or any one of them, either separately or together, with the Celtic language and literature; mathematics, including arithmetic and book-keeping; natural sciences; and such other subjects of secular education as the Board may from time to time prescribe.[78]

Three grades of examinations were set – junior, middle and senior – and results fees were paid on a sliding scale to those schools where pupils had attended for not less than 100 days in the year. Exhibitions and prizes were awarded to individual boys and girls for the best examination performances. In the first year (1879), a total of 3,473 boys and 798 girls applied to sit the examinations. For boys, the preferred subjects were Latin, English, arithmetic, algebra, and French while for girls, English, French, arithmetic, drawing and music were most popular. There were separate examinations centres for boys and girls in towns around the country: in 1879 there were forty-three for boys and thirteen for girls.[79] Rivalry developed between schools over which could gain the best results and earn the highest results fees. Among those which entered their pupils were the major Catholic boys schools in Dublin (Belvedere College, the Catholic University School, Blackrock College, St Vincent's College, Castleknock and six schools run by the Christian Brothers, namely Francis Street, James's Street, North Brunswick Street, Synge Street and Westland Row). Entrants also came from diocesan colleges such as St Mel's in Longford, St Finian's in Mullingar, St Peter's in Wexford and St Patrick's, Armagh. The Christian Brothers in particular benefited from grants paid by the Intermediate Board and they entered a large number of pupils from their schools around the country including CBS Wexford, CBS Armagh, CBS Newry and CBS Tralee. Successful Protestant boys' schools included the High School, the King's Hospital, Wesley College, and the Masonic School (all in Dublin); the Belfast Academy, the Royal Academical Institution and the Methodist College (all in Belfast), and Bishop Hodson's School in Elphin, Galway Grammar School, and the Royal School, Armagh.

---

78 By the 1890s other subjects added included drawing, music, shorthand with domestic science and botany for girls only.   79 *Report of the Intermediate Education Board in Ireland for 1879* [C 2600], H.C. 1880, xxiii, 31.

While the number of girls' schools entering candidates was smaller, they were nonetheless successful. These included Catholic girls' schools, notably the Loreto Convent schools in Dublin, Kilkenny, Navan and Omagh; the Dominican College in Dublin; the St Louis Convent in Monaghan and the Convents of Mercy in Macroom, Tullamore and Arklow. Protestant girls' schools which entered candidates for the examinations included Alexandra College, Rutland School and the Masonic School for Girls (all in Dublin); Rochelle School in Cork and Cork High School for Girls; the Ladies Collegiate School, and the Methodist College (both in Belfast) and the Friends' School in Mountmellick, Co. Laois.[80]

The Intermediate Board presented annual reports to parliament which contained information about examination of each subject, the numbers entering, the pass/fail rates and amounts paid out in results fees, prizes and exhibitions. The names of examiners and extracts from their reports were also included. As a result, it is possible for historians to trace the development of a school subject in the curriculum and to track numbers taking the subject. For example, in 1879, out of a total of 4,271 candidates, French as a subject was taken by 1,602 boys and 477 girls. By 1900, out of a total of 7,608 candidates, French was taken by 4,810 boys and 1,832 girls; and by 1910 out of a total of 11,900 candidates, 7,294 boys and 3,709 girls took the examination, thus demonstrating the increased popularity of the language, especially in girls' schools.[81] The examiners' reports reveal the achievements of candidates. The examiner for middle grade boys' papers in 1900 reported:

> The work of looking over papers has, on the whole, been a pleasant one, for an unusual number of them were very good indeed, and bore eloquent witness to the fact that French is a favourite study, pursued *con amore* throughout Irish schools. Moreover, gleams of sunshine, more especially in the translations and the historical allusions connected with two set books, brightened the road for the examiner when at times it threatened to become a little monotonous.[82]

---

80 *Appendix to the report of the Intermediate Education Board for Ireland for 1885*, p. 33 [C 4688], H.C. 1886, xxvi, 21; Mary Cullen (ed.), *Girls don't do honours: Irish women in education in the nineteenth and twentieth centuries* (Dublin, 1987); Marie O'Connell, 'The genesis of convent foundations and their institutions in Ulster, 1840–1920' in Janice Holmes & Diane Urquhart (eds), *Coming into the light: the work, politics and religion of women in Ulster, 1840– 1940* (Belfast, 1994), pp 179–201; Catríona Clear, *Nuns in the nineteenth century* (Dublin, 1987); Tony Fahey, 'Nuns in the Catholic Church in Ireland in the nineteenth century' in Cullen (ed.), *Girls don't do honours*, pp 7–30. **81** See the published reports of the Intermediate Education Board of Ireland for the period 1879–1921 in [C 2600], H.C. 1880, xxiii, 31, to [C 1388], H.C. 1921, xxxiv, 397; see especially *Report of the Intermediate Education Board for Ireland for 1900* [Cd 588], H.C. 1901, xxi, 417; *Report of the Intermediate Education Board for Ireland for 1910* [Cd 5768], H.C. 1911, xxi, 47. In addition, the Board published annually *Rules and programme of examinations* which had to be approved by the lord lieutenant and these were published in the parliamentary papers. Copies of the Intermediate Board examination papers are available for consultation in the NLI. **82** *Report of the Intermediate Education Board for Ireland for 1900* [Cd 588], H.C. 1901, xxi, 417.

In addition, results fees paid out to individual schools are listed in the annual reports so it is possible to examine the growth and provision of secondary education in a local area. For instance, in 1900 in Kilkenny City there were four boys' schools in receipt of result fees (the Christian Brothers, Kilkenny College, St Kieran's College and the Pococke School) and one girls' school, the Loreto Convent. At the same time in Galway city there were three boys' schools in receipt of fees (Galway Grammar School, St Ignatius College and St Joseph's Seminary) and two girls' schools (the Dominican convent and the High School). Schools advertised their results figures in the local press in order to impress parents and encourage attendance.

Although schools benefited greatly from the result fees earned by their pupils, and thus were able to improve their facilities and teachers' salaries, the Intermediate examination system imposed a core academic examination curriculum on the schools, which caused considerable stress on both teachers and pupils.[83] On the other hand, the system allowed voluntary schools to remain autonomous institutions, employing their own staff and controlling their own finances and admissions. Under the 1878 Act the powers of the Intermediate Education Board were limited – it could not plan the location of schools, nor provide capital grants for building, nor control the appointment and salaries of teachers. It did not have the power to appoint an inspectorate to examine the schools, thus creating an alternative to the system of payment by results. Rather, the Board's remit was confined to paying examiners and results fees to schools as well as granting prizes and exhibitions to successful individual candidates. In 1890 the Board was assigned an additional source of money under the Local taxation (customs & excise) Act. Commonly known as 'whiskey money' this annual grant was fixed at £46,566 in 1911 and it allowed the Board to pay result fees to the increasing number of schools that entered for the examinations.[84] Despite its drawbacks, this system lasted until 1924 when under the Irish Free State government secondary schools were paid a capitation fee for each registered pupil studying the State examination course. Patrick Pearse, leader of the 1916 Rising and pioneering educationalist, was very critical of the intermediate examination system on the grounds of its English content and what he viewed as its narrow ranged, cramming effect on pupils and teacher alike. In his best known pamphlet *The murder machine* he wrote:

> One if the most terrible things about the English education system in Ireland is its ruthlessness. I know no image for that ruthlessness in the natural order. The ruthlessness of a wild beast has in it a certain mercy – it slays. It has in it a certain grandeur of animal force. But this ruthlessness is literally without pity and without passion. It is cold and mechanical, like the ruthlessness of an immensely powerful engine … It grinds night and day; it

83 See P.H. Pearse, *A significant Irish educationalist: the educational writings of P.H. Pearse*, ed. Séamus Ó Buachalla (Dublin & Cork, 1980). **84** *Report of the Council of Education on the curriculum of the secondary school, 1962*, pp 48–50.

obeys immutable and predetermined laws; it is as devoid of understanding, of sympathy, of imagination, as any other piece of machinery that performs an appointed task. Into it is fed all the raw human material in Ireland; it seizes upon it inexorably and rends and compresses and re-moulds.[85]

Attempts to reform the secondary education system, 1898–1922
In secondary education the next two decades were dominated by four key issues – the search for a system of funding other than payment by results; broadening of the school curriculum to include more science, mathematics and modern languages as opposed to classical languages; provision of increased salaries and professional registration for teachers and lastly, development of closer co-operation between primary and secondary education. By 1900 there were three separate boards providing education in Ireland, namely the commissioners of national education located in Marlborough Street; the commissioners of intermediate education, in Hume Street; and the Department of Agriculture and Technical Instruction, located in St Stephen's Green (in 1911 it moved premises to nearby Merrion Street). Each operated separately with its own finances and there was no formal mechanism for joint planning and co-operation.

Palles commission on intermediate education, 1898
Dissatisfaction with the classical examination curriculum and with the system of payment by results led to the setting up in 1898 of the Palles commission on intermediate education.[86] The intermediate commissioners asked for an independent commission of inquiry but the government did not oblige, responding that if they wished, the commissioners could set up their own commission of inquiry consisting of members of the Intermediate Education Board. Thus, Christopher Palles, lord chief baron and chairman of the Intermediate Board, chaired the commission.[87]

The Palles commission reviewed in detail the working of the intermediate examination system during its first twenty years. It therefore offers an in-depth insight into the problems and achievements of that system. The commission took evidence from six women witnesses, though there were, as yet, no women members of the Intermediate Board. The girls' schools had, on the whole, benefited from the Intermediate system as it had raised academic standards and provided grants to develop facilities. The headmistresses of the country's more prominent girls' schools such as Margaret Byers of Victoria College, Belfast and Henrietta White of Alexandra College, Dublin supported retention of the examination system and the payment by results policy, despite (as they admitted) the considerable strain it

---

85 Quoted in Proinsias MacAonghusa & Liam Ó Réagáin (eds), *The best of Pearse* (Cork, 1967), p. 33; Pearse, *A significant Irish educationalist*, ed. Ó Buachalla, p. 373.   **86** *First report of the commissioners on intermediate education (Ireland), with appendix* [Palles report] [C 9116, 9117], H.C. 1899, xxii; *Final report* [C 9511], H.C. 1899, xxii; *Evidence* [C 9512], H.C. 1899, xiii: *Part II of Appendix to final report* [C 9513], H.C. 1899, xxiv.   **87** V.T.H. Delany, *Christopher Palles* (Dublin, 1960).

placed on staff and pupils alike.[88] In addition, the commission received many written submissions from Catholic and Protestant schools, expressing support for the work of the Intermediate Board and these were summarized in the report. The Palles commission recommended that, despite its limitations, the payment by results system ought to continue because schools supported it and because there was resistance to an alternative of a system of State inspection with capitation grants.[89] While the commission recommended that a 'public general examination of students be retained as the basis for the calculation of the school grant', it stated that these grants should be paid to schools as a block grant payment rather than being based on individual examination results. It was proposed that a gradual change should be made to 'a normal school grant', based on the triennial average performance of each school in the examination. In addition, the Palles report recommended changes in the curriculum aimed at encouraging the teaching of science and mathematics. It advised that two distinct courses should be introduced, firstly, a grammar school course for pupils intending to enter university or higher posts in the civil service, and secondly, a modern course which included natural sciences and modern languages for those who wished to pursue a career in industry or commerce.

Permanent inspectorate, 1909

If the system of payment by results were to be changed, a system of evaluation by a State inspectorate was needed to replace it. In 1900 an Intermediate education Act[90] was passed which gave the Board permission to appoint inspectors. However, although a number of temporary inspectors were appointed in 1902, it was not until 1909 that a permanent inspectorate was appointed. That system remained ineffective and inadequate as the government was not prepared to finance both an inspectorate and a payment by results system. Strong opposition to the introduction of a secondary school inspectorate came from the Catholic Headmasters' Association (CHA), who considered their schools to be private institutions which were not open to State inspection. A joint resolution of the CHA and heads of convent intermediate schools provided a clear indication of their position:

> while we are prepared to accept inspection as defined in paragraphs 11 to 14 of
> the general summary of the recommendations of the vice-regal commission of

---

88 Susan M. Parkes, 'Intermediate education for girls' in Raftery & Parkes, *Female education in Ireland*, pp 69–104. The Catholic religious heads of convent schools were not allowed to give evidence so James Macken, an examiner in English, was asked by Loreto schools to present their case in person: see *Report of the commissioners on intermediate education (Ireland), with appendix* [Palles report], *Evidence* [C 9512], H.C. 1899, xiii, pp 472–81.   89 *Report of the commissioners on intermediate education (Ireland), with appendix* [Palles report], *Final report* [C 9511], H.C. 1899, xxii, 629.   90 See *Bill to amend law relating to intermediate education in Ireland* [C 210], H.C. 1900, ii, 511, amended in committee [C 3315], H.C. 1900, ii, 515.

1898, we regard as outside the legal powers of the Board any extension of the scope of inspection so defined, and in particular, the inspection of the residential departments of boarding schools, of academic degrees, or diplomas, of teachers and of the financial arrangements of the schools.[91]

An attempt was made in 1902 to introduce payment of a 'normal school grant' but overall it ended in failure and the Board retained payment by results.[92] The only area where the 'normal school grant' was adopted was in the preparatory grade but in 1913 the preparatory grade examinations were abolished (as recommended by the Palles commission) and schools were paid instead an 'inspection grant' for their junior pupils aged between twelve and fourteen years.[93] Payment by results, therefore, continued as the system of financing secondary schools down to 1924.[94]

Dale & Stephens report, 1905
Throughout the early decades of the twentieth century the government still sought to find a way of re-organizing secondary education and improving teachers' salaries and conditions. In 1905, following publication of the Dale report on primary education (1904), F.H. Dale and his fellow HMI inspector, T.A. Stephens from London, were invited by the government to conduct a survey of Irish secondary education. They were asked to afford particular attention to co-ordination of intermediate education with primary, secondary and technical education; the staffing and equipping of schools; the allocation of funding, the role of an inspectorate and the salaries and registration of teachers. Their influential report on intermediate education, which was published in 1905, recommended abolition of the payment by results system, a reduction in the number of school examinations to two (intermediate and school-leaving certificates), and the introduction of local authorities with responsibility for intermediate education, with an overarching central education board. Although these proposals were not implemented immediately, they were to have considerable influence on Irish education policy over the next two decades.[95] The increased finance required to improve teachers' salaries and equip schools depended upon a restructuring of the administration of Irish education, but strong opposition from both the Catholic Church and voluntary secondary schools made this a difficult task.[96]

91 McElligott, *Secondary education*, pp 78–86.   **92** *Report of the Intermediate Education Board for Ireland … 1903*, pp ix–xiii [C 2113], H.C. 1904, xx, 847.   **93** Áine Hyland, 'An analysis of the administration and financing of national and secondary education in Ireland, 1850–1922' (PhD thesis, TCD, 1982).   **94** Áine Hyland, 'The setting up of the intermediate inspectorate, 1900–1909' in *Proceedings of the Third Annual Conference of the Educational Studies Association of Ireland, New University of Ulster, 1978* (Dublin, 1979), pp 159–70.   **95** *Report of Messrs F.H. Dale and T.A. Stephens, her majesty's inspectors, Board of Education, on intermediate education in Ireland* [Cd 2546], H.C. 1905, xxviii, 709.   **96** Titley, *Church, State & the control of schooling*, pp 35–43; Ó Buachalla, *Education policy in the twentieth century in Ireland* pp 49–59, 108–121.

Teachers' salaries grant, 1913

In 1909 the Association of Secondary Teachers of Ireland (ASTI) was founded to lobby for better conditions and pay for lay secondary teachers.[97] Teachers needed professional recognition of their qualifications, security of tenure, a living wage and pensions. In an effort to provide part of the necessary extra finance, the chief secretary, Augustine Birrell, introduced a teachers' salaries grant of £40,000 which was to be paid directly to schools for lay staff. That same year the Secondary Teachers' Registration Council was established to oversee the professional qualifications of secondary teachers.[98] In 1919 the first register of intermediate teachers was published. It listed the names of all registered teachers along with their degree qualifications and education diplomas, where relevant.[99] Also listed were schools where each teacher had obtained the necessary qualifying experience. This register is useful for identifying individual religious and lay teachers and their schools and it points to the emergence of a professional graduate teaching force. The prominence of women teachers listed in the register reflects the increasing number of women graduates and the growth of girls' schools.

Molony vice-regal committee, 1918

The issue of salaries came to a head when in 1918 the Molony vice-regal committee on teacher salaries and conditions and 'on the distribution of grants made from public funds for intermediate education' was established.[1] The committee's report was published in March 1919 and although technically its brief was confined to salaries and finance, in fact it ranged over much wider educational issues. It advised that the minimum salary for teachers should be raised and that incremental payments and a pension scheme ought to be introduced. In order to co-ordinate provision of education at all levels, it was recommended that a single central board of education be established along with local education authorities.

MacPherson education bill, 1919

Influenced by the two major reports on educational provision (Killanin and Molony) which appeared in 1918 and which advised the setting up of a central

---

97 See John Coolahan, *The A.S.T.I. and post-primary education in Ireland, 1909–1984* (Dublin, 1984); the Dale and Stephens report noted that that average salary of a male secondary lay teacher was £82 6s. 7d. and that of a female secondary lay teacher was £48 2s. 7d. Since the majority of teachers in Catholic secondary schools were members of religious orders, the status of lay teachers was low. 98 *Bill to amend the law relating to secondary education in Ireland*, H.C. 1912–13 (219), ii, 879; H.C. 1914 (161), iii, 477; *Bill to amend the law relating to secondary education in Ireland*, H.C. 1912–13 (219), ii, 1879; H.C. 1914 (161), iii, 477. 99 *Register of the intermediate school teachers in Ireland* (Dublin, 1919). The postgraduate university higher diploma in education, which became the required professional qualification for secondary teachers was, as yet, not compulsory and only a minority of teachers in 1919 had obtained this diploma. The university education courses dated from 1898 in TCD and in the RUI, and from 1909 in the colleges of the NUI and QUB. 1 *Report of the vice-regal committee on the condition of service and remuneration of teachers in intermediate schools, and on the distribution of grants from the public funds for*

education authority, the government introduced the ill-fated MacPherson education bill in 1919.[2] Had it become an act of parliament, this bill would have abolished both the National and Intermediate Education Boards and placed primary and secondary education under a central education board, backed up by local education authorities. However, it was strongly opposed by the Catholic Church which feared a loss of its power and control over schools and also by nationalists who viewed the proposed central authority as another 'English board' and eventually the bill was withdrawn. Consequently, the Intermediate Board continued to operate until 1922 when its functions were subsumed into the Secondary Branch of the new Free State Department of Education. In Northern Ireland responsibility for secondary education passed to the new N.I. Ministry of Education and to the local education authorities established under the Londonderry Education Act, 1923.[3]

VIII. ENDOWED SCHOOLS

Wyse report, 1835 and Kildare endowed schools commission, 1857–8
As early as 1835, Thomas Wyse (1791–1862), MP for Waterford, chaired a parliamentary committee on the state of endowed schools.[4] The Wyse report presented a far-sighted plan for the development of Irish education, recommending that there should be a school in every parish, an academy in each county and a provincial college and agricultural school in each province. The report advised that the curriculum taught in these latter schools should include classical, commercial and scientific courses to meet the needs of the middle classes since

> to a well-educated and middle order the State must mainly be indebted for its intellectual and moral progress. Such a class is especially desirable in the present time in Ireland. Our Committee are of the opinion that a liberal, judicious and appropriate system of education for the middle class is the only means by which they can be enabled to acquire and maintain that proper position in society to which they are entitled, and by the maintenance of which the community can be fully protected against the chaos of internal disorder. They are further of the opinion that such a system is not likely to be provided as rapidly or extensively as may be required by voluntary effort; and that it thus becomes the duty of the legislature to intervene.[5]

intermediate education in Ireland [Molony committee] [Cmd 66], H.C. 1919, xxi, 645. The publication of the report coincided with that of the Killanin vice-regal committee on primary teachers' salaries.   **2** *Bill to further provision with respect to education in Ireland, and for other purposes connected therewith*, H.C. 1919 (214), i, 407; H.C. 1920 (25), i, 563. Macpherson was the Irish chief secretary in 1919.   **3** Education Act (Northern Ireland) 1923; Farren, *Politics of Irish education*, pp 59–85.   **4** Auchmuty, *Sir Thomas Wyse*; *Report from the select committee on foundation schools and education in Ireland*, H.C. 1836 (630), xiii, 1 (evidence); see also *Report from the select committee on foundation schools and education in Ireland* [Wyse report], H.C. 1837–8 (701), vii, 345.   **5** *Report from committee on foundation schools* [Wyse report], H.C. 1837–8 (701), vii, 64.

Among those interviewed were Revd Reuben Bryce, principal of Belfast Royal Academy and James Simpson, the Scottish educationalist. Although the Wyse report had little immediate effect, it probably influenced Robert Peel's decision to establish the provincial Queen's colleges in 1845.[6]

A further parliamentary report, the Kildare commission, was undertaken in 1857–8.[7] This commission was concerned with both primary and secondary school endowments and so schools of both levels were included. Secondary schools examined included diocesan free schools, royal free schools, Incorporated Society schools, grammar schools at Ballyroan, Bandon, Clonmel and Kilkenny, and grammar schools of the Erasmus Smith Trust at Drogheda, Ennis, Tipperary and Galway.[8] The diocesan colleges of Armagh, Belfast and Cavan were visited, as were Christian Brothers schools at Cork, Limerick and Tralee. The Belfast Academy and the Belfast Royal Academical Institution were also examined. The overall report was critical of the narrow classical curriculum taught in the schools:

> We are obliged to record our disapproval of the classical instruction hitherto pursued in grammar schools in Ireland, which, in our opinion, requires alteration in two important respects. In the first place, we think that the amount of time devoted to the study of dead languages has been so great; and in the second, that the knowledge of them ordinarily attained is very imperfect, and quite disproportionate to the labour expended upon the acquisition.[9]

The report recommended that more geography, history, mathematics and science should be included in the curriculum so as to provide the strong basis of a commercial education to which both Catholic and Protestant middle classes aspired.

The Kildare commission took evidence on the endowments in public courts held in towns across the country and witnesses were called. This evidence provides detailed information on a number of endowments and is useful for studying the origins of schools in specific localities. For example, in the public court at Waterford, a number of witnesses were called to give evidence on Bishop Foy's School (est. 1707). These included the Church of Ireland bishop of Cashel and the dean of Waterford, both trustees of the school, the master, physician, housekeeper/matron, parents and ex-pupils. Thus a graphic picture of conditions at the school in the mid-nineteenth century emerges.[10] The commissioners were critical of the poor

6 Moody & Beckett, *Queen's University, Belfast*, 1, lvii–lx.   **7** *Report of her majesty's commissioners appointed to inquire into the endowments* [Kildare commission], H.C. 1857–8 (2336–I–IV), xii, pts i–iv; *Separate report by Archibald John Stephens, Esq., one of the commissioners, conveyed in a letter to the Secretary of State for the Home Department*, H.C. 1857–8 (2345), xlvi, 409 (hereinafter *Separate report by Archibald John Stephens, Esq.*, H.C. 1857–8 (2345), xlvi, 409).   **8** See Wallace, *Faithful to our Trust*.   **9** *Report of her majesty's commissioners appointed to inquire into the endowments* [Kildare commission], H.C. 1857–8 (2336–I), xxii, pt i, 204.   **10** *Report of her majesty's commissioners appointed to inquire into the endowments* [Kildare commission], i, *Evidence taken before her majesty's commissioners of inquiry into the state*

standard of the buildings, which were described as dirty and unkempt. They criticized the lack of supervision by the governors, the bishop and dean of Waterford. Yet the picture of the school was neither entirely consistent nor negative as can be gleaned from the comments of Mr Arthur Sharman Crawford, one of the assistant commissioners, who visited the school in November 1855. He remarked:

> The amount of instruction professed to be given in this school is rather limited. When I visited it, I found the establishment in general good order, and in clean condition. A considerable sum of money has, within the last three months, been expended in putting the house in good condition; and I have no reason to suppose that, at the present time, the rules for the government which have been framed for the institution are not carried out. The bishop of Cashel informed me that the school is in much better order than it used to be, and that he had found it necessary to remonstrate with the master for neglect of duty. The bishop of Cashel himself pays frequent visits to the school when in Waterford and inquires into the management of the establishment and the progress of the pupils in secular and religious learning.
>
> The pupils answered … in English history as far as the reign of Edward I, but had not advanced farther. They answered well in mental arithmetic; one boy was able to answer satisfactorily in the first book of Euclid, but he was the only one who could do so …

Crawford suggested that the school's efficiency would be greatly enhanced if membership of the board of governors were increased to include a number of the city's residents. At the time when he was reporting there were only two members, namely the bishop and the dean, who were occasionally absent from Waterford. In their absence, nobody had authority to enforce proper discipline, or to inspect the school, and the master was unsupervised. Notwithstanding these difficulties, however, Crawford remarked

> with reference to the result of my examination into the secular instruction, that it appears that within the past few months, six of the oldest boys in the school, and who formed the first class, have been bound as apprentices. And therefore that the most advanced boys in the school at present, are only entering on the course of instruction given in the first class.[11]

In addition to calling public witnesses, the Kildare commission carried out a survey of endowed schools in each parish and this is particularly valuable for local studies. The survey listed details of the foundation of the endowment, acreage of

of the endowed schools in Ireland, H.C. 1857–8 (2336–II), xxii, pt ii, 861–913.   **11** *Report of her majesty's commissioners appointed to inquire into the endowments* [Kildare commission], iii, *Papers accompanying the report (tables of schools and endowments)*, H.C. 1857–8 (2336–IV), xxii, pt iv, 409.

the school site, names of trustees, the course of instruction, the appointment and salary of the teacher, the size of the school building, and the number of children on roll along with an indication of their religious denomination. Where it is relevant, a cross reference is provided to evidence given by witnesses in the public court of the commission. The commission appointed five assistant commissioners to visit the schools and collect relevant data regarding the endowments. Typically the endowed schools were managed by the local Church of Ireland rector, parish priest or local landlord. The salary was paid out of the endowment and often apartments and some land were included. The curriculum was limited to basic literacy in English and numeracy with some geography and religious instruction, either Catholic or Church of Ireland. A key feature of the 1850s was irregular attendance at school; the average daily attendance was sometimes below fifty per cent of those on roll. The children were often kept at home to work on the farm, to help with the harvest, or to look after younger children. Occasionally they were permitted to stay at home when inclement weather prevented them from walking to school. Some of the larger endowed schools enjoyed substantial endowments that were under-utilized, while others had poorly paid teachers and few facilities.

Mercer's School in Castleknock, Co. Dublin was founded in 1735 in fulfilment of a bequest made by Mary Mercer in her will. Additional provision was made for the school in the wills of Robert Lightbody in 1796 and Mary Lightbody in 1804. The acreage of the school lands was 747 acres, 2 perches, 15 roods and the annual income from the land was £531 3s. 5d. The school was established 'for the maintenance of as many Protestant children as the residue of the income will afford, after paying £92 6s. 2d. to the sick poor of the parishes of St Peter, St Bridget, St Nicholas Without and St Luke'. The course of instruction included reading, writing, grammar, arithmetic, English and Roman history, and, because it was a girls' school, plain and fancy needlework and knitting. Religious instruction consisted of 'Scripture history and Church catechism'. The matron in charge received a salary of £80 per annum, which was paid out of trust funds by the dean of Kildare, who was one of the trustees, and free 'apartments, fuel, candles and garden' were provided. The schoolroom was estimated to accommodate 160 girls and there was room for 28 boarders. When the assistant commissioner visited the school in October 1856 there were only 33 girls on roll, all of whom were of the United Church (Church of Ireland). The school was free but four pupils paid £12 per year. The assistant commissioner, F.W. McBlain, found the school to be in satisfactory order and he examined the girls in reading, geography, English history and grammar. However, he was very critical of the school premises and the lack of washing facilities, remarking that the school had 'no bathroom or water-closet'.[12]

---

12 *Report of her majesty's commissioners appointed to inquire into the endowments* [Kildare commission], iii, *Papers accompanying the report (tables of schools and endowments)*, H.C. 1857–8

The foundation and condition of the schools were recorded at parish level. Protestant parish schools were often found to be poor and offered a very limited curriculum. For example, in the parish of Rosenallis in Queen's County, there was one school, which had been founded in 1822 with a grant of £73 16s. 11d. from the lord lieutenant's fund, subscriptions totalling £36 18s. 5 ½d., and a grant from the marquis of Drogheda. The site of the school was one rood only and it was valued at £3 11s. 6d. The purpose of the school was 'for [a] resident schoolmaster to teach children, selected by the minister of the parish or the master, English and arithmetic under the regulation of the minister'. The course of instruction was 'reading, writing, English grammar, geography [and] arithmetic'. The master was paid a salary of £12 by the rector; the average attendance was sixteen but there were twenty-two on roll, of whom twenty were Church of Ireland and two were Catholics. The assistant commissioner found the school to be 'very unsatisfactory' because 'the girls in this school seem to receive very little instruction. Their reading is a mere attempt and they are not expected to parse. The arithmetical test textbook ([by] Thompson) is never used, and the school is altogether in a state of very imperfect efficiency'.[13] By contrast, in the parish of Rathdowney in the same county, Erill National School received a much more favourable report. Having established a connection with the National Board, this school was much better financed. It was founded in 1823 with a grant of £92 6s. 2d. from the lord lieutenant's fund, plus subscriptions of an equal amount and a grant of land from the local landlords, the Fitzpatricks. It had a site of one acre with an annual value of £6 11s. Here, the core curriculum consisted of 'reading, writing, English grammar, geography, arithmetic' and the 'Roman Catholic catechism for Roman Catholic children'. The master was appointed by the 'proprietors of the estate' and was paid a salary of £33 10s. of which £26 came from the National Board while the landlord, Mr Fitzpatrick, paid the remaining £7 10s. The master was also provided with 'apartments and land' valued at £5, plus school fees amounting to £5. The Erill schoolroom could accommodate 100 pupils. Average daily attendance was sixty. There were 151 children on roll, of whom 147 were Catholics and four Church of Ireland. The state of the school was reported to be satisfactory though it was remarked that the 'principles of arithmetic were not well known'.[14]

Despite the detailed work of the Kildare endowed schools commission, it had little immediate effect. The main concerns expressed in the report were the lack of provision of education for the middle classes, the narrow classical curriculum taught in the grammar schools and the lack of qualified candidates to attend the new colleges of the Queen's University. However, the report foundered on the issue of

(2336–IV), xxii, pt iv, 161–7, 41.   **13** *Report of her majesty's commissioners appointed to inquire into the endowments* [Kildare commission], iii, *Papers accompanying the report (tables of schools and endowments),* H.C. 1857–8 (2336–IV), xxii, pt iv, 206–7, 212. Thomson's *Arithmetic* was a standard school text of the period.   **14** *Report of her majesty's commissioners appointed to inquire into the endowments* [Kildare commission], iii, *Papers accompanying the report (tables of schools and endowments),* H.C. 1857–8 (2336–IV), xxii, pt iv, 204–5.

non-denominational education as it recommended the establishment of a State-supervised system of intermediate schools and a new central board with a supervisory role of schools and of endowments.[15] Concerned at these proposals, the Catholic Church stepped up its campaign for providing Catholic denominational education in the three sectors of primary, secondary and university.[16]

Reform of endowed schools

In 1878, along with setting up of the Intermediate Education Board and in a further effort to appease Catholic opinion, another endowed schools commission, this time chaired by Lord Rosse, was established to examine once again the existing educational endowments with a view to reforming and redistributing them more equitably.[17] The commission collected evidence from a range of endowed schools, most of which had been reviewed by the 1857–8 commission. Consequently, it is possible to trace the history of an individual school through these two commissions. The reports show how State accountability was slowly increasing, making these essentially private institutions conform to certain regulations regarding the proper use of their endowments. For example, in the case of Bishop Foy's School in Waterford, evidence was taken from the bishop of Cashel, from Mr Henry Mackesy, agent and treasurer for the Bishop Foy charity and from the headmaster, William Henry Smith.[18] In gathering evidence for Mercer's School in Castleknock, Co. Dublin, evidence was taken from three witnesses – Miss Kate Curtis, assistant mistress, Revd M.W. Jellett, secretary to the school and B.W. Rooke, agent for the Mercer estate.[19] The school was also visited by one of the assistant commissioners, Mr Hugh Keys Moore, who reported:

15 *Report of her majesty's commissioners appointed to inquire into the endowments* [Kildare commission], H.C. 1857–8 (2331–I), xxiii, pt 1, 267–84. Two of the commissioners, Archibald John Stephens and Henry George Hughes, refused to sign the report on the grounds that they considered the 'mixed education' of Catholics and Protestants unacceptable: see *Separate report by Archibald John Stephens*, H.C. 1857–8 (2345), xliv, 409. **16** Norman, *Catholic Church in the age of rebellion*, pp 52–85. A book published in 1859 by James Kavanagh, entitled *Mixed education: the Catholic case stated* significantly strengthened the Catholic campaign. Kavanagh had been a head inspector of the National Board and his book was highly critical of the national school system. **17** *Report of the commissioners appointed by the lord lieutenant of Ireland* [Rosse commission] [C 2831], H.C. 1881, xxx, 1. The Taunton Commission on endowed schools (see [C 3966], H.C. 1867–8, xxviii, pts i–xvii) had examined the endowed schools in England in 1867 and this report led to an Endowed Schools Act, 32 & 33 Vict. c. 56 (1869) which authorised major reform of endowed schools. **18** *Report of the commissioners appointed by the lord lieutenant of Ireland* [Rosse commission] [C 2831], H.C. 1881, xxxv, 976–90. The Rosse evidence is indexed both by person and by institution so it is easy to track an individual school. In addition each school was asked to submit a written report to the commission and these papers are deposited in the National Archives, Bishop Street, Dublin). **19** *Report of the commissioners appointed by the lord lieutenant of Ireland* [Rosse commission] [C 2831], H.C. 1881, xxxv, 230–4.

The institution impresses me as being in a highly satisfactory condition – both regards the education and the household arrangements. The answering of the thirty girls present, in all the English subjects, including history was excellent, while they were well instructed in music and drawing and a few in Latin. Six girls passed at the last intermediate examinations, two being on the prize list. The house is in good repair and the internal arrangements satisfactory with the exception of the infirmary and the lavatory.[20]

Tables of schools and endowments were listed for each county, giving details of the endowment, the trustees, course of instruction offered, the appointment of the master and his salary, the school-buildings and numbers of pupils attending with an indication of their religious denomination.

One of the more valuable sections of the Rosse commission is the critical report on endowed grammar schools penned by Dr J.P. Mahaffy of Trinity College Dublin.[21] Mahaffy visited a range of Protestant schools including the royal schools, the four Erasmus Smith grammar schools as well as smaller grammar schools such as Bishop Hodson's school in Elphin, Viscount Weymouth's in Carrickmacross and also new boarding schools such as Foyle College, Derry,[22] St Columba's College in Rathfarnham and the Methodist College, Belfast. The Catholic schools that he visited included St Malachy's in Belfast, the French College in Blackrock, Co. Dublin, and seven schools run by the Christian Brothers. Mahaffy was critical of the dissipation of endowments, the lack of inspection, the elderly headmasters and inexperienced assistant teachers, and the heavy weight that the intermediate examinations placed on students and teachers.[23]

As a result of the Rosse report and unlike the outcome to the earlier Kildare commission (1858), legislative powers were given to educational endowments commissioners by the Educational Endowments Act of 1885. These commissioners were empowered to investigate and to reconstitute the endowments of schools. The work was to take ten years to complete and included the division of the royal school endowments to provide for both Catholic and Protestant schools in Ulster.[24] The commissioners published annual reports, which contained the new schemes of endowments drawn up under the 1885 act. Evidence was given in open court by witnesses drawn from managers of educational trusts, principals and staff of the

---

20 Ibid., p. 268.   **21** W.B. Stanford & R.B. McDowell, *Mahaffy: a biography of an Anglo-Irishman* (London, 1971).   **22** Maurice Hime, headmaster of Foyle College, was author of a number of books on Irish schools including *Home education: Irish schools for Irish boys* (London, 1887).   **23** *Report of the commissioners appointed by the lord lieutenant of Ireland* [Rosse commission] [C 2831], H.C. 1881, xxxv, appendix A, 233–62. Mahaffy also visited a number of public schools in England including Winchester, Marlborough and Uppingham to compare them with Irish schools.   **24** *Bill entitled 'an Act to reorganize the educational endowments of Ireland'*, H.C. 1884–5 (176), i, 445; Wilkinson, 'The Educational endowments (Ireland) Act and its implication in intermediate schools of public foundation in Ulster, 1885–1900'; idem, 'Educational endowments Act (Ireland) 1885 as part of nineteenth-century educational reform' in *Irish Educational Studies*, 3:2 (1983), pp 98–121.

schools.[25] Schools that benefited from the re-organized endowment schemes included Alexandra College and School in Dublin, which was incorporated in 1887 (scheme no. 10), the Gilson Endowed School in Oldcastle, Co. Meath (scheme no. 56),[26] Monaghan Collegiate School (scheme no. 19), Kilkenny College (scheme no. 46)[27] and Rochelle School in Cork (scheme no. 52).[28] By far the most important scheme drawn up by the commissioners was no. 34 which divided the endowments of the Ulster royal schools with Catholic schools in each Ulster county. Local Protestant and Catholic boards of education were established to administer the endowments and Catholic schools benefited from a portion of the endowment.[29] These local boards were supervised by the commissioners of education, who inspected the schools and reported each year on their management and funding.[30]

IX. TECHNICAL EDUCATION

Technical education in Ireland received little State finance throughout the nineteenth century. The lack of industrial growth, except in the north-east around Belfast, and the high dependence on agriculture, meant that technical education was seen to have little practical value. In rural areas the failure of the National Board's scheme for agricultural schools during the 1860s and 1870s and the introduction of a classical academic curriculum by the Intermediate Education Board in the 1880s

---

25 See *Reports of the educational endowments (Ireland) commissioners, with proceedings; evidence and appendices: First report for 1885–6* [C 4903], H.C. 1886, xxvi, 89 to *Final report for 1894* [C 7517], H.C. 1894, xxx, pt 1, 469. These reports contain the minutes of evidence taken from witnesses in open court. From the 1870s the endowed schools are listed under a separate heading 'Endowed schools' in the index to the British parliamentary papers. Michael Quane published several articles on individual endowed schools and these are listed in R.J. Hayes (ed.), *Sources for the history of Irish civilization: articles in Irish periodicals* (9 vols, Boston, MA, 1970), iv, 546–7, for example, 'Dundalk Grammar School' in *Louth Arch. Soc. Jn.*, xvi, no. 2 (1966), pp 91–102; 'Drogheda Grammar School' in *Louth Arch. Soc. Jn.*, 15:3 (1963), pp 207–48; 'Hibernian Marine School' in *Dublin Hist. Rec.*, 21:2 (1967), pp 67–78; 'Celbridge Collegiate School' in *Kildare Arch. Soc. Jn.*, 14 (1969), pp 397–414. **26** Christopher F. McCormack, *The Gilson Endowed School, Oldcastle Co. Meath: the story of a school's search for identity* (Kells, 2002). **27** Howard Welch, 'A history of Kilkenny College, 1538–1903' (unpublished PhD thesis, TCD, 2002); Whiteside & Whiteside, *History of Kilkenny College.* **28** W.R. Wilkinson, *Our good school upon the hill: Monaghan Collegiate School, formerly Monaghan Diocesan School* (Monaghan, 1982). **29** The Ulster Royal schools were Armagh, Dungannon, Portora, Enniskillen, Cavan, Raphoe and there were two further endowments, Carysfort Royal, Co. Wicklow and Banagher Royal in King's County. The Catholic schools which benefited from the divided Royal endowments were St Patrick's College in Armagh, St Patrick's College in Cavan, St Macarten's Seminary in Monaghan, St Patrick's College in Dungannnon, St Eunan's in Letterkenny, and St Michael's College in Enniskillen. The Carysfort royal endowment was divided among schools in Arklow, Co. Wicklow. **30** See, for example, *Annual report of the commissioners of education in Ireland for the year 1903*, pp 21–39 [C 2078], H.C. 1904, xx, 807.

resulted in the creation of a separate technical education structure. However, the main impetus for establishing technical schools did not come until after the setting up of the Department of Agriculture and Technical Instruction (DATI) in 1899.[31] Technical education, therefore, developed on a county authority basis with the establishment of local technical instruction committees (TICs), which received guidance and financial support from the DATI. The presence of a technical school in a town had a marked influence on the expansion of educational opportunities within a locality. It offered further education opportunities to those aged fourteen and older as well as adult evening classes. In addition, a group of peripatetic teachers travelled around the county, offering a range of practical and literary courses. As a consequence, after 1900 'the tech' as these technical schools were commonly known, represented an important element in the development of educational provision in local communities throughout Ireland.

The leading scientific and technical institution in Ireland was the Royal Dublin Society, founded in 1713 'to improve husbandry, manufactures and useful arts'. It encouraged the development of agriculture, opened the Botanic Gardens in Glasnevin, founded a school of art in 1746 and housed a large library in Leinster House, Kildare Street, where it had its offices from 1810 onwards.[32] In the 1830s mechanics institutes, which offered education to artisans in the scientific principles underlying the trades, were established in Belfast, Dublin, Cork and Galway.[33] In 1845 the Museum of Irish Industry was founded in St Stephen's Green. It hosted lectures in science and sponsored a number of professorships and eventually developed into the College of Science in 1867.[34]

The British government's establishment of a new Science and Art Department at South Kensington in 1856 was significant for the promotion of education in Ireland as the department offered Irish students grants for attendance at science and art classes and provided a series of examinations in science and art. In Ireland the grants were taken up by primary and secondary schools and encouraged teaching in these areas. The department's annual reports contain lists of the Irish

31 *A bill for the establishing of a Department of Agriculture and other industries and technical instruction in Ireland, and for other purposes connected therewith*, H.C. 1899 (180), i, 55. **32** T. Meenan, *The Royal Dublin Society, 1731–1931* (Dublin, 1970). **33** Kieran Byrne, 'Mechanic Institutes in Ireland, 1825–1850' in *Proceedings of the Educational Studies Association of Ireland Conference, 1979* (Dublin, 1980), pp 32–47. **34** J.J. Lee, 'Technical education and change in Irish society' in John Logan (ed.), *Teachers' Union of Ireland: the T.U.I. and its forerunners in Irish education, 1899–1994* (Dublin, 1999), pp 1–15; W.P. Coyne, 'Science teaching and technical instruction' in idem (ed.), *Ireland: industrial & agricultural*, pp 155–74. Sir Robert Kane was the first director of the museum and author of the influential book, *The industrial resources of Ireland* (Dublin, 1844). He later became president of Queen's College, Cork: see Deasmumhan Ó Raghallaigh, *Sir Robert Kane, first president of Queen's College, Cork: a pioneer in science, industry and commerce* (Cork, 1942); *Report of select committee on scientific institutions (Dublin)*, H.C. 1864 (495), xiii, 1; *Report of the commission on the College of Science, Dublin*, H.C. 1867 (219), lv, 771; Clara Cullen, 'The Museum of Irish industry, Robert Kane and education for all in the Dublin of the 1850s and 1860s' in *History of Education*, 38:1 (Jan. 2009), pp 99–114.

schools in receipt of grants along with their examination results. Such was its success that in 1868 a commission was appointed to examine whether a separate science and art department should be set up in Dublin to serve Irish schools. The report decided against it, much to the disappointment of the Irish lobby. It was argued that the 'imperial' qualifications offered by London would have higher academic status that examinations based in Dublin.[35] In 1867 the Museum of Irish Industry was transformed into the (Royal) College of Science and was taken over by the Science and Art Department. Ten years later the Royal Dublin Society School of Art and Drawing passed under the department's control and became the Metropolitan School of Art.[36]

The Samuelson royal commission on technical education (1881–4) stressed the urgent need for support for technical education in Ireland and submitted a separate Irish report.[37] This report, which situated Irish technical education within the context of technical education in Britain, showed the great need for technical development to support the Irish economy. The Technical instruction Act (1889) that followed empowered local authorities to raise a technical education rate and, in the absence of a county council administrative structure, the municipal authorities of Dublin, Belfast, Galway, Limerick and Cork opened technical schools.[38] Soon after, the Local Government Act (1898), which established urban and county authorities, allowed technical education (unlike primary or secondary education) to be structured on a local county basis.

However, the most significant development in advancing technical education in Ireland did not occur until after the establishment in 1899 of the Irish Department of Agriculture and Technical Instruction as a central funding and administrative board. In 1896 Sir Horace Plunkett, the pioneer of technical education and founder of the co-operative movement in Ireland, set up a conference of his fellow Irish

---

35 *Report of the commission on the Science and Art Department in Ireland* [C 4103–I], H.C. 1868–9, xxiv, 2 vols –1, *Report, 2, Minutes of evidence, appendix and index*.   **36** John Turpin, *A school of art in Dublin from the eighteenth century, 1746–1995* (Dublin, 1995).   **37** *First report of the royal commission on technical instruction* [C 3171], H.C. 1881, xxvii, 153; see also further reports with evidence and appendices [C 3981], H.C. 1884, xxix, xxx, xxxi, xxxi, pt 1. The second report of the commission ([C 3981], H.C. 1884, xxx), contains a special section on Ireland; volume iii (1884, xxxi) features an article by Professor W.R. Sullivan, president of University College Cork, while volume iv (1884, xxxi, pt i) is devoted solely to evidence from Ireland. Witnesses called included Sir Patrick Keenan, resident commissioner of national education and Br James Burke, the science and technical pioneer teacher of the North Monastery Christian Brothers School, Cork: see Kelleher, *James Dominic Burke*. **38** The schools included Kevin Street Technical School, Dublin, Hastings Street Technical School, Belfast, and Crawford Municipal Schools of Science and Art and Technical Schools, Cork. See Kieran Byrne, 'Laying the foundations: the voluntary and State provision for technical education, 1730–1930' in Logan (ed.), *Teachers' Union of Ireland*, pp 16–36; Seán MacCartáin, 'Technical education in Ireland, 1870–1899' in McMillan (ed.), *Prometheus's fire*, pp 188–210; Jim Cooke, *Technical education and the foundation of the Dublin Trades Council, 1886–1986* (Dublin, 1987); Dublin Institute of Technology, *Kevin Street Technical College: one hundred years, 1887–1987* (Dublin, 1987).

members of parliament to examine Ireland's economic development and the role of technical education. This recess committee, so-called because it met during the parliamentary recess, recommended the establishment of a ministry of agriculture and industries for Ireland that would co-ordinate the work of scientific development and technical education.[39]

The DATI made marked progress under the leadership of its first vice-president, Sir Horace Plunkett, and its first secretary, T.P. Gill and by 1924 there were sixty-five technical schools operating under county and urban technical instruction committees.[40] The department also supported the teaching of science in secondary schools, gave grants to equip science laboratories and drew up a joint examination programme with the Intermediate Education Board.[41] Technical instructions committees were set up gradually in each county, each local scheme being sent first to the department for approval and sanction. In the first year twenty-four counties submitted schemes and five of these (Carlow, Fermanagh, Galway, Meath and Waterford) were approved by 1901. The City of Dublin Technical Instruction Committee became locked in a dispute with the DATI regarding the appointment of the principal of the new Bolton Street Technical School and consequently did not obtain sanction and funding for their scheme until 1912.[42]

---

39 *The Agricultural and Technical instruction (Ireland) Act*, 62 & 63 Vict., c. 50 (1899); *Report of the recess committee on the establishment of a Department of Agriculture and Industries in Ireland* (Dublin, 1896). The recess committee suggested that there should be seven departments in the new ministry whose priorities included 'promotion of agriculture and industries' and 'practical education'. Jim Cooke, 'Dublin Corporation and the development of technical education in Ireland' in McMillan (ed.), *Prometheus's fire*, pp 424–45. **40** Trevor West, *Horace Plunkett, co-operation and politics: an Irish biography* (Gerrards Cross & Washington, DC, 1986); W.P. Coyne, *Ireland: agricultural and industrial* (Dublin, 1902), W.P. Hoctor, *The Department's story: a history of the Department of Agriculture* (Dublin, 1971); *Technical education: essays in memory of Michael Clune* (Dublin, n.d.). The DATI took over the supervision of the institutions that had been previously under the control of the Science and Art Department, South Kensington. These were the Royal College of Science, the Metropolitan School of Art, the Science and Art Museum, the Botanic Gardens, the National Library, and the Royal Zoological Gardens. The DATI consisted of six branches – agricultural, technical instruction, fisheries, statistics and intelligence, veterinary, and accounts. An Agricultural Board and Technical Instruction Board comprised elected representatives of interest groups to oversee policy and finance. The members of the Technical Instruction Board were drawn for the county boroughs, provincial committees, urban councils of Dublin County, the commissioners of national education, the Intermediate Education Board and the Department itself. Members of the first board included Professor George Fitzgerald, the TCD physicist, Revd T.A. Finlay, political economist of University College, Dublin and Dr W.J. Starkie of the Board of National Education. **41** *First report of the Department of Agriculture and Technical Instruction in Ireland, 1900–01*, 51–72, 180–203 [CD 833], H.C. 1902, xx, 511. **42** Ibid. The annual reports of the DATI are listed under the heading of 'Agriculture' in the British parliamentary papers. The records of local technical instruction committees are to be found in local authority archives such as those of Dublin City and Galway City. See also Jim Cooke, 'The dispute between the Department of Agriculture and Technical Instruction and the City of Dublin Technical Instruction Committee, 1901–12' in *Technical education: essays dedicated to the memory of Michael Clune*, pp 47–61.

The DATI (commonly called 'the Department') developed its own series of technical examinations and published annual reports which listed the technical schools in receipt of grants along with their examination results and reported on the institutions of science and art that were under its care. It also published a journal featuring short articles written by DATI staff among others. For example, George Fletcher, DATI's assistant secretary for technical instruction, contributed a series of articles on the teaching of science and the role of technical education in industrial growth. (See, for example, 'The place of science in a general education' (1906) and 'A decade of technical instruction in Ireland' (1912).) Another series of articles, which dealt with the building of new technical schools and the adaptation of other older buildings, incorporated photographs of the specialist rooms for science, domestic economy, art and woodwork. The articles, written by school principals, were intended 'to be of interest and value in view of future developments in towns in which permanent buildings have not yet been provided'. Among the technical schools featured were those at Ballymena, Newry, Newtownards, Clonmel and Queenstown where old buildings had been adapted[43] and also new, larger municipal schools such as the Central Technical Institute in Waterford, Dundalk's Municipal Technical School and the Municipal Technical School in Londonderry.[44] The fact that some of these new schools had expensive purpose-designed buildings helped raise the status of technical education within the local community. Annual reports on the work of the Albert College in Glasnevin, and the opening of the Royal College of Science building on Merrion Street in 1911, published in the journal, were also relevant to technical education.[45]

Digby committee of inquiry, 1907
Despite its efforts, the DATI came under criticism for the impoverished nature of technical education, the slow progress made by the local technical instructions committees and the policy of employing a large number of Englishmen on its staff.[46]

---

43 P.F. Gillies, 'Technical instruction in Ballymena' in *Journal of the D.A.T.I.*, 8:2 (Jan 1908), pp 260–72; E. Holden, 'Technical instruction in Newry' in ibid., 9:1 (Oct. 1908), pp 76–91; Philip A. Cole, 'Technical instruction in Newtownards' in ibid., 11:3 (Apr. 1911), pp 462–71; Cecil Webb, 'Technical instruction in Clonmel' in ibid., 11:4 (July, 1911), pp 687–96; George Thompson, 'Technical instruction in Queenstown' in ibid., 8:3 (Apr. 1908), pp 465–78. **44** F.C. Forth, 'Technical instruction in Belfast' in ibid., 7:3 (Apr. 1907), pp 457–73; B. O'Shaughnessy, 'Technical instruction in Waterford' in ibid., 8:4 (July 1908), pp 666–79; J. Pyper, 'Technical education in Bangor, Co. Down' in ibid., 12:1 (Oct. 1911), pp 41–51; A.E. Easthope, 'Technical instruction in Dundalk' in ibid., 8:4 (July 1908), pp 666–79; G.E. Armstrong, 'Technical instruction in Londonderry' in ibid., 11:1 (Oct. 1910), pp 32–46; J. Comerton, 'Technical education in Limerick' in ibid., 12:3 (Apr. 1912), pp 532–49; J. Grindley, 'Technical education in Cork' in ibid., 12:4 (July 1912), pp 720–31; T. Clearkin, 'Technical education in Larne' in ibid., 13:1 (Oct. 1912), pp 60–75. **45** Anon., 'Opening of the Royal College of Science building' in ibid., 12:1 (Oct. 1911), pp 3–10. The records of the Royal College of Science for Ireland (1867–1926) and of the Albert Agricultural College (1838–1926) are held in the Archives Department, University College, Dublin. **46** The first assistant secretary in respect of technical instruction in the DATI was an

It came to be seen as an attempt to 'kill home rule by kindness' and so was unpopular among nationalists. In 1907 a government inquiry, chaired by Sir Edward Digby, was set up to conduct a critical examination of the department's work and in particular the role of its president, Sir Horace Plunkett.[47] Evidence was taken from a large number of witnesses drawn from each county on the work of local technical instruction committees, and thus the report provides a detailed survey of the progress of technical education at grassroots level. Among the witnesses called were F.C. Forth, principal of Belfast Municipal Technical Institute, Sir James Henderson, chairman of the Belfast Library and Technical Instruction Committee, John Mulligan, chairman of the City of Dublin Technical Instruction Committee and Mr Harry Clifton, representative of the Association of Technical Institutes of Ireland.[48]

Though the Digby report itself vindicated the work of the department and of its president, Plunkett chose to resign even before the final report was published, and the momentum of the department's work slowed down. T.W. Russell became vice-president and T.P. Gill continued as secretary until his retirement in 1919.[49] In 1924 the Department of Agriculture was set up and responsibility for technical education was transferred to the technical branch of the new Department of Education.[50]

X. UNIVERSITY EDUCATION IN THE NINETEENTH CENTURY

University education in nineteenth-century Ireland was the privilege of a male elite and until the growth of secondary education in the mid-century, demand remained limited. While the development of university education has little specific

Englishman, Robert Blair, who later became the first chief executive officer of the Education committee of the London County Council. See D.W. Thoms, *Policy making in education: Robert Blair and the London County Council* (Leeds, 1980). Blair was followed as assistant secretary in 1904 by George Fletcher from Derby who had been an inspector with the Science and Art Department, South Kensington. Unlike Blair, Fletcher worked with the DATI in Dublin throughout his career, making a major contribution to the development of Irish science and technical education. See Susan M. Parkes, 'George Fletcher and technical education in Ireland, 1900–27' in *Irish Educational Studies*, 9:1 (1990), pp 13–30; Jim Cooke, *A history of the Irish Vocational Association, 1902–2002* (Dublin, 2009). **47** *Report of the departmental committee of inquiry into the provision of the Agriculture and Technical instruction Act, 1899* [Digby committee] [Cd 3572], H.C. 1907, xvii, 799; *Minority report* [Cd 3575], H.C. 1907, xxvii, 963; *Evidence* [Cd 3574], H.C. 1907, xxvii, 1; *Appendix* [Cd 3573], H.C. 1907, xviii, 501. A minority report was presented by W.A. Micks of the Local Government Board, demanding the setting up of a new development board to take over part of the work of the DATI. **48** *Report of the departmental committee of inquiry into Agriculture and Technical instruction Act, 1899* [Digby committee], *Evidence* [C 3574], H.C. 1907, xvii, 1, pp 527–32, 521–4, 756–62, 762–3. **49** T.P. Gill was author of a number of pamphlets including *The needs of technical education Ireland: address at Blackrock Technical School prizegiving* (Dublin, 1917), *Character and educational efficiency in Ireland: address to the British Association at Dublin, September 7, 1908* (Dublin, 1908) and *Education and citizenship: with special reference to the labour problem* (Dublin, 1913). **50** In 1930, under the Vocational

relevance for researchers interested in the history of most localities in Ireland, the existence of a university college in a town or city inevitably influenced the life of the local community whether in Dublin, Belfast, Cork or Galway. A university college attracted educated teaching staff, gave employment to ancillary staff, and drew in students from the surrounding catchment area. The founding of the secular, non-residential and State-funded Queen's colleges in Belfast, Cork and Galway in 1845 marked the beginning of a plan to broaden access to third-level education to a much greater number of students. However, it also marked the beginning of a long political struggle between Church and State, commonly known as 'the Irish university question', whereby each party fought for control over the provision of university education for the Catholic laity. This bitter controversy hindered the growth of university education in the nineteenth century and a compromise solution was not reached until the Universities' Act of 1908.[51]

Trinity College, Dublin, University of Dublin
In 1800 there was only one university in Ireland, Trinity College, Dublin, University of Dublin, founded in 1592. After repeal of the penal laws at the end of the eighteenth century Catholics and dissenters were allowed to enter, but the college remained a privileged Protestant institution.[52] Meanwhile in Belfast there was growing prosperity among the middle class, and in 1810 the Belfast Academical Institution was founded. Although efforts were made to develop it into a university-style college for the city, these were slow in yielding results.[53] Following on his 1837 report on foundation schools, Sir Thomas Wyse, MP wrote to the government in 1841, stressing the need for provincial colleges of higher education.[54]

Queen's colleges, 1845
In 1845 a major attempt was made to provide both general and professional education for the middle classes, Catholic and Protestant, through the foundation of the three Queen's colleges in Belfast, Cork and Galway which together comprised the Queen's University of Ireland. These colleges were less expensive to attend than Trinity College, Dublin. However, the Catholic Church, under the leadership the new Catholic archbishop of Dublin, Dr Paul Cullen, objected to

Education Act, the technical instruction committees were replaced by the Vocational education committees, which had extended powers including the provision of continuation education. See *Department of Education report, 1930–31* (P. 733), pp 5–67. **51** *Bill to enable her majesty to endow new colleges for the advancement of learning in Ireland*, H.C. 1845 (299) (400), i, 357, 365; Moody & Beckett, *Queen's, Belfast, 1845–1949*. **52** McDowell & Webb, *Trinity College, Dublin*; *Report of the commissioners to inquire into the state, discipline, studies and revenues of the University of Dublin, and Trinity College*, H.C. 1852–3 (1637), xlv, 1: *Bill to abolish tests in Trinity College, Dublin, and the University of Dublin*, H.C. 1873 (no. 3) (124), vi, 375. **53** Moody & Beckett, *Queen's, Belfast, 1845–1949*, I, xliv–liii; *Fourth report of the commissioners of Irish education inquiry, Belfast Academical Institution*, H.C. 1825 (89), xiii, 157. **54** *Letter to Lord Morpeth by T. Wyse, M.P., May 1841, relative to the establishment of provincial colleges*, H.C. 1843 (446), li, 339.

these so-called 'godless colleges' and in 1850 the Queen's colleges were condemned by the Catholic Synod of Thurles and by a papal rescript. Catholics were forbidden to attend or to teach in them.[55] Attendance at the Queen's colleges, therefore, remained low, except for Belfast where the Presbyterian community supported the college. As State-funded institutions the Queen's colleges were required to present annual reports to parliament and these reports by the three presidents provide valuable details of the attendance figures of students along with an indication of their religious persuasion, the names and salaries of staff, academic achievements of graduates and finances.[56] For example, in the decade 1849–59, the average attendance at the three colleges was 421 students, of which 189 were at Belfast, 147 were at Cork and 85 at Galway. For the decade 1896–7 the average attendance had risen to 806, of whom 400 were at Belfast, 211 at Cork, and 128 at Galway. The annual reports of the Queen's University contain the names of graduates and the degrees awarded.[57]

The cost of running these colleges which had such low attendance rates led to public criticism and a government inquiry was set up in 1857. It concluded that the reasons for low attendance were the aftermath of the 1845 Great Famine, the lack of secondary education and opposition from the Catholic hierarchy.[58] However, the colleges survived and continued to offer limited third-level educational opportunity in the three provincial cities.[59] The Catholic Church's opposition to 'secular education' became a united campaign against the National Board's model schools, the Marlborough Street Training Institution and the Queen's colleges. The Catholic hierarchy made a determined effort to provide alternative educational institutions, particularly in cities such as Galway where State-funded institutions were located. In 1865 only nineteen Catholic students were among the forty-nine entrants to Queen's College, Galway, while at the model school no Catholic student attended.[60]

55 *Battersby's Catholic directory* (Dublin, 1853), pp 148–9; John Murphy, *The college: a history of Queen's/University College, Cork* (Cork, 1995); Tadhg Foley, *From Queen's College to National University: essays on the academic history of QCG/UCG/NUI* (Dublin, 1999). **56** *Report of the president of Queen's College, Belfast, for the academic year 1849–50*, H.C. 1850 (1272), xxv, 715; *Report of the president of Queen's College, Cork, for the academic year 1849–50*, H.C. 1850 (1272), xxv, 717; *Report of the president of Queen's College, Galway, for the academic year 1849–50*, H.C. (1272), xxv, 719. **57** Moody & Beckett, *Queen's, Belfast, 1845–1949*, i, 140; *Report on the condition and progress of the Queen's University in Ireland for the year 1852*, H.C. 1852–53 (1561), xliii, 477; *Report on the condition and progress of the Queen's University for the year 1881–82*, H.C. 1881–2 (3289), xxiv, 535. **58** *Report of the commissioners appointed to inquire into the progress and condition of the queen's colleges at Belfast, Cork and Galway, with minutes of evidence, documents, table and returns*, H.C. 1857–8 (2413), xxi, 53. **59** There was a further report on the queen's colleges in 1884; see *Report of the commissioners appointed by the lord lieutenant to inquire into certain matters affecting the well being and efficiency of the queen's colleges in Ireland* [C 4313], H.C. 1884–5, xxxv, 1. **60** *Report of the president of Queen's College, Galway, for the session, 1902–03* [Cd 1871], H.C. 1904, xx, 111.

Catholic University of Ireland, 1854

In 1854, in an important effort to provide acceptable higher education for Catholics, the Catholic hierarchy established the Catholic University of Ireland with the Oxford movement academic (Cardinal) John Henry Newman as the first rector.[61] However, the university failed to flourish, due partly to a lack of qualified young Catholic students who could attend, and partly owing to differences about management between Newman and the Irish hierarchy led by Archbishop Cullen. Consequently, in 1858 Newman retired back to England. However, Newman's ideals of a liberal university education, which he articulated in his now famous lectures, 'The idea of a University', delivered in Dublin in 1852, became an inspiration to future generations of educators.[62] The most successful department of the Catholic University was the medical school in Cecilia Street, Dublin.[63] The Catholic University continued to exist but ultimately failed in its efforts to obtain a charter from the government. Therefore, the 'university question' reached an impasse and became a major political issue throughout the following fifty years.[64] In 1873 Gladstone's government attempted to find a solution to the 'university question' by creating a single University of Dublin which would have included Trinity College, a Catholic University College and the three Queen's colleges. However, the bill met with strong opposition, particularly from Trinity College, which would have lost its historic autonomy as the only college of the University for Dublin, and it was decisively defeated.[65]

Royal University of Ireland, 1879

In a compromise measure, the Royal University of Ireland (RUI) was established in 1879 as an examining university only, which meant that students from the three Queen's colleges and from the Catholic University in St Stephen's Green could enter for its degrees. Limited resources for teaching fellowships were made available to the four colleges and the numbers attending slowly increased. The Catholic University College was placed under the direction of the Jesuit order from 1883 and later became a flourishing institution under the leadership of Fr William Delany, S.J.[66]

61 F. McGrath, *Newman's university: idea and reality* (Dublin, 1931); Louis McRedmond, *Thrown among strangers: John Henry Newman in Ireland* (Dublin, 1990). **62** J.H. Newman, *The idea of a university* (London, 1857), ed. with notes by I. Ker (Oxford, 1976). **63** William Doolin, 'Catholic University school of medicine, 1855–1909' in Michael Tierney (ed.), *Struggle with fortune: a miscellany for the century of the Catholic University of Ireland, 1854–1954* (Dublin, 1954), pp 61–79. The records of the Catholic University of Ireland (1854–1911) are deposited in the Archives Department, University College, Dublin. **64** William Walsh, *The Irish university question: the Catholic case – selections from the speeches and writings of Archbishop William Walsh, archbishop of Dublin* (Dublin, 1897); T.W. Moody, 'The Irish university question in the nineteenth century' in *History*, 43:148 (1958), pp 90–109; Larkin, *Making of the Roman Catholic Church in Ireland.* **65** *Bill for the extension of university education in Ireland*, H.C. 1873 (55), vi, 329. **66** Thomas J. Morrissey, *Towards a national university: William Delany, S.J. (1853–1924). An era of initiative in Irish education* (Dublin, 1983); Tierney

RUI degrees were open to women for the first time and this had an important influence on the development of women's higher education.[67] The first women students graduated in 1884 and became leaders in the campaign for women to gain admission to men's colleges.[68] Reports of the Royal University of Ireland were published annually and contained lists of the degrees awarded along with numbers of men and women taking examinations. However, the RUI was regarded as a 'stop-gap' measure only and the Catholic hierarchy's demand for recognition of a Catholic University continued to be a major political issue.[69]

Irish Universities Act, 1908

In 1903 the Robertson commission on university education was established to examine once again the structure of university education. Although the commission could not agree on a single solution, the report recommended that the RUI should become a federal teaching university for both men and women.[70] The Universities' Act of 1908 established the National University of Ireland with three non-denominational and co-educational constituent colleges at Dublin, Cork and Galway. Queen's College, Belfast was elevated to become the Queen's University, Belfast.[71] Although both universities were legally non-denominational, the National University was accepted as 'a university for Catholics' while Queen's University, Belfast was seen as 'a university for Protestants'.[72] Trinity retained its privileged position as the sole college of the University of Dublin and admitted women to degree programmes in 1904.[73]

At the beginning of the twentieth century, therefore, a complex system of educational administration had evolved in Ireland in which there was little co-operation between the different sectors, each having responsibility for its own finance and administration. Following the struggle between Church and State in the nineteenth century for control and provision of education, a partnership had emerged: the State laid down the rules governing the distribution of central State

(ed.), *Struggle with fortune.*   **67** Raftery & Parkes, *Female education in Ireland,* pp 105–44. **68** Maria Luddy, *Women in Ireland, 1800–1918: a documentary history* (Cork, 1995); Eibhlín Breathnach, 'Charting new waters: women's experience in high education, 1879–1908' in Cullen (ed.), *Girls don't do honours,* pp 55–78.   **69** Thomas J. Morrissey, *William J. Walsh, archbishop of Dublin, 1841–1921* (Dublin, 2000).   **70** See *Report of the royal commission on university education (Ireland)* [Cd 825–6], H.C. 1902, xxxi, 21; *Second report* [C 899–900], H.C. 1902, xxxi, 459; *Third report* [Cd 1228–9], H.C. 1902, xxxii, 1; *Final report* [Cd 1483–4], H.C. 1903, xxxii, 1. The administrative records of the RUI are held in the offices of the National University of Ireland, Merrion Square, Dublin, including the minutes of the Senate, copy of letter books (1880–1908), calendars and examination papers.   **71** *Bill to make further provision with respect to university education in Ireland,* H.C. 1908 (184), ii, 1057; *Irish universities bill as amended by standing committee,* H.C. 1908 (35), ii, 1075; *Lords amendment to the Irish universities bill,* H.C. 1908 (358), ii, 1097; Irish Universities Act, 1908, 8. Edw. VII, c. 38. **72** Donal McCartney, *UCD: a national idea. The history of University College Dublin* (Dublin, 1999).   **73** Kenneth Bailey, *A history of Trinity College, Dublin, 1892–1945* (Dublin, 1945); Susan M. Parkes (ed.), '*A danger to the men? The history of women in Trinity College, Dublin, 1904–2004* (Dublin, 2004).

funding while responsibility for management and provision of education rested at local level. Primary national schools were based on Church parishes, secondary schools on voluntary bodies and religious orders, and technical education on local authorities. The failure of the 1919 bill to re-organize the structure of Irish education meant that this triple-level structure was inherited by the Irish Free State government and by the Northern Ireland Ministry of Education in 1922. A Department of Education headed by a minister for education was established in 1924 with separate branches responsible for primary, secondary, and technical education. The partnership of Church and State was retained. The most radical changes made by the Free State government were in the school curriculum as the Irish language, Irish history and geography became compulsory core subjects. In Northern Ireland there was greater degree of structural change: a Ministry of Education was established in 1923 along with new local education authorities which had responsibility for the three sectors, primary, secondary and technical education.[74]

74 Farren, *Politics of education.*

CHAPTER 2

Primary sources for the history of Irish education

I. PRINTED GUIDES

There are a number of useful guides which provide a good introduction to the primary sources available for the history of education. These are to be found in most public and college libraries. The most useful general guide to sources is Seamus Helferty and Raymond Refaussé (eds), *Directory of Irish archives* (4th ed., Dublin, 2003) which lists the archival repositories in Ireland, both north and south, with a summary of their contents. The guide also lists the address, e-mail, opening hours and contact telephone number/website of each depository. (For many of the private archive collections it is necessary to make a prior appointment to visit.) The directory outlines the major collections in public archives such as the National Library of Ireland and the National Archives of Ireland as well as in local authority archives such as Dublin City Archives, Cork Archives Institute and Cavan County Archives. The libraries of the universities, the Royal Irish Academy and Archbishop Marsh's Library, Dublin, as well as in the educational archives of religious orders, including for instance, the Mercy Congregational archives, the Irish Jesuit archive and the Holy Ghost Congregation archives, all in Dublin, are listed. The archives of individual schools such as Alexandra College, The King's Hospital, The High School (all in Dublin), Glenstal Abbey, Limerick, St Kieran's College, Kilkenny and those of diocesan colleges such as St Patrick's College, Thurles and St Finian's College, Mullingar also feature in this directory.

Another useful guide for educational sources is R.J. Hayes (ed.), *Manuscript sources for the history of Irish civilisation* (12 vols, Boston, MA, 1964) and *Manuscript sources for the history of Irish civilisation: first supplement* (3 vols, Boston, MA, 1979). These volumes are organized under both person and place so the relevant manuscript sources for a specific area can be easily located. Hayes's *Sources for the history of Irish civilisation: articles in Irish periodicals* (9 vols, Boston, MA, 1970), which lists articles published in Irish periodicals, is also useful for identifying articles of interest and relevance to historians. The entries are arranged by county, and within each county, places are listed in alphabetical order. It is important to consult relevant articles relating to the entire county as well as to a specific place within the county.

Susan M. Parkes's *Irish education in the British parliamentary papers in the nineteenth century and after, 1801–1920* (Cork, 1978) contains details of the important education bills and parliamentary education reports, including the reports of royal commissions such as the Powis commission on national schools (1870), the Palles commission on intermediate education (1898) and the Robertson commission on university education (1902). Also listed is a selection of the 'accounts and papers' referring to education which were presented to parliament. These short reports are listed under various headings such as 'school books', 'training and model schools', 'university education', 'convent schools', and so on. The British parliamentary papers are one of the main official sources for the study of Irish education in the nineteenth century and copies are to found in the major libraries such as the National Library and the university libraries. Parkes's guide lists the education sources under six headings – primary, intermediate, technical and university education as well as reformatory and industrial schools and the decennial population census returns for education. Reference numbers for parliamentary papers consist of four distinct elements: the date of the session, the paper command number (in parenthesis), the volume number (in roman numerals) and the page number; for example, *First report of the commissioners of Irish education inquiry*, HC 1825 (400), xii, 1. These reference numbers are essential for locating a particular report or paper. While the Parkes guide is a useful finding aid, researchers are advised to consult the official *General indexes to the British parliamentary papers* for a complete list of the education material available. There are nine volumes of these indexes: *General index to bills, estimates, accounts, 1801–52; General index to accounts and papers, 1801–52; General index to reports and select committees, 1801–52; General index to bills, reports, estimates, accounts and papers printed by order of the House of Commons, 1852–1869; General index to bills, reports, estimates, accounts and papers, printed by order of the House of Commons, 1870–79; General index of bills, reports estimates, accounts and papers, printed by order of the House of Commons, 1880–89; General index of bills, reports, estimates, accounts and papers printed by order of the House of Commons, 1890–99; General index to bills, estimates, reports accounts and papers, 1900–20.*[1] A database of the parliamentary papers relevant to Ireland is available on line from the Enhanced British Parliamentary Papers Project (www.eppi.ac.uk) and the full text of the parliamentary papers (H.C.P.P.) in available online.[2]

---

1 The general indexes for British parliamentary papers spanning the period 1800–1900 were reprinted by the Irish University Press (Shannon, 1968). The House of Commons parliamentary papers are also available on microfiche, published by Chadwyck-Healey (Cambridge, 1987) and essential guides to the microfiche edition are Peter Cockton's *House of Commons parliamentary papers, 1801–1900: guide to the Chadwyck-Healey microfiche edition* (Cambridge, 1991) and Cockton's *Subject catalogue of the House of Commons parliamentary papers, 1801–1900* (Cambridge, 1988), section iv, ch.13, sub-section 'education' which includes papers relating to Ireland; see also P. & G. Ford, *Select list of British parliamentary papers, 1833–1899* (Oxford, 1953; repr. Shannon, 1969). The texts of parliamentary papers are now available online at http//:www.eppi.ac.uk. 2 For full text see http://parlipapers. chadwyck.co.uk/home.do.

A useful collection of printed documents relating to the history of Irish education is the three-volume *Irish educational documents* edited by Áine Hyland and Kenneth Milne (Dublin, 1987–8).[3] The first volume features material from earliest times to 1922; volume two covers the period from 1922 to 1990 and the third, edited by Áine Hyland, Kenneth Milne, Gordon Byrne and John Dallat, focuses on sources relating to Northern Ireland during the years 1922 to 1990. These collections contain extracts from official public documents of the nineteenth and twentieth centuries such as the Stanley Letter of 1831, the Intermediate Education Act of 1878, Irish Universities' Act of 1908, each with a short commentary, placing the document in its historical context. The extracts, which are taken from official papers, include education bills, acts, parliamentary commissions, annual reports and programmes of curriculum such as the payment by results programme of 1872 and the Revised programme of 1900. They are arranged under topic headings e.g. national education, intermediate education, technical education etc. Volume one also contains a short guide to research in the history of education by Kenneth Milne, and a guide to sources for educational history in the Public Record Office of Ireland (National Archives) by Ken Hannigan and in the Public Record Office of Northern Ireland by Trevor Parkhill. These volumes provide a very useful introduction to education sources.

Maria Luddy's *Women in Ireland, 1800–1918: a documentary history* (Cork, 1995) contains a section relating to women's education (pp 89–156) which includes a wide variety of extracts from contemporary pamphlets such as Isabella M. Tod's *On the education of girls of the middle classes* (London, 1874), personal memoirs of school and university such as Mary Colum's *Life and the dream* (London, 1947), and extracts on the conditions of schools taken from the reformatories and industrial schools commission of 1884. *The national school system, 1831–1924: facsimile documents* (Dublin, 1984), published by Public Record Office of Ireland (now the National Archives), is a useful short guide to the type of records available in the public archives. The facsimile documents include a contemporary copy of the Stanley Letter of 1831, an application form for aid for building a national school in Rathmines in Dublin (1832) and a section of the annual results report for the male national school in Gort, Co. Galway in 1877.

The Women's History Project, under the direction of Professor Maria Luddy, published *A directory of sources for women's history*, together with a CD–ROM and internet database, which is a valuable finding aid. The directory can be searched by topic such as 'female education' or by name of person.[4] Lists of research theses on education (including history of education) are to be found in the *Register of theses on educational topics in universities in Ireland* compiled by the Educational Studies Association of Ireland (ESAI). These lists indicate the range of topics in the history of Irish education which have been the subject of masters and doctoral

3 Hyland & Milne (eds), *Irish educational documents*, ii; Hyland, Milne, Byrne & Dallat (eds), *Irish educational documents*, iii. **4** The database of the directory of sources for women's history can be accessed at http:// www.nationalarchives.ie/wh/sources.html.

dissertations and these can be accessed through university libraries and by inter-
library loan. Much research has been undertaken in the history of education field
in recent years, particularly national education. The first ESAI register of theses
was produced in 1980 and contained a list of postgraduates' research topics for the
period 1911 to 1979. The second volume covered the decade 1980 to 1990 and
also features a bibliography of articles published in the *Irish Educational Studies*
journal from 1976 down to 1990. This journal is published by ESAI and by
Routledge/Taylor and Francis and features papers presented at the society's annual
conference. Articles on aspects of the history of education have appeared regularly.[5]
Among these are Deirdre Raftery's article 'Home education in nineteenth-century
Ireland: the role and status of the governess' (2000) which views the education and
duties of governesses and the work of the Governesses' Association of Ireland,
founded in 1866. Other relevant contributions include Maura O'Connor's 'Theories
on infant pedagogy of Dr Timothy Corcoran, professor of education, University
College, Dublin' which examines the influence of Professor Corcoran on the Irish
primary curriculum (2004); Margaret Ó hÓgartaigh's 'Books and baths and
run all the way: the cultural formation of female primary teachers in the early
twentieth century' which examines the daily life and routines of women's training
colleges (2004); and Thomas Walsh's 'The revised programme of instruction,
1900–22' which assesses implementation of the programme, its successes and
shortcomings (2007). The website of the Educational Studies Association of Ireland is
www.esai.ie, and plans are afoot to publish the register of theses on this site.

    The international journal *History of Education*, published by the History of
Education Society and Routledge/ Taylor and Francis, mostly contains articles on
British and European education but a number of articles relating to Irish
education have been published, notably those by Sean Farren on model schools
and Judith Hartford on the movement for the higher education of women in
Ireland.[6] In addition, the History of Education Society publishes the *History of
Education Researcher* (formerly *Bulletin*) and a recent article on Irish education is
Judith Harford's 'The movement for the higher education of women in Ireland:
the role of Margaret Byers and Victoria College'.[7] The *History of Education*

---

5 Many of these are listed under 'history of education' in Pádraig Hogan and Donald
Herron's bibliography of articles featured in *Irish Educational Studies* during the period 1976
to 1990: see this bibliography in *Register of theses on educational topics in universities in Ireland*,
ii, 1980–90 (Dublin, 1992), pp 97–126. Recent articles include Maura O'Connor, 'The
theories of infant pedagogy of Dr Timothy Corcoran, professor of education, University
College, Dublin' in *Irish Educational Studies*, 23:1 (spring/summer 2004), pp 35–48;
Margaret Ó hÓgartaigh, 'Books and baths and run all the way: the cultural formation of
female primary teachers in the early twentieth century' in ibid., 23:2 (autumn 2004), pp
55–64 and Thomas Walsh, 'The revised programme of instruction, 1900–22' in ibid., 26:2
(June 2007), pp 127–44.   6 Farren, 'Irish model schools, 1833–70: models of what?', pp
45–60; Judith Harford, 'The movement for the higher education of women in Ireland:
gender equality or denominational rivalry?' in *History of Education*, 34:5 (Apr. 2005), pp
473–92.   7 *History of Education Researcher*, 75 (May 2005), pp 39–47.

Researcher contains useful details of the activities of History of Education Society as well as book reviews, information on education archives and on research centres in history of education. Further details of the Society may be accessed at www.historyofeducation.org.uk

II. MANUSCRIPT SOURCES

(a) Public repositories

The National Archives of Ireland, Bishop Street, Dublin 8

www.nationalarchives.ie
The National Archives of Ireland (NAI) is the main public repository for sources relating to the history of Irish education. It holds an extensive collection of the records of the national school system as well as those of the Intermediate Education Board and endowed schools. The Chief Secretary's Office Registered Papers relate to government policy from 1800 onwards, as do as the Official Papers and the Council Papers. Records of the commissioners of charitable donations and bequests contain material on endowed schools; those of the Office of Public Works feature material on school buildings and public institutions, and the census returns for 1901 and 1911 include educational and literacy statistics.

The most extensive records in the National Archives are those of the commissioners of national education in Ireland from 1831 down to 1922. As outlined in chapter one, the national school system was administered from a central office in Marlborough Street, Dublin. Each national school, as it entered the system, was allocated a roll number and all correspondence relating to the school was filed under that number. Files pertaining to individual schools include initial applications, appointment, names and salaries of teachers, correspondence between the school manager and the National Board central office, and therefore are very useful for researching the history of a locality. There is a consolidated card index for all national schools, which contains details of the sources relating to each school in the ED/1, ED/2, and ED/9 files. The following are the main categories of material stored in this ED collection.

The ED/1 files are comprised of the initial applications for aid for schools made in the period 1832–90. They are bound chronologically by county and contain detailed information relating to the locality and to the existing educational provision there. Under the terms of the Stanley Letter the proposed site, size and layout of the school building and the terms of the lease had to be stated, along with the names of the local trustees. The estimated pupil attendance and the location of the other nearest schools in the district had to be given. Since the national system was intended to encourage interdenominational education, the signatures of both Protestant and Catholic supporters of the application, usually local clergy and gentry, were required.[8] Thus it is possible to ascertain from these applications the extent of support and opposition to the national system in an area and the names of the local landowners. In certain localities Protestant clergy and landlords refused to sign the sheet as they did not support the national system.[9] By the 1840s the application query sheet was changed so that joint signatures were no longer required and single denominational applications could be submitted. The Presbyterian clergy in particular were opposed to joint applications and to the clause in the application which gave consent to access to the school for all clergy to teach separate religious instruction. It was largely due to their opposition that the joint signatures requirement was dropped. Donald H. Akenson argues that failure of the National Board to insist on joint applications was one reason why the national system became denominational.[10]

There were two types of query sheet, one for 'the fitting-up of schools, the paying of teachers, and the obtaining of school requisites' and one for the 'building of a schoolhouse'. For example, the application form for the fitting-up of a school in Rosenallis and Reary, in Queen's County, was made in 1832. The two schools were already in existence (Rosenallis opened in 1830 and Reary in 1831). Both schools were under the direction of the parish priest, Revd John Byrne and his curate, Revd Timothy Dunne. It was recorded that the Rosenallis school house was 'ceiled and plastered, has a lime and sand floor, and wants to be dashed, is slated', while Reary school house was 'plastered and dashed but not ceiled, but has a bad earthen floor'. Rosenallis had fifteen desks and seats but Reary had no desks or seats apart from three borrowed ones. The teacher at Rosenallis was Florence McCarthy, who 'had learned the system' in Graignamanagh, Co. Kilkenny. She could teach reading writing 'both plain and ornamental', as well as arithmetic, book keeping, English grammar, geography, construction and drawing. At Reary, the master, Martin Fogarty, who 'learned the system' in Mountmellick, Queen's County, could teach reading, writing, and arithmetic. No mistress was employed in either school owing to a lack of resources. Other schools identified in the area included one 'only a few perches distant' which was connected with the Kildare Place Society and its patron was the Revd Thomas Pigott. The other was a hedge school, and the master was John Dunne. The school was '74th of a mile distant from Rosenallis and Reary distant 2¼ miles'. The poverty of this area was stressed in the appeal for funding:

> We humbly beg leave to state to your honourable board, that the bulk of the
> people in this parish are wretchedly poor and that the schools have not been

8 The National Board stated that it would look 'with peculiar favour' on joint applications from Protestant and Catholic clergymen, or from a clergyman of one denomination and laymen of the other, or laymen of both denominations. 9 See Hannigan (ed.), *The national school system, 1831–1924: facsimiles documents*, p. 30 for an example of a public notice, dated 1834, which was addressed to tenants in Co. Tyrone by Protestant landlords protesting strongly against the introduction of national schools. 10 Akenson, *Irish education experiment*, pp 161–87.

conducted on the improved system (though the teachers understand it) owing to want of books and school requisites. Therefore we would expect immediately for both schools, books and school requisites – about £14, to furnish Reary schools with desks and seats and to make the ceiling and floor, £5 to dash and repair Rosenallis, and in future a decent subscription for 2 masters and one mistress …[11]

The application query form was signed by fifteen Protestants of the neighbour-hood and by eleven Catholics, as was required by the National Board. However, the parish was granted only six pounds for salary and requisites for Rosenallis and the same for Reary with an addition of eight pounds for the purchase of forms and desks.[12]

Another example of an early application is one from Fethard, Co. Tipperary.[13] In 1825 there were thirteen schools in this town, the best being the Church of Ireland parish school. When the national school system came into operation, the rector, Mr Woodward, was so opposed to it that he refused to support applications tendered by others. However, Dr Michael Laffan, the parish priest of Fethard and Killusty, very quickly submitted an application to the Board in 1832, stressing that the parish schools had no other support than the parish funds. The master, Robert Blunden in Fethard, was paid only £20 per year, which sum was taken from the priest's salary. The schoolhouse was described as 'a thatched private house, 26ft x 16ft with two windows' and there were only three desks, three benches and some 'borrowed seats'. Nevertheless, the curriculum taught was quite extensive; among the books being used were Davis's English grammar, Voster's Arithmetic, Shannon's Geography lessons, Scott's Lessons, and Dr Butler's Catechism. Laffan requested aid for a salary for the teacher, plus three desks and forms which he estimated would cost around 100 shillings. Attached to the query sheet, written in fine copperplate hand, was the following note:

> We, the undersigned request to call your attention to the Catholic parish school established in this town, that the teacher thereof may get a salary from the government. There are 100 poor scholars educated in it (none for payment) for the tuition of whom the master is paid by Rev Dr Laffan, P.P.[14]

---

11 The 'improved system' was the monitorial system of class management. Desks were required for half the pupils who were writing while the other half stood for reading and spelling. See applications for aid towards building and fitting up schools, paying teachers and obtaining books and school requisites, 13 Apr. 1832 (NAI, ED 1/73/nos 11/12). **12** The Board's decision to grant (or refuse) aid was often noted on the query sheet by one of its officials. The decision to grant only partial aid shows that the Board was trying to encourage local initiative and co-operation (Ibid.). **13** Applications for aid towards building and fitting up of schools, etc., 10 Dec. 1832 (NAI, ED 1/81/no. 24); see Susan M. Parkes, 'Sources for the history of education in Co. Tipperary: a case-study from Fethard' in *Tipperary Historical Journal*, 5 (1992), pp 116–21. **14** Applications for aid towards the building and fitting-up of schools, etc., 1832 (NAI, ED 1/81/no. 24).

The initiative to apply so early to the National Board may have come from the teacher, Robert Blunden himself. In the 1825 report he was described as 'being educated by his father who superintended an excellent mathematical school in Fethard' and was therefore a well-educated man. Seventeen local men, both Protestants and Catholics, signed the application form, but the rector was not among the signatories.

Laffan failed to secure aid for the Fethard school in 1832 but was successful when next he applied in 1840. The school entered the national system as roll no. 2459 and Robert Blunden was awarded a salary grant of £8 per annum, plus a free stock of the National Board's lesson books for 125 children. The official reply to this successful application stated that 'local parties must provide at their own expense adequate furniture'. On the other hand, Laffan's application in 1832 for aid for Killusty school was positively received. In this instance, he applied for furniture, textbooks and a salary grant for the teacher 'to enable him to instruct a certain number of poor children, 40–50, who were destitute of the benefit of education'.[15] As in Fethard, the application form was signed by both Protestant and Catholic local men. However, in its response to the initial application, the Board demanded to know what furniture was required, and more seriously, why the signatures on the form had been all written in the same hand. Somewhat impatiently, Laffan replied to the 'Chief Secretary, Education, Dublin Castle', listing the furniture required as 'one desk and form 20 ft in length, six desks with forms attached 9 ft each, and four forms each 12 ft in length'. On the matter of the signatures, he explained: 'With regard to the signatures attached to the official queries, I beg to state that they were not written by the individuals themselves but with their approbation'. Although this was not in line with the National Board's guidelines, Killusty school nevertheless entered the national system as roll no. 598, making it one of the first national schools in the country.[16]

15 Applications for aid towards the building and fitting up of schools … etc., 2 Sept. 1832 (NAI, ED 1/81/no. 18 – Killusty National School).   **16** Ibid. Another early application came from nearby Cloneen (roll no. 548). Here, the schoolmaster took the initiative and completed and corrected the query sheet which was then submitted to the Board by the parish priest, Revd Fr Cornelius O'Brien. The submission requested aid not only for 'six desk and forms' and 'a desk for the master' but also for a grant to install an upper floor in the schoolhouse and build an outside stone staircase for the female pupils. The school's close proximity to the chapel displeased the Board; it was thought that such an arrange-ment would lead to the school being identified with one denomination. In its response to the application, the Board requested a 'plan of the chapel, chapel, schoolhouse' and queried the need for a stone staircase. The form was signed by one Protestant and by twelve Catholics. (The Revd Woodward refused to sign it 'as he discountenanced a system formed on such as basis'.) By 1852 there were 147 pupils on roll in Cloneen, 121 in Killusty and 119 boys in Fethard. A separate national school for girls (roll no. 6384) had been opened which had 116 pupils on roll. See *Appendix to the nineteenth report of the commissioners of national education in Ireland, for the year 1852*, 1, H.C. 1852–3 (1688), xliii, pt i, 508–11. See also Applications for aid towards the building and fitting up of schools … etc., 22 Mar. 1834 (NAI, ED 1/81/no. 48 – Cloneen National School).

Details recorded on these application query sheets show the difficulties that beset the national school system in its early days. Local opposition and lack of support militated again the preparation of joint applications. The lengthy application process and uncertainty around the prospect of obtaining a grant did little to encourage poor parishes, where schools were in greatest need of assistance, to apply. In an effort to consider applications in the form in which they were presented, the Board was prepared to overlook its own rules such as the requirement that a national school would not to be placed in close proximity to the church (particularly in instances when this was the only site available) and the stipulation that signatories of the application form had to be from both Catholic and Protestant denominations in the locality.[17] The Board did not have the authority to decide where schools ought to be built; it could only refuse an application for aid if there was another national school located within a three-mile radius. Therefore a network of small schools developed with little centralized planning and on a separate denomination basis, although on the positive side, this system afforded applicants autonomy at local level and helped foster a sense of parish ownership of the schools.

The ED/2 files contain school registers for the period 1835–1905. In these books, the National Board summarized its dealings with individual national schools. For the period 1835 to 1855, the schools are arranged by county and thereafter by inspectorial district. The registers contain Board orders, letters, and other communications with individual schools. Details for each school include its parish and town location, its proximity to religious houses, date of establishment and when it came under the supervision of the Board. Also listed are the names of clerical applicants (Church of Ireland, Presbyterian or Roman Catholic) and the number of lay applicants, together with an indication of their religious denomination. The history of a specific school can, therefore, be traced using these registers. Inspectors' comments on the schoolhouse or on pupils' attendance were recorded and correspondence with the manager summarized.[18]

The ED/3 files are registers of the district model schools, which similarly summarize the Board's dealings with each of these individual schools. In total Ireland had twenty-six district model schools and the files contain details of the building and construction of these schools, as well the names of teachers, their date of appointment and their salaries. The first district model schools were opened in 1849, two in Ulster (Newry and Ballymena) and two in Munster (Clonmel and Dunmanway). The last was built at Enniskillen in 1867. These registers contain preliminary correspondence regarding the lease of the proposed site and building of the schools. District model schools were built in response to local requests in towns where a suitable site could be found. Once established,

17 The National Board abandoned the query sheet in the 1840s and instead a Board inspector was sent to make a report on the application. 18 The state of repair of schoolhouses was a frequent problem as the responsibility for maintenance rested with the local manager: see NAI, ED/2, registers of National schools.

details of the running of the schools were recorded, including names, salaries, religious denomination, dates of appointment and resignation of teachers.[19] For example, a request for a model school in Waterford was first made in July 1851 in a memorial signed by the clergy, the mayor, and leading professional men in that city. The National Board replied that it was unable to respond positively to their request as during that year, model schools were being opened in Limerick and Kilkenny. Waterford would have to wait. To maintain the pressure, the Grand Jury of Waterford sent a second memorial to the National Board, stressing their support for the school. However, by December 1851, the Catholic bishop, Dr Nicholas Furlong, had stated his objections to the proposed model school and an address to that effect was circulated to Catholics in the city. Letters from Mr John Aloysisus Blake (later mayor of Waterford), assured the National Board of the general support for the school and so the plans went ahead. The model school eventually opened in 1855, albeit without the support of the city's Catholic community.[20]

The ED/4 and ED/5 files relate to teachers' salaries. ED/4 comprises salary books of the National Board that record salary payments to teachers in all national schools during the period 1834–1918. The teachers are listed under the name of their school and details of their appointment and earnings are given. Information concerning a teacher's previous work experience is also often recorded, thereby making it possible to trace an individual teacher's career. The costs of school requisites provided are also recorded. The ED/5 files record the same details for teachers in the country's model schools as does ED/6, which has been amalgamated with it.

The ED/7 files comprise twenty-six newspaper-cutting books, spanning the years 1854 to 1922, and relating to education. Compiled in the National Board Office in Marlborough Street, Dublin, these volumes are indexed and serve as a

---

19 Other district model schools were located in Trim, Coleraine, Bailieborough (1850), Galway, Athy (1852), Kilkenny (1854), Limerick, Waterford (1855), Ballymoney (1856), Belfast (1857), Londonderry, Enniscorthy (1862), Sligo (1863), and Cork (1865). In addition the Board built seven smaller minor model schools at Omagh, Parsonstown (1860), Carrickfergus, Monaghan, Newtownstewart (1861), Newtownards (1862) and Lurgan (1863). Files relating to the model schools in Ulster are held in PRONI (ED/8 and ED/12). **20** See *Royal commission of inquiry into primary education (Ireland)* [Powis commission], vii, *Returns from National Board* [C 6–VI], H.C. 1870, xxviii, pt v, 534–6. Waterford Model School made progress, but the attendance of Catholic pupils remained small. In 1863 there were 357 pupils on roll, of whom 180 were Catholics, 135 were Church of Ireland, 27 were Presbyterians and 15 were classed as 'others'. Quoting the *Waterford Mail*, the inspector commented on the achievements of the school: 'Were all national schools in Ireland as complete in every respect as the Waterford model school, it would leave but little to be looked for in the way of education for the lower classes. Each child receives not only a good secular education but religious instruction is given separately to each religious denomination every day, and the clergy each persuasion are specially invited each Friday to give such further religious as they may consider necessary …'. See *Appendices to the thirtieth report of the commissioners of national education in Ireland, for the year 1863*, i, H.C. 1864 (3351), xix, pt i, 144–9.

useful guide to educational topics covered in nineteenth-century newspapers. As such, they provide valuable insights into education policy issues of the day and contemporary attitudes of the press towards education. ED/8 is a miscellaneous collection of documents covering the period 1861 to 1912, which includes an index of teachers who qualified at the country's training colleges (1893–1907) and a list of teachers deemed competent to teach Irish in the years 1895 to 1916. The ED/9 school files represent a particularly important collection for scholars researching the history of individual schools since they contain references to the Board's correspondence relating to each national school. In addition to documents that deal with routine matters such as the appointment of school managers, these files often contain fascinating material concerning more colourful or controversial characters and events in a school's history, such as allegations of misconduct made against teachers. ED/10/1–5 is a contemporary index to the ED/9 files, which are numbered consecutively, but the consolidated card index of schools is the most useful finding aid.[21]

A growing number of records of individual national school have been deposited in the National Archives. These records, which can include registers and roll books, are of immense value to scholars researching the history of a specific school. Among records recently deposited in the National Archives are those relating to Ardara (Wood) National School, Co. Donegal (1949–94), Lettermacaward National School, also in Co. Donegal (1886–1979), and Dangan National School, Co. Roscommon (1865–1948).[22]

The National Archives also hold the papers generated by the royal commission on primary education (Powis).[23] These contain minute books concerning the drafting of the report as well as three volumes of written submissions sent in to the commission. The commissioners – seven Catholics and seven Protestants – hired ten assistant commissioners to work for them and the report, which took two years to complete, represents a valuable record of the workings of the national system. The historical sketch of the national school system was drafted by the chairman, Lord Powis, together with two other members of the commission – Revd B. Cowie and Mr N. Stokes, both school inspectors for England. The minute books offer a valuable insight into the slow, detailed work of the commission and point to the differences between different religious denominations on education matters.

Files relating to the Board of Intermediate Education (est. 1878)[24] are not as comprehensive as those for the national education system since the Intermediate

---

21 Files from the central registry from the Department of Education, dating from 1919, have been transferred to the National Archives, Bishop Street, Dublin and these are an extension of the ED/2 and ED/9 files for schools. There are three volumes of index and files are listed by county and school. In 1922 the commissioners of national education in Ireland were replaced by the Department and a Minister for Education in the Irish Free State who took charge of national schools. In Northern Ireland a ministry of education was established and took responsibility for primary (formerly national) schools. 22 National school records may be deposited in the National Archives of Ireland for safe-keeping (subject to the availability of the NAI's resources). 23 See NAI, OP/1870/4 A & B. 24 Records of

Board was concerned only with examinations and grants. This NAI collection contains minutes of Board meetings, school rolls, claims for school grants and notices of intention to present for examinations. Also useful are papers relating to the endowed schools' commission (Ireland) (1878–81), and minute books, letters and completed questionnaires relating to the work of educational endowments commissioners (1885–90) which are to be found in the Official Papers of the Chief Secretary's Office collection (see below).

Substantial amounts of material pertaining to Irish education are contained in two of the NAI's most important collections – the Chief Secretary's Office Registered papers (CSORP), which span the period 1818 to 1924, and the Official papers of the Chief Secretary's Office. The Chief Secretary's Office in Dublin Castle was the centre of the British government throughout the nineteenth century and down to 1922. In the National Archives reading room, researchers can consult the finding aids for the CSORP papers, namely the annual registers of incoming correspondence. Each item was entered daily and allocated a file number. However, the files were often carried forward for several years and were allocated a fresh file number each time a new item was added. As a result, researchers can experience difficulties in locating the file required. Among the most important files relating to education are CSORP 1873/12782 (Powis commission), CSORP 1904/10032 (Dale report of 1904) and CSORP 1896/6999, which details attempts to accommodate the Christian Bothers schools within the national school system following the Irish Education Act of 1892.

Researchers will also find material relevant to education in the letter books of the Chief Secretary's Office which cover the period 1801 to 1921 as these contain copies of out-going mail. Regrettably there is no comprehensive index to these volumes. It is, therefore, advisable to search for an out-going letter using the dates of incoming letters as a guide.

The Official Papers, spanning the period 1790 to 1880 and comprising incoming material often generated by government departments or officials, contain correspondence relating to educational matters. Papers dating from 1790 to 1831 are numbered consecutively and a calendar and card index serve as finding aids. In some years material is grouped under the subject heading 'Education' and relevant papers are listed in the calendar under the heading 'Education, 1823–31'. Official papers for the later period (1832–80) are arranged in chronological order with a calendar and card index. Official Papers referring to education include a letter from Joseph Lancaster, dated 1813 (OP334/4), concerning his proposed new system of education; a report compiled by a parliamentary committee set up to

the commissioners of intermediate education, 1897–1918, school rolls, 1890–1915 (NAI, ED/101), claims for school grants, 1910–17 (NAI, ED/102), Choir and orchestra bonus claims, 1913–17 (NAI, ED/103), inspection and grant claims, 1917–18 (NAI, ED/104), birth certificates and candidates at examinations, 1879–99 (NAI, ED/105), notices of intention to present for examinations, 1915–18 (NAI, ED/106); see also Minutes of commissioners of intermediate education, 3 vols, 1878–1922 (NAI, 2001/98/1–24).

consider a petition for support from the Society for Promoting the Education of the Poor in Ireland (OP426/3); and part of the original Stanley Letter of 1831 (OP590).[25] This collection also contains applications for aid made in the 1820s to the lord lieutenant's school building fund, established in 1819 in an attempt to channel funds to poor schools. These applications, which came from teachers and managers of schools, often give details of the individual school seeking aid, including plans of the buildings. These constitute an especially valuable record for the study of education in the 1820s, prior to the establishment of the national school system.[26]

Among the other important collections held in the National Archives are business records as it is here that researchers will find records generated by institutions such as Wilson's Hospital in Mullingar, Co. Westmeath (BR WM 1) and Inchicore Railway model school (BR DUB 52). Among papers of the commissioners of charitable bequests, who were responsible for endowed and charitable institutions, researchers will find files (CHAR 2) relating to individual school endowments schemes. The CHAR 2 series also contains papers relating to the commissioners of the Board of Education for the years 1809–13 and material pertaining to the Endowed schools commission (1856–7). Also useful are the household census returns for 1901 and 1911 which contain data on literacy, knowledge of the Irish language, and names of occupants of boarding schools, orphanages and residential institutions.[27]

The records of the Office of Public Works (OPW) which are available for consultation in the NAI contain drawings and plans for national schools and other public education institutions. Responsibility for school buildings was transferred from the architectural department of the National Board to the OPW in 1856. The latter's records relating to national schools are to be found in OPW 1 (secretarial branch) under OPW 1/15, which comprises twenty-seven volumes of letter books covering the years 1856 to 1881. Under OPW 5/7 are registers relating to national schools for the period 1859 to 1935. Individual school files contain records concerning the site, the amount of the grant paid towards construction of the building, its repair and maintenance, together with detailed drawings and specifications. In addition the OPW was responsible for building the later model schools such as Galway (1852), Enniscorthy (1862), and Monaghan

25 Hannigan (ed.), *The national school system, 1831–1924: facsimiles documents.* **26** K. Hannigan, 'Guide to sources in the National Archives' in Hyland & Milne (eds), *Irish educational documents*, i, 367–78. Notes were made on the applications to the lord lieutenant's fund as to whether a grant was made or not. One also finds in the substantial Official papers collection in the NAI, a valuable statistical return relating to educational standards in the goals and workhouses undertaken in 1849 (see NAI, OP 1849/99, OP1849/159). **27** The 1911 census of Dublin became available online in 2007 (www.census/ireland.ie). Hard copies of the forms relating to individual counties are now available for consultation in county libraries throughout Ireland.

(1861), and for constructing the central model schools and the Central Training Institution on Marlborough Street, Dublin. Plans for Talbot House, the female training establishment (1842–3), and for the infant model school building (1858), on Gardiner Street, in Dublin city, are all held in the archive. The OPW's architectural records for public educational buildings include those for the Queen's colleges in Belfast, Cork, and Galway (1845), St Patrick's College, Maynooth (1845), the Royal University of Ireland (1879), University College, Dublin (1908), the Royal College of Science (1904–11) and the Meath industrial schools in Blackrock, Co. Dublin (1902–7).[28]

The Public Record Office of Northern Ireland, Balmoral Avenue, Belfast
www.proni.gov.uk/education/edindex.htm

The Public Record Office of Northern Ireland (PRONI) holds education files (ED/1–12) relating to national/elementary schools in the six counties of Northern Ireland from 1832. These files were transferred in 1922 from the Public Record Office in Dublin. These ED files are arranged in a similar pattern to those in the National Archives, Dublin. They are divided into sub-groups dealing with various aspects of the work of the commissioners of national education, the Intermediate Education Board and the area of technical education. The ED/1 files are comprised of grant-in-aid applications for national schools for the period 1832–89. ED/2 consists of National Education Office files dealing with individual schools, and the ED/3 collection holds national school building files. All three are very useful for studying the history of a specific school.[29] The ED/5/1–8 files deal with recruitment and service of teachers, pupil-teachers and monitors, and also contain inspectors' reports. The ED/8 files are dedicated to model schools in Ulster,[30] while ED/12 files are comprised of plans and drawings of these schools. ED/6 files are the school registers from 1835. ED/7 holds the salary books of teachers covering the years 1899 to 1905.

Material relating to other aspects of the education system in the North include the ED/10 files on the public examination system of the Intermediate Board of Education (1878–1922): these include minute books, printed annual reports, rules, examination papers and prize lists, inspectors' and examiners' reports. The ED/14 files on technical education relate to the work of local technical instruction committees and technical schools. Printed records of the Department of Agriculture and Technical Instruction (DATI) from 1899, including copies of the journal

---

28 Rena Lohan, *Guide to the archives of the Office of Public Works* (Dublin, 1994). The OPW archives also may be accessed on the website of the National Archives of Ireland (www.nationalarchives.ie). **29** Jonathan Bardon, *A guide to local history sources in the Public Record Office of Northern Ireland* (Belfast, 2000). **30** See Robin Wylie, *Ulster model schools* (Belfast, 1997). There are detailed plans of the Belfast model school in the *Twenty-fourth report of the commissioners of national education in Ireland for the year 1857*, H.C. 1859 (2456–I), vii; Farren, 'Irish model schools', pp 40–66. The ED/8 files include records of Ballymoney Model School, 1856–96 (PRONI, Sch/12) and of Lurgan Model School, 1863–1945

produced by the DATI, are in ED/10. Also available to researchers are printed copies of the major parliamentary reports on education including the Irish education inquiry (1825), the Powis commission on primary education (1870), and the Belmore commission on manual and practical instruction (1898). Collections of papers pertaining to individual schools include those of Belfast Royal Academy (est. 1785), the (Royal) Belfast Academical Institution (est. 1814), the Erasmus Smith Trust and other private charity institutions. The Foster-Massereene papers contain material relating in particular to the Erasmus Smith grammar school in Drogheda. The personal papers of Vere Foster, publisher of the writing copy books and a founder member of the Irish National Teachers' Organization,[31] are of interest, as are those of Thomas O'Hagan, lord chancellor of Ireland in the years 1868–74 and 1880–1 and a commissioner of national education (1858–85). A high profile Catholic, O'Hagan encouraged his fellow Catholics to avail of the educational opportunity offered by the founding of the Royal University in 1879.

The National Library of Ireland, Kildare Street, Dublin 2
www.nli.ie

The National Library of Ireland (NLI) holds a substantial collection of material relating to Irish education, in both manuscript and printed form. Using the library's online catalogues it is possible to search for both under subject headings such as 'Education', 'Schools', and 'Textbooks' as well as under persons and authors. Among the library's most important manuscript collections relating to education are the minutes of the commissioners of national education in Ireland which span the years 1831 to 1922. (Researchers should note that the volume for the period February 1837 to June 1840 is missing.)[32] These minutes provide an essential record of central educational policy decisions and issues throughout the nineteenth century. Also available are minutes of the proceedings of the commissioners of national education in Ireland (private and confidential, 1900–21). The library holds important collections of the personal papers of leading Irish figures involved in education, including the Bolton papers which contain the education papers of Thomas Orde, chief secretary of Ireland during the years 1784–7 and author of *Mr Orde's plan of an improved system of education in Ireland* (Dublin, 1787).[33] Also useful are the newspaper cutting books of Thomas Larcom (1801–79), the Irish under-secretary from 1853 down to 1868. This body of material drawn from national and provincial newspapers is very revealing on major contemporary issues and developments in Irish education ranging from the work of the endowed school's commission (1857–8) and advances in intermediate

(PRONI, Sch/482). **31** O'Connell, *A hundred years of progress*, pp 5–7; Mary McNeill, *Vere Foster: an Irish benefactor* (Newton Abbot, 1971). **32** Minutes of the commissioners of national education in Ireland, 1831–1922 (NLI, MSS 5518–5528 (index), 5529–43). **33** A copy of Orde's 'plan for an improved system of education in Ireland; submitted to the house of commons, April 12 1787; with the debate which arose thereon' (NLI, MS 15,885/2); see also Hyland & Milne (eds), *Irish educational documents*, i, 55–8.

education to the foundation of Queen's colleges and the campaign for a charter for the Catholic University.[34] The papers of the earl of Mayo, chief secretary of Ireland (1866–8) together with those of William Monsell (1812–94), earl of Emly, MP for Limerick County, contain material relating to the university education question, notably correspondence with the Catholic hierarchy regarding a proposed charter for the Catholic University.[35] Mayo, as chief secretary, put forward a plan in 1867–8 to establish a single university of Ireland joining TCD, the Queen's colleges and the Catholic University. However, his proposal failed to win support. Monsell, a leading political Catholic spokesman and a strong supporter of Gladstone's ill-fated university bill of 1873, was representative of lay Catholic opinion on intermediate and university education in the 1860s and 1870s.[36] The Bonaparte-Wyse papers contain relevant material on Thomas Wyse (1791–62), the Waterford MP and educationalist.[37] This collection also includes a letter book covering the years 1904–5 which belonged to A.R.N. Bonaparte-Wyse (1870–1940), who served as secretary of the National Board and transferred to the Ministry of Education Northern Ireland in 1922.[38]

Among other personal papers of interest to the historian of education are those of Patrick Pearse (1879–1916), the nationalist leader and founder of Scoil Eanna in south Co. Dublin[39] and of T.P. Gill, secretary of the DATI (1899–1922).[40] The papers and diary of Mary T. Hayden (1862–1940), female academic and first professor of modern Irish history at University College, Dublin (1911–38) are also very revealing, especially as Hayden diary is the personal record of a leading figure in the campaign for the admission of women to higher education.[41] The papers of Michael Quane, of the endowed schools branch in the Department of Education

34 Newspaper cutting books of Thomas Larcom (NLI, Larcom papers, MSS 7648, 7659, 7668).   **35** NLI, Mayo papers, MS 11,017. Mayo was appointed viceroy of India in 1868; see W.W. Hunter, *Life of the earl of Mayo* (London, 1875) and Norman, *Catholic Church in the age of rebellion*; see also *Memorials by the Roman Catholic prelates in Ireland on the subject of university and national education and correspondence in relating thereto; and Copies of memorials addressed to the secretary of state by the Roman Catholics prelates in Ireland on the subject of university education in Ireland*, H.C. 1865–6 (84), lv, 242; *Correspondence relative to the proposed charter to a Roman Catholic University in Ireland*, H.C. 1867–8 (288, 380), liii, 779.   **36** NLI Monsell papers, MSS 8317, 8319; *Bill for the extension of university education in Ireland*, H.C. 1873 (55) vi, 329.   **37** 'Political observations by Sir Thomas Wyse, 1820–1828' (NLI, MS 34,222/1–3); Miscellaneous material of the Bonaparte-Wyse family (NLI, MS 36,008). **38** Letter book of A.R.N. Bonaparte-Wyse, 1904–5 (NLI, MS 34,232); Farren, *Politics of Irish education*, pp 42, 79, 103.   **39** *A significant Irish educationalist: the educational writings of P.H. Pearse*, ed. Ó Buachalla.   **40** T.P. Gill papers (NLI, MSS 13,478–13,526).   **41** Diary of Mary Hayden, 1878–1903 (NLI, MS 16,641). Hayden was a graduate and a junior fellow of the Royal University of Ireland (1895). She was a founder member of the Irish Association of Women Graduates, established in 1902, and she gave evidence to the Robertson Commission on University Education, 1902; see *Third report of the commissioners on university education (Ireland), minutes of evidence* [Cd.1228–9], H.C. 1902, 357–9; Joyce Padbury, 'Mary Hayden: first president of the Women Graduates Association' in Anne Macdona (ed.), *From Newman to Newwoman: UCD women remember* (Dublin, 2001), pp xii–xvii; Conan Kennedy, *The diary of Mary T. Hayden, 1878–1903* (5 vols, Killala, 2007).

SEQUEL NO. II.

TO THE

SECOND BOOK OF LESSONS.

MONDAY MORNING, ᴏʀ GOING TO SCHOOL.

4 'Monday morning' – an extract from the *Second sequel to the second book of lessons* (1866) published by the National Board. The text emphasizes the benefits of going to school and of cleanliness and neatness of person.

and author of many articles on the history of endowed schools contain useful material on Midleton College, D'Israeli School and Hewetson School among others.[42]

The National Library also holds an extensive collection of contemporary Irish textbooks, in both English and Irish, which provide insights into the curriculum of the hedge schools of the eighteenth century as well as that of the nineteenth-century national school system. These include chapbooks and readers dating from the 1820s as well as the lesson books introduced by the commissioners of national education and those used by the Christian Brothers.[43] The graded series of five national lesson books, published in the 1830s, formed the original basis of the national school curriculum. By the 1850s further lesson books had been added, including *Sequel to the second book no. 1*, *Sequel to the second book no. 2*, *Supplement to the fourth book*, *Reading book for girls*, *Biographical sketches of eminent British poets*, *Selection of British poets*, *English grammar*, *First book of arithmetic*, *Epitome of geography*, *Agricultural classbook*, and *Directions for needlework*. The Board also sanctioned the use of books published by individual authors of whom it approved. Among these were Professor Robert O'Sullivan's *English grammar*, *Spelling book superceded*, and *Geography generalized*; Professor McGawley's *Lectures on natural philosophy*, Dr Thomson's *Treatise on arithmetic* and Hullah's *Manual of vocal music*.[44]

Lastly, the National Photographic Archive of the National Library, located on Meeting House Square, Temple Bar, Dublin 2, contains photographs of Irish school children with their teachers, often formally posed outside their school-house, which offer rare contemporary glimpses of the buildings and of the children's clothing and demeanour.[45]

---

42 Michael Quane, 'Midleton School, Co. Cork' in *Jn. R.S.A.I.*, 82:1 (1952), pp 1–27; idem, 'D'Israeli School, Rathvilly' in ibid., ser. 7, 18 (1948), pp 11–23; idem, 'Hewetson endowed school, Clane' in *Kildare Arch. Soc. Jn.*, 14:1 (1964–5), pp 56–85. For a list of Quane's articles on endowed schools see Hayes, *Sources for the history of Irish civilization: articles in periodicals*, iv, 546–7. Quane's papers in the NLI include minutes of the Board of Education for the period 1806 to 1812 (MS 16,927) and those of the commissioners of education for the years 1814 to 1826 (MS 16,918).   **43** See McManus, *Irish hedge school*; Dowling, *Hedge schools of Ireland*; R.R. Adams, 'Swine-tax and eat-him-all-Magee: the hedge schools and popular education in Ireland' in James S. Donnelly and Kerby Miller (eds), *Irish popular culture, 1650–1850* (Dublin, 1998), pp 97–117; John P. Walsh, 'A comparative analysis of the reading books of the commissioners of national education and of the Christian Brothers' (MA thesis, UCD, 1983); John Coolahan, 'The Irish and others in the nineteenth-century textbooks' in J.A. Mangan, *The imperial curriculum* (London, 1993), pp 54–63; David Fitzpatrick, 'The futility of history: a failed experiment in Irish education' in Ciaran Brady (ed.), *Ideology and the historians* (Dublin, 1991), pp 168–86; *Appendix to the nineteenth report of the commissioners of national education in Ireland for the year 1852*, 1, H.C. 1852–3 (1688), xliii, 91–4.   **44** Professor Sullivan and Professor McGauley were on the staff of the Marlborough Street Training Institution. For a full list of national school books see *Royal commission of inquiry into primary education (Ireland)* [Powis commission], i, pt 1, *report of the commissioners; with an appendix* [C 6], H.C. 1870, xxviii, 1.   **45** See Sarah Rouse, *Into the light: an illustrated guide to the photographic collections of the*

The Royal Irish Academy, Dawson Street, Dublin 2

www.ria.ie

The Royal Irish Academy library collection contains valuable printed material for the history of Irish education, particularly for the nineteenth century. The Haliday Pamphlets are a large collection of bound printed works relating to Ireland's political, social, economic, ecclesiastical and educational history. Part of this collection is now searchable on line, while an index to each bound volume is available in the Reading Room. The index to each bound set of pamphlets can be searched under the headings 'education' and 'miscellaneous'. For example, for the years 1803–11, there are pamphlets relating to the Charter schools, the Incorporated Society, the monitorial system, the Kildare Place Society and school textbooks. These include *Report of the education committee appointed by the Society for Discountenancing Vice* (1803) (HP 839: 6); Charles Fletcher M.D.'s *Thoughts on the national importance of Protestant Charter schools* (1807) (HP 865: 9); *Rules governing Charter schools in Ireland* (1808) (HP 953: 8); Andrew Bell's *Pamphlet on an experiment in education, Egmore near Madras* (3rd ed., 1807) (HP 909: 1); *Spelling book for use of the Hibernian School Society* (1812) (HP 1015: 8) and Paul Deighan's *Complete geography of Ireland* (1810) (HP 1015: 8).[46]

Material relevant to the history of Irish education may also be found in the Academy Tract Collection which contains material dating from the sixteenth to the nineteenth centuries and in the collection of Irish language manuscripts (the world's largest). Researchers should note that admission to the RIA library is restricted and that a letter of introduction from a member of the RIA or from a recognized institution must be presented when applying for a reader's ticket. Members are listed on the RIA website.

(b) University archives and libraries

In addition to the archival collections of individual universities and colleges (see Helferty & Refaussé (eds), *Directory of Irish archives*), researchers may find material pertinent to their studies in the following repositories.

Trinity College Dublin, Library, Manuscripts Department

www.tcd.ie/library

The Trinity College Dublin Library Manuscript Department holds the muniments that cover the university's history from the sixteenth century. The main sources are

National Library of Ireland (Dublin, 1998). For examples see Michael C. Coleman, *American Indians, the Irish and government schooling: a comparative study* (Lincoln, 2007), pp 176–7. The National Folklore Collection, University College, Dublin also contains national school photographs. **46** Revd Andrew Bell was one of the inventor of the monitorial system of school organization, commonly known as the 'Madras' system; see Mary Sturt, *The*

the university Board registers (Mun V/5), the companions to those registers (Mun V/6), the entrance books (Mun V/23–5), and the general P/1 files of letters, pamphlets and so on. One particular section in the muniments relates to the admission of women in 1904 (Mun/women). Other records relevant to the history of Irish education held in the TCD collection include the entrance and leaving books of Kilkenny College, founded in 1538 (MS 2019). The Kilkenny registers contain the dates and names of boys entering the school and these can be followed through using the printed alumni register of the University of Dublin, which lists the schoolmasters who sponsored the boys entering the university.[47] The TCD collection also contains the archives of the Incorporated Society for Promoting Protestant Schools in Ireland (est. 1733). These comprise Board and committee books as well as the rolls and accounts of individual charter schools and the general register of apprentices. For the purposes of a study of a specific charter school these records provide useful data relating to individual schools masters and pupils. For example, in the report book for Farra School, Co. Westmeath, one finds a visitor, writing in 1815, informing the central committee:

> I beg leave to observe to the committee of fifteen that on my visit to the school on Sunday last, an order came for any two boys to be apprenticed as servants to Mr Christopher Adamson. I examined those fixed on in reading, arithmetic, etc. and thought them too deficient in education for apprentices and was of the opinion [that] their age of thirteen and a half years would admit them of half a year's instruction ...[48]

Another important archive in the TCD collection is that of the Central Association of Irish Schoolmistresses (CAISM), founded in 1882, whose object was

> to promote the higher education of women in Ireland: to afford means of communication and co-operation between school mistresses and other ladies interested in education, and to watch over the interests of girls, specially with regard to Intermediate and University education.

education of the people (London, 1967). **47** *Alumni Dublinenes: a register of the students, graduates, professors and provosts of Trinity College in the University of Dublin*, ed. G.D. Burtchaeli and T.U. Sadleir (Dublin, 1935); Howard Welch, 'A history of Kilkenny College, 1538–1903' (unpublished PhD thesis, TCD, 2002). **48** Quoted in Milne, *Irish charter schools*, p. 162. Reports on pupils from individual schools were recorded: for instance, 'When Moses Lyddy was apprenticed from the Clonmel School, where he had been pupil for six years, it was discovered he could scarcely read or write' (TCD, MS 5238, 20 Sept. 1786; Milne, *Irish charter schools*, p. 162). In a report on apprentices of Ray school in Donegal, two were apprenticed to Mr Walker, a schoolmaster in Raphoe. One of these, William Colgan, was 'kept constant in the schoolroom' while the other, Patrick Leggett, was 'doing business in the schoolroom with great diligence' (TCD, MS 5786/9b), quoted in Milne, ibid., p. 165 (Raphoe). See also Michael C. Coleman, '"The children are used wretchedly": pupil responses to the Irish charter schools in the early nineteenth century' in *History of*

The minute books of the executive committee of CAISM (MS 9722) run from 1889 down to 1981, when the association was dissolved, and these contain details of correspondence and matters relating to the higher education of women and to teachers, school curricula and examinations. There are also typescript copies of the CAISM annual reports from 1921.[49]

The Starkie papers (MSS 9209–9212) include the diaries and some correspondence of William J.M. Starkie, resident commissioner of national education from 1893 to 1919. The diaries, which cover the years 1903 to 1918, feature comment on key issues of the day such as implementation of the revised programme of 1900, the Dale report (1904) and the vice-regal Dill committee of inquiry (1913). Starkie was called to give evidence to the Dill committee and to defend his policies as resident commissioner. He had difficult relations with the Catholic Church, the government, the inspectorate and the national school teachers and as a consequence, many of his efforts to reform the system of national education failed.[50]

The Department of Early Printed Books in the TCD Library contains the valuable Pollard collection of children's books, chapbooks and school textbooks of the eighteenth and nineteenth centuries, including the lesson books of the National Board and those of the Christian Brothers schools, Vere Foster copy books and school readers produced by British school publishers such as Blackies. (The books can be located under the heading 'Textbooks – Irish' in the Early Printed Books online catalogue).[51] Among other valuable education material available in the library are sets of Pestolozzian reading and arithmetic charts for children, published by the Roundwood Press in the 1820s.[52] These were the work of John Synge (1788–1845) of Glanmore castle, Co. Wicklow, who founded a Pestalozzian school and a printing press on his family estate in an attempt to encourage the spread of Pestalozzi's educational ideas in Ireland.[53] Researchers should be aware that access to the TCD Manuscripts Department is restricted to bona fide scholars.

Education, 30:4 (July 2001), pp 339–57. **49** Copies of the printed reports of CAISM are in the Early Printed Books Library, TCD. The first president of CAISM was Isabella Mulvany and the first secretary was Alice Oldham, who lead the campaign to gain admission of women to TCD. See Lucinda Thomson, 'The campaign for admission, 1870–1904' in Parkes (ed.), *A danger to the men?*, pp 19–54. **50** W.J.M. Starkie, *Recent reforms in Irish education* (Dublin, 1902); idem, *The history of Irish primary and secondary education in the last decade* (Dublin, 1911); C.T. O'Doherty, 'William Starkie (1860–1920), the last resident commissioner of national education' (PhD thesis, University of Limerick, 1997); Áine Hyland, 'Educational innovation – a case history'; for a personal memoir of Starkie, see his daughter Enid Starkie's autobiography *A lady's child* (London, 1941). **51** The books were the lifetime collection of Mary 'Paul' Pollard, librarian in the TCD Early Printed Books Department. The collection is comprised of children's books before 1914, with an emphasis on books for girls. Part of it came to TCD in 1984 and a further collection followed on Pollard's death in 2005. Charles Benson & Siobhan Fitzpatrick (eds), *That woman: studies in Irish bibliography – a festschrift for Mary 'Paul' Pollard* (Dublin, 2005). **52** The charts are listed in the online catalogue under the name of 'John Synge'. **53** J.H. Pestalozzi (1746–1827) was a Swiss educator whose ideas of child development and education influenced significantly the educational methods of the child-

University College Dublin, Archives Department, Belfield, Dublin 4
www.ucd.ie~/archives

In addition to the records of University College Dublin from 1908, the UCD archives collection contains records of the Catholic University of Ireland (1854–1911)[54] and those of other predecessor institutions, namely the Royal College of Science (1867–1926), the Museum of Irish Industry (1846–70), the Albert Agricultural College (1838–1926) and the Royal Veterinary College (1900–60). Records relating to the Irish Association of Women Graduates (IAWG), founded in 1902 to espouse the women's campaign for admission to the universities, are also held here. These include the minute book of the IAWG, some correspondence, photographs of early women graduates of University College, and a copy of a printed memorial by the association addressed in 1910 to the Senate of the National University of Ireland, expressing its opposition to recognition by the university of lectures being delivered in the Catholic women's colleges. There is also a copy of a typed address by the association in 1910 to the Governing Body of University College, expressing again its opposition to a possible recognition by the university of separate women's colleges. Personal papers in the archive which have particular pertinence to the history of Irish education include those of Revd Professor T.J. Corcoran S.J., first professor of education at UCD, Eoin McNeill, Minister for Education (1922–5), John Marcus O'Sullivan, Minister for Education (1926–32) and Richard Mulcahy, Minister for Education (1954–7). Minutes of meetings, reports of conferences and printed material generated by the Teachers' Union of Ireland, founded in 1973, are also deposited in the archive.

Delargy Centre for Irish Folklore and the National Folklore Collection, University College Dublin, Belfield, Dublin 4
www.ucd.ie/irishfolk

The archive of the former Irish Folklore Commission (1935–71) contains manuscripts, photographs, drawings, and other material, collected through the national schools during the 1930s. Particularly relevant are several personal accounts of school life and photographs of national schools.[55]

---

centred schools of the German educator Friedrich Froebel; see K. Silber, *Pestalozzi: the man and his work* (London, 1960). For details of John Synge see Clive Williams's 'Pestolozzi and John Synge' in *Hermathena*, 106 (1968), pp 23–89; Clive Williams, 'Pestalozzi John: a study of the life and educational work of John Synge' (PhD thesis, TCD, 1966); *'An Irish traveller (John Synge)': a biographical sketch of the struggles of Pestalozzi to establish his system, compiled and translated chiefly from his own work* (Dublin, 1815). The Roundwood Press Pestalozzian charts were printed by Thomas Collins, the famous first pupil of the Claremont Institute for the Deaf and Dumb, founded by Charles Orpen in 1816; see Rachel Pollard, *The Avenue: a history of the Claremont Institution* (Dublin, 2006), pp 44–8. **54** The Catholic University of Ireland papers include minute books of the Catholic University Committee (1850–56), the register of students (1854–79), the building fund register (1862–6) and minutes of the Academic Council and University Council. **55** For an example of use of this material see Coleman's comparative study of the education of American Indians and Irish children,

The library of the Church of Ireland College of Education, Rathmines, Dublin 6

www.cice.ie

The Church of Ireland College of Education (CICE) holds the archives of the Kildare Place Society (KPS) or Society for Promoting Education of the Poor in Ireland (est. 1811). These records were stored in Kildare Place when the Church of Ireland Training College took over the buildings in 1884, and they were transferred and listed when the College moved to new premises in Rathmines in 1968.

The KPS archive is a large one, containing general correspondence, proceedings, accounts, minute books of the book committee and of the model school committee as well as a collection of chap books and textbooks published by the Society. Of particular interest for local studies are the provincial schools ledgers (MSS 346–63) which summarize correspondence between individual schools in receipt of grants and the central office in Dublin. These schools were entered into the ledgers sequentially as they received grants from the Society and all subsequent correspondence and grants were recorded, including documentation concerning the appointment of teachers and gratuities paid to teachers. Orders for school effects such as slates, reading charts, quill pens and so on were also recorded, making it possible to trace the progress of an individual school.

Furthermore, the registers of the Kildare Place Training Institution (MSS 680–7) list the name and the school of each student teacher (male and female) who came to Dublin to be trained. Student teachers were recommended for training by a patron or clergyman whose name was also recorded in the register. The students usually stayed at the training institution for six to eight weeks only before returning to their schools, having been instructed at the Society's model schools in the monitorial method of Joseph Lancaster. The Society published its *Schoolmaster's manual* in 1825,[56] and each teacher received a copy as he or she left the training institution. The manual provided practical advice on setting up and organizing a school, and featured model building plans, model timetables, discipline and methods of teaching arithmetic, reading and writing.[57]

American Indians, the Irish, and government schooling. **56** See *Schoolmaster's manual recommended for the regulation of schools, compiled by the Society for Promoting the Education of the Poor in Ireland* (Dublin, 1825). The monitorial method of Joseph Lancaster was based on his *Improvements in education* (London, 1803) and his *Hints and directions for schools* (London, 1811). See also Mona Dickson, *Teacher extraordinary: Joseph Lancaster, 1778–1838* (Sussex: Book Guild, 1986), David Salmon (ed.), *The practical parts of Lancaster's 'Improvements' and Bell's 'Experiment'* (Cambridge, 1932). A large monitorial schoolroom was used, with fixed desks down the centre for writing and standing circles of ' reading drafts' down the sides. The discipline and order was rigid and the pupils moved silently to the command of the teacher. Older pupils, called monitors, were taught by the master and then in turn taught the pupils. The system became very popular in the nineteenth century as it was both cheap and efficient, it allowed large numbers to be taught the basis 3'Rs and it imposed obedience and order on the children. **57** See Karen Willoughby, *Slates up! Schools and schooling in the nineteenth century* (Dublin, 2005). This history workbook for schools was

The KPS regarded the training of teachers and the reform of schools as the most important features of its work:

> At present, in the majority for schools for the instruction of the poor, there is total neglect of the morals, of cleanliness, of decency of conduct and of order and regularity; the only object endeavoured to be attained by the masters, being able to instruct their schools in reading, writing and arithmetic. In order to remedy those evils, and supply those defects, the Society for Promoting the Education of the Poor in Ireland are desirous to promote the establishment of schools and assist in the support of schools, in which the rudiments of knowledge may be obtained in less time, and at less expense, than can be offered in the schools existing in this country ...[58]

The KPS archive also contains copies of the textbooks and library books published by the Society from the 1820s. Two of these, *The Dublin spelling book* (1813) and *The Dublin reading book* (1813) were popular Irish pioneer readers for schools. They contained graded reading and spelling exercises and short stories, which carried a moral and social message. The value of education itself was emphasized:

> Take thy book and read with care,
> Keep thy place, nor play the fool,
> Wash thy face, then mind thy book,
> Play with good boys, talk not so loud,
> Hold up thy head, go to thy seat
> Come in at two, go home at four.[59]

In addition, the KPS published an extensive series of library chapbooks for both children and adults. Regarded as 'improving' reading, these contained useful knowledge and moral tales of travel, adventure and the wonders of the natural world and were intended as a contribution towards a liberal utilitarian education. By 1832 the Society had published a range of eighty titles and sets of these chapbooks were distributed free of charge to all schools in receipt of KPS grants.

based on material in the *Schoolmaster's manual* and on pictures and charts in the KPS archive. **58** *Schoolmaster's manual*, p. 15; Joyce H. Reid (ed.), *Balleer School, Co. Armagh. Copy-book of letters* (Belfast, 1977). Balleer School was one of twenty-six schools in County Armagh which were granted-aided by KPS. The master, Robert Reid, wrote quarterly reports to the school patron, Thomas Wilson. The letter book contains draft copies of these letters, which provide a graphic and personal insight into the running of a rural school in the 1820s. Reid attended at the KPS Model School in 1821–2, was awarded the Society's annual gratuities and received a medal for teaching in 1833. (The original manuscript of the letter book is deposited in PRONI.) **59** *The Dublin spelling book*, p. 33. Other textbooks published by KPS include *A dictating arithmetic, Elementary treatise on the principles of geometry, General geography* and a needlework manual. The Society also supplied three

The titles included *The new Robinson Crusoe; an instructive and entertaining history for the use of children* (1819), *The history of Little Jack, a foundling* (1824), *The cottage fireside* (1826), *The discovery of America by Christopher Columbus* (1820) and *The life of Captain Cook* (1820).[60] The books were illustrated with woodcuts and sold in great numbers and it is interesting to compare them with the national school lesson books published a decade later.[61]

Along with the manuscript records of the KPS, the archives contain the Society's annual printed reports from 1812 to 1840, which summarised the work of the Society. Letters from grateful patrons of schools and from schoolteachers (see below) were included (anonymously) in the appendix of reports:

> Sir,
> ... I had conducted schools in divers parts of Ireland, for 16 years previous to my admission into your model school in April last, and I can candidly confess that I render more service, and with less trouble to my self, to the 300 children, who are in attendance under me, in three months than I could to 50 in the ordinary manner of teaching, in nine.
>
> > I have the honour to be yours and the Society's most humble servant.[62]

The library also holds a valuable collection of Irish primary school textbooks dating from the nineteenth and twentieth centuries. Permission to consult the KPS records should be sought in the first instance by writing to the librarian at the Church of Ireland College of Education. One's research topic should be clearly identified.

The records of the Church of Ireland Training College from 1884 and of Coláiste Moibhí, the preparatory college, from 1926 are also held in the CICE archives. These include governors' minute books, student registers, annual reports, teaching method books with critical reports of students' lessons, newspaper-cutting books and photographs.[63] Permission to consult these records should be sought from the governors of the college by writing in the first instance to the college principal. Researchers should note that access to some of these records may be restricted.

The National University of Ireland, 49 Merrion Square, Dublin 2
www.nui.ie

The office of the National University of Ireland holds the records of the Royal University of Ireland (RUI) for the period 1879–1908, including financial records,

books in Irish – a spelling book and two readers.   **60** Hislop, 'Kildare Place Society', pp 98–117.   **61** Ibid., pp 109–10. In 1824 an estimate of distribution was one million books, and a million-and-a-half of books printed by Society.   **62** Letter dated 23 Dec. 1820 in *Appendix to the ninth annual report of the Society for Promoting the Education of the Poor in Ireland for 1821* (Dublin, 1822), p. 75.   **63** Parkes, *Kildare Place*; Kingsmill Moore, *An*

copy letter books, applications for matriculation, printed annual calendars and examination papers. The RUI calendars are particularly valuable as they feature lists of all graduates and prize winners, along with matriculation, first and second year examinations results. Candidates are listed together with their place of study, such as Queen's College, Belfast, University College, St Stephen's Green and, in the case of women, Alexandra College, St Mary's Dominican College, and so on. As a consequence it is possible to trace the growth of these higher education institutions.

The records of the National University of Ireland from 1908 are also held here and these contain minutes of the NUI Senate. Archives relating to the Queen's colleges and to constituent colleges of the National University of Ireland (namely University College, Dublin, National University of Ireland, Cork, National University of Ireland, Galway, National University of Ireland, Maynooth) are held in the libraries of the respective university colleges. These collections include college charters and statutes, college council minutes, letters books, property deeds, architectural plans and photographs.[64]

(c) Local authority archives and libraries

Local archives and libraries are often the most accessible repositories holding material that is relevant to the history of educational provision in a locality, be it a county, town or village.[65] When embarking upon a research project, it is advisable to inquire whether county and local libraries, archives and museums have relevant source material. Their most important collections often include records of the Poor Law Guardians, workhouse schools and county Agriculture and Technical Instruction committees (1899–1930). These committees worked closely with the central Department of Agriculture and Technical Instruction from which they received an annual grant and to which they submitted an annual report, detailing courses run in the technical schools and the numbers attending. For example,

unwritten chapter in the history of education; Valerie Jones, *A Gaelic experiment: the preparatory system, 1926–1961 and Coláiste Moibhí* (Dublin, 2006). **64** See Mary Ann Lyons, 'Maynooth; a select bibliography of printed sources' in *Irish Historical Studies*, 29:116 (Nov. 1995), pp 441–74. For a list of available archives for University College, Dublin see McCartney, *UCD: a national idea*, pp 453–63; for Queen's College, Cork and University College, Cork, see J.A. Murphy, *The College: a history of Queen's/ University College, Cork, 1845–1995* (Cork, 1995), pp 439–41; for University College, Galway, see Tadhg Foley (ed.), *From Queen's College to National University: essays on the academic history of QCG/ UCG/ NUI, Galway* (Dublin, 1999); for Queen's College/ University, Belfast, see Moody & Beckett, *Queen's, Belfast*, ii, 563–868. Material relating to the building of three Queen's colleges is to be found in the National Archives of Ireland in the Chief Secretary's Office Registered papers (CSORP) and in the OPW Board of Works Provincial colleges letter books. **65** See Helferty & Refaussé (eds), *Directory of Irish archives* for details on holdings in local authority archives.

Donegal County Archives (www.donegal.ie) contain the records of the county's Poor Law Unions (1841–1923), minutes of the county council from 1899, those of the County Committee on Agriculture (1901–30), local national school roll books and registers (*c.*1880–1960s) and records of Lifford endowed schools for the years 1879 to 1992. Galway County Council Archives include records of that county's Poor Law Unions as well as material relating to the county council education committee (1911–64) and Galway Mechanics Institute (1826–1977). Cork Archives Institute holds records relating to both Cork city and county, including those of the Poor Law Unions and the Cork model school (est. 1861), while the city's Crawford Municipal Art Gallery (www.crawfordartgallery.com) has the minute books of the Cork Technical Instruction Committee and student registers.

Printed records of the Dublin City Technical Instruction Committee (est. 1899) may be consulted in the Dublin City Archives, Pearse Street (www.dublincity publiclibraries.ie). The minute books of the municipal council of the city of Dublin, which span the period from 1841 to 1918, contain decisions made by the Council regarding the work of the Technical Education Committee (TEC). The latter's annual reports to the Council feature in the reports and printed documents of Dublin Corporation (1869–2003). The minutes are numbered and are cross referenced to the reports, making it is easy to locate material relevant to technical education. Each Corporation Committee report has a sequential number.[66] For example, minute no. 623 of the Council meeting of August 1911 reads: 'That the standing order no. 12 be suspended to enable the Council to take into consideration the report of the Technical Education Committee (no. 147), submitting a scheme of technical instruction for the County Borough of Dublin'. The Dublin Technical Education Committee had a long-running dispute with the central DATI over the appointment of an educational director and the DATI withheld its funding. In 1910 the TEC claimed that that the DATI was acting '*ultra vires*'.[67] Records of the Dublin County Committee of Agriculture and Technical Instruction covering the period 1908 to 1942 are held in Fingal County Archives, Parnell Square, Dublin 1. Material relating to Bailieborough model school, dating from the 1860s down to the 1900s, is in Cavan County library.[68] Researchers should consult Helferty and Refaussé (eds), *Directory of Irish archives* (4th ed., Dublin, 2003) for listings of major collections held by local repositories.

66 *Report of the Technical Education Committee on the subject of the excessive and illegal control sought by the DATI over the working of the system of technical education in the County Borough of Dublin, and over the personnel of the staff employed by the Corporation* (report no. 190), committee reports (1910), iii, 45–82 and Council minute no. 773 (Oct. 1910); see Jim Cooke, 'The dispute between the Department of Agriculture and Technical Instruction and the City of Dublin Technical Instruction Committee, 1901–12' in *Technical education: essays dedicated to the memory of Michael Clune* (Dublin, n.d.), pp 47–61.   **67** *Reports, Dublin Corporation, 1911, Report of the Technical Instruction Committee*, pp 757–66.   **68** Donegal County Archives, Lifford, County Donegal; Galway County Archives, Cathedral Square, Galway City; Cork Archives Institute, South Main Street, Cork; Dublin City Archives,

(d) Selection of recommended private repositories and archives

Private collections containing important material for the history of Irish education may be found in the archives of various Churches and religious orders, education societies and trusts, as well as those of individual colleges and schools. Those orders involved in education generally have their own archives relating to the work of their schools. In all cases it is necessary to make an appointment to consult papers. Further details and addresses can be found in Helferty & Refaussé (eds), *Directory of Irish archives*.

Agriculture House Library, Kildare Street, Dublin 2

www.agriculture.ie

The Department of Agriculture Library is not a public library and therefore access is limited. Permission to consult the technical education material must be sought in writing from the librarian, who will facilitate requests from specialist researchers.

The library contains education papers relating to the work of the Department of Agriculture and Technical Instruction from 1900 to 1921. The most important of these are minutes of proceedings of the Board of Technical Instruction (volumes 1–7 covering the period 1900 to 1921) which had responsibility for the technical education policy of the Department. These minutes were printed and given to Board members on a confidential basis. Decisions regarding progress of the county boroughs and county council technical instruction schemes, the Board's finances, and staff appointments were recorded. The first meeting of the Board was held on 18 July 1900 and the last on 18 December 1919. The Board was accountable for administration of technical education grants and the sanctioning of and payment to the county technical education committees. For instance, at its meeting on 19 October 1900 the Board expressed its confidence in Sir Horace Plunkett continuing as president of the DATI:

> [The Board] considered it of very greatest importance that he should continue to act in that capacity in order that the work of the department shall be started on the proposed lines, and that it shall command the confidence of the country.[69]

Other matters considered at this meeting were arrangements made for training science teachers at the Royal College of Science, the inspection of schools, the series of Pioneer Lectures on the importance of scientific and technical education that the new department had delivered around the country, and plans for giving

Pearse Street, Dublin 2.   **69** Minutes of proceedings of the Board of Technical Instruction, 17 Oct. 1900. Plunkett lost his parliamentary seat in the 1900 election. It was considered by some that the vice-president of the DATI should be an MP as this strengthened the Department's political influence. Plunkett's popularity was further diminished by the publication of his book *Ireland in the new century* (Dublin, 1904) which was critical of the grants for science laboratories to secondary schools. The Board also received a memorandum on technical schools in England, Scotland and France. The schemes drawn up by the county councils were recorded in full in the appendix to minutes and these are useful for researching the historical development of local technical education committees. For example, the scheme for County Armagh, presented in October 1902, proposed the opening of a central technical school which would start in temporary accommodation in the town. A salary of £200 per annum would be paid to a headmaster of £200. Because industries in the area were related to the linen trade, the school would offer (in addition to science) manual instruction and commercial subjects, the making of linen and damask, bleaching and flax spinning.[70]

The high hopes and aspirations of the DATI were reflected in the Board of Technical Instruction minutes, and those recorded at the Board's final meeting in December 1919 showed its members' sadness and anger at the losses and failures they had experienced. In 1919 the MacPherson Education bill proposed that technical education should be separated from agriculture and become a branch of the proposed new central education department. Members of the Board were incensed by such a proposal:

> We confess we cannot comprehend how a scheme of such wholesale destruction of the most successful and popular education machinery in Ireland can be seriously contemplated by the government. We respectfully protest against such a proposal, and most earnestly request the government to re-consider this part of the bill.[71]

In addition to the minutes of proceedings, the Agriculture Library holds reports from county Agriculture and Technical Instruction committees. These reports, published annually by the DATI, contain progress reports on the work of these local committees and as such represent an especially valuable source for historians focusing on specific localities. For instance, reports generated by the Clare County Council Committee for Agriculture and Technical Instruction during the period

influential role of the Catholic Church in Ireland. **70** Ibid. Appendix to meeting of 29 Aug. 1902. Other subjects taught in the schools included building construction and drawing, machine construction and drawing, carpentry, cookery, laundry-work, dress-making, and commercial subjects – shorthand, type-writing, and book-keeping. **71** Ibid., Minutes, vii, 18 Dec. 1919. The 1919 Education bill ([C 214], H.C. 1919, i, 407) which proposed a new central education department with control over primary, secondary and technical education, was defeated. However, after 1922 under the Irish Free State government, the DATI was dismembered and technical education was transferred to the new Department of Education with a minister for education. Some of the staff of the Technical Department were transferred to the Department of Education, including George Fletcher, the assistant secretary, Robert Turnbull, who had been a junior and later senior inspector with the DATI since 1902, and John Ingram, senior inspector, who later chaired the Ingram Committee on Technical Education, which led to the Vocational Education Act of 1930.

1901 to 1904 feature accounts of Ennis Technical School, Ennis Convent Technical School, Kilrush Convent Technical School and the Christian Brothers Technical School. Details of the committee of management, of the local scheme, the staffing and subjects taught in the schools are also listed. Records of the occupations of young men and women enrolling for courses are particularly useful to social historians.[72]

Office of the commissioners of charitable donations and bequests for Ireland, 12 Clare Street, Dublin 2

The records of schemes for educational institutions and trusts framed under the Educational Endowments (Ireland) Act, 1885 are held in this office. Files contain material relating to the history and administration of endowed schools that are still in operation. Both W.R. Wilkinson's *Our good school on the hill: Monaghan collegiate school* (Monaghan, 1982) and Christopher F. McCormack's *The Gilson endowed school, Oldcastle: the history of a school's search for identity* (Kells, 2003) draw upon this archival collection (schemes nos 19 and 26 respectively). Other schools which operate under the endowment schemes, instituted by the 1885 act, include Midleton College (no. 16), the Robertson endowments (no. 35)[73] and the Incorporated Society for Promoting Protestant Schools in Ireland (no. 210). Permission to consult files in this repository must be obtained first in writing and the purpose of the research clearly stated.

Dublin Diocesan Archives, Drumcondra, Dublin 9

The archives of Dublin archdiocese, which include papers of Catholic archbishops of Dublin, are among the most significant for the history of education in the nineteenth century, particularly on Church–State relations. As the nineteenth century progressed the role of the Catholic Church hierarchy in education became increasingly important and the leadership of the archbishops of Dublin was very influential. As outlined in chapter one, the government sought the support of the Church for the implementation of its educational policies, and consulted and bargained with the Catholic Church prior to the introduction of the national school system in the 1830s, the intermediate examination in the 1870s and the foundation of the Queen's colleges in the 1840s. This continued down to the 1890s when attempts were made to reach a solution to the 'university question'.[74]

---

72 *Annual reports of Clare County Clare Council Committee of Agriculture and Technical Instruction, 1901–04* (Dublin, 1904). Similar county reports survive for Derry and Monaghan. In later years the county reports are mostly concerned with agriculture. **73** The Robertson endowment was founded in 1790 by Colonel Robertson to support Church of Ireland schools in the diocese of Raphoe. It made provision for purchasing books 'as well of entertainment, as of instruction' and for paying a gratuity to schoolmaster. The schools were subject to the bishop's annual visitation. In 1856 twenty-three schools were in receipt of Robertson grants (see *Report of her majesty's commissioners appointed to inquire into the endowments* [Kildare commission], iii: *papers accompanying the report (tables of schools and endowments)*, H.C. 1857–8 (2336–IV), xxii, pt iv, 534–5. **74** See Norman, *Catholic Church*

The papers of Archbishop John Thomas Troy (1786–1823) deal with the founding of St Patrick's College, Maynooth (1795) and the Catholic education debate that took place during the early years of the nineteenth century. The papers of Archbishop Daniel Murray (1823–50), who supported the national school system and who was one of the first commissioners of national education, feature material on crucial educational issues of the 1830s and 1840s. These included the founding of the Queen's colleges in 1845, the opening of district model schools of the National Board in 1849, the Irish colleges in Europe, diocesan relations with religious orders, and the bitter controversy between Murray and Archbishop John McHale of Tuam (1834–81) regarding the Church's support for the national education system in the 1830s. There is a complete list of Murray's papers published in *Archivium Hibernicum* from volumes xxxvii (1981) to xli (1987) and the index in the latter serves as an invaluable finding aid for researchers intending to consult this collection. In addition, the papers of John Hamilton, Murray's personal secretary, are available for the same period and these too are listed in *Archivium Hibernicum*, volumes xliii (1988) to liv (2000).

The papers of Paul Cardinal Cullen (1852–78), a strong advocate of Catholic education, cover contemporary developments and point to his key influence in shaping educational policy. These include issues such as the university question from 1850 and the founding of the Catholic University (1854), the Synod of Thurles (1850) and condemnation of the Queen's colleges and the model schools, the demand for denominational secondary education and the introduction of the Intermediate Education Act (1878). The papers of Dr Bartholomew Woodlock, who was rector of the Catholic University (1854–79), relate chiefly to the university question. Those of Archbishop Edward McCabe (1878–85) cover the setting up of denominational teacher-training colleges in 1883. Those of Archbishop William Joseph Walsh (1885–1921) relate to the demand for a university that was acceptable to Catholics and provide an insight into Walsh's major input in setting up the National University of Ireland in 1908 as a compromise measure with the government. Walsh served as the first chancellor of the NUI from 1908.[75] Applications to consult the diocesan archives should be made in writing to the archivist or by e-mail at archives@dublindiocese.ie.

The Representative Church Body Library, Braemor Park, Dublin 14

www.library.ireland.anglican.org

The Representative Church Body (RCB) Library holds parish and diocesan records of the Church of Ireland (Anglican) and of Protestant educational societies.[76] Among the most important education societies records are those of the

in the age of rebellion; Larkin, *The Catholic Church and the emergence of the modern Irish political system*; Akenson, *Irish education experiment*. **75** See David C. Sheehy, 'Dublin Diocesan Archives – an introduction' in *Archivium Hibernicum*, 42 (1987), pp 39–47; David C. Sheehy & Patrick J. Corish, *Catholic Church records* (Maynooth research guides for Irish local history, no. 3, Dublin, 2002). **76** Raymond Refaussé, *Church of Ireland records* (Maynooth research

Church Education Society (CES) founded in 1839 to provide aid for Anglican primary schools. The collection contains minute books, letters, inspectors' reports, applications from parish schools for teachers and registers of the CES training college in Kildare Place.[77] The following letter of application for a teacher shows the importance of the teacher possessing a good character. It also indicates an expectation that the teacher would also fulfil the role of parish clerk and that his wife would be employed as a teacher of needlework to the girls:

> Rev John Powell of St Anne's Newtown Forbes, in the diocese of Ardagh wants a schoolmaster with a wife or sister to teach needlework. The master is to act as parish clerk, and therefore sing well. Both must be active, diligent, neat and cleanly in their habits and pious. The school is 2 miles from the church. The emolument is £50, a house and about English acre of land value. A gratuity is given for children promoted at inspection and £3 for school fuel.[78]

Records of other Protestant education societies include those of the Incorporated Society for Promoting Education of English Protestant schools in Ireland (est. 1733),[79] the Sunday School Society of Ireland (est. 1809), the Association for Promoting Christian Knowledge (est. 1792), the Island and Coast Society established in 1833 to support remote Protestant schools on the outlying coasts and islands,[80] and the Female Orphan House, North Circular Road, Dublin (later Kirwan House) which was founded in 1790.[81] Annual reports of the London Hibernian Society are to be found in the papers of the Incorporated Society.

Among the RCB's collection of records pertaining to individual Protestant schools are those of endowed schools such as Bishop's Hodson's School in Elphin (est. 1685),[82] the Ralph Macklin School, Dublin (est. 1821),[83] the Diocesan School

guides for Irish local history, no. 2 (Dublin, 2000; 2nd ed., 2006). Note that restricted access applies in the case of some of the RCB collection (marked 'R'), hence prior permission to consult these files must be sought. Researchers may consult the manuscript collection index and a card catalogue, searching under 'schools'. It should also be noted that the RCB Library does not hold old national school registers or roll books. Instead, these are deposited in the National Archives of Ireland.   **77** Committee proceeding book, 1873–1901 (RCB Library, CES MS 8); Subcommittee proceedings book, 1839–54 (RCB Library, CES MS 19); Register of male and female students (RCB Library, CES MS 47); Applications for school masters and school mistresses (RCB Library, CES, MS 49).   **78** Applications for school masters (RCB Library, CES).   **79** The Society's main collection is in Trinity College Library.   **80** Most of the Island and Coast Society's records are in Trinity College Library.   **81** The Female Orphan House was founded 'for the maintenance and education of poor female orphans, and for apprenticing them as servants'. See C.T.A. Carter, *Kirwan House, the foremost Irish charity, 1790–1995* (Dublin, 1996).   **82** In 1685 provision was made 'for the maintenance of a grammar school in the town of Elphin, to be approved by the bishop of Elphin, for the benefit of the children of the inhabitants of Elphin; those of them whose parents are poor to be taught gratis'. See *Report of her majesty's commissioners appointed to inquire into the endowments* [Kildare commission], iii: *Papers accompanying the report (tables of schools and endowments)*, H.C. 1857–8 (2336–IV), xxii, pt iv, 718–19.   **83** Ralph Macklin Schools (one for boys and one for girls),

for Girls, Dublin (est. 1902), the School for the daughters of Irish clergy (est. 1843), the School for the sons of Irish clergy (est. 1854), Drogheda Blue Coat School (est. 1813),[84] Bishop Foy's School in Waterford (est. 1707) including registers for the years 1711 to 1826,[85] the Merchant Tailors' Schools Charity (est. 1642), and the Meath Protestant industrial schools (est. 1876). The library's collection also contains material relating to Mountjoy School, Dublin, the Hibernian Marine School,[86] Bandon Grammar School, and Sligo Grammar School. A number of miscellaneous papers relating to other Protestant schools are also listed in the catalogue index. Records of the Irish Church Missions, which had schools in the west of Ireland, are held in the offices of the Irish Church Missions, Bachelor's Walk, Dublin 1, as are those of the Irish Society for Promoting the Education of the Native Irish through the medium of their own Language, established in 1818. Material relating to Thomas Pleasants's school for the education of Protestant orphans, Camden Street, Dublin (est. 1818), is held in the National Library.[87]

The RCB Library also holds both Church of Ireland parish and diocesan records that contain material relating to parochial schools and the annual diocesan visitations by the bishops. These often feature observations on parish schools and schoolmasters. Records of Dublin diocese include minute books and roll books for schools in parishes including St Peter's, St Michan's, St Catherine's, St Luke's, St Mark's, St Audoen's, St Mary's and St Andrew's. Also of interest are the minute books of the Dublin School Managers' Association, which was established in 1902 to support Church of Ireland national schools.

were founded in compliance with the terms of the last will and testament of Ralph Macklin. He provided 'for the establishment of an institution to be denominated Ralph Macklin Sunday and Thursday Poor School under the direction of governors of the Magdalen Asylum, aided by the curates of St Anne's, St Andrew's and St Werburgh's parishes'.   **84** Drogheda Blue School was founded in 1836 by the Drogheda Corporation as a charity school for St Peter's parish. The Corporation paid the schoolmaster's salary and free apartments, coal and candles were provided. See *Report of her majesty's commissioners appointed to inquire into the endowments* [Kildare commission], iii: *Papers accompanying the report (tables of schools and endowments)*, H.C. 1857–8 (2336–IV), xxii, pt iv, 172–3. The Drogheda school endowment was revised by scheme no. 150 under the Educational endowments Act, 1885.   **85** Bishop Foy's School in Waterford was founded in 1707 'for apprenticing to members of the United Church, sons and daughters of the inhabitants of Waterford, nominated by bishop, dean and an mayor, or any two of them; and for teaching fifty children of the inhabitants of Waterford to read, write and cast accounts, and to say the Church catechism …'. See *Report of her majesty's commissioners appointed to inquire into the endowments* [Kildare commission], iii: *Papers accompanying the report (tables of schools and endowments)*, H.C. 1857–8 (2336–IV), xxii, pt iv, pp 398–9, 409.   **86** Papers relating to the Hibernian Marine Society are also in the National Library of Ireland and in Trinity College Library.   **87** In his will Thomas Pleasants made provision 'for the maintenance, clothing and appropriate education of poor orphan Protestant girls in some branch of industry, such as knitting, straw-hat making, or whatsoever else could be thought of to be the best'. See *Report of her majesty's commissioners appointed to inquire into the endowments* [Kildare commission], iii: *Papers accompanying the report (tables of schools and endowments)*, H.C. 1857–8 (2336–IV), xxii, pt iv, pp 60–1. Pleasants' Asylum was merged with the Female

Religious Society of Friends Historical Library, Stocking Lane, Dublin 16
The Quaker Historical Library contains records relating to Quaker education and schools as well as details of individual Quakers, including Anne Jellicoe (1823–80), foundress of Alexandra College, Dublin (1866).[88]

Irish Architectural Archive, 45 Merrion Square, Dublin 2
www.iarc.ie
The IAA Library contains photographs and architectural plans of some schools buildings and public educational institutions.[89] In the database, photographs are catalogued under place within each county and are cross-referenced under 'Buildings – Schools'. There are biographies of architects such as Jacob Owen (1778–1870) who served as architect to the Board of National Education (1832–56). He was responsible for the National Board's Marlborough Street central model schools and designed the Female Training School on Talbot Street, Dublin (1844). His son, James H. Owen (1822–91) designed some of the later district model schools, including those at Enniskillen, Monaghan, Omagh, and Parsonstown.

Frederick Darley (1798–1873) was architect to the National Board from 1848 to 1856 and he designed early district model schools including Newry, Ballymena and Belfast. The IAA Reading Room has copies of major architectural journals such as *The Dublin Builder, The Irish Builder* and *The Civil Engineer and Architect's Journal*, which contain contemporary articles on new school buildings, for example, Talbot Street Female Training School (est. 1844),[90] Londonderry Model School (est. 1860) and Enniscorthy Model School (est. 1861).[91] These large model school buildings were admired for their style and specialist features such as ventilation, light and hygiene. An article published in 1859 in the *Dublin Builder* commented on the new school, then under construction, on Marlborough Street:

> A[n] important building, designed for the 'practising schools' is being built by the Commissioners of National Education at the rear of the Central Model Schools. One elevation will face on to Lr. Gardiner's Street, and another on to the existing buildings in Marlborough Street, though access from front to rear being maintained by an open and lofty ground passage, 14 ft wide with splayed, moulded, and semi-circular headed entrances placed in

Orphan House, North Circular Road (later Kirwan House) in 1949; see Carter, *Kirwan House*, p. 27. **88** O.C. Goodbody, *Guide to Irish Quaker records, 1654–1860* (Dublin, 1967). Anne V. O'Connor, 'Anne Jellicoe, 1823–80' in Mary Cullen & Maria Luddy (eds), *Women, power and consciousness* (Dublin, 1995), pp 125–60. **89** For example, see Edward McParland, *Public architecture in Ireland, 1680–1760* (New Haven & London, 2001), pp 143–75; Carole Scully, 'The history of the development of primary school building in the nineteenth century' (MEd thesis, TCD, 1987). **90** See *Civil Engineer and Architect's Journal*, 7 (1844), p.18. **91** See *The Dublin Builder*, 1:9 (1859) and ibid., 3:35 (1861). Working drawings of Enniscorthy Model School are in the National Archives in the OPW papers

a two-storey projection, which forms a chief feature. The total length of the building is 212 ft, the wings and connecting portions being only one storey high and the general plan of oblong form …[92]

Archives of religious orders: a select list

The archives of the Sisters of Mercy are in the Catherine McAuley Centre, Herbert Street, Dublin 2. These include records of the order (1778–1870), an extensive collection of material on Our Lady of Mercy Training College, Carysfort, Blackrock spanning the period 1883 to 1955, records relating to the Convents of Mercy including Baggot Street (1870–1950), Arklow (1876–1950), Naas (1860–1950), Borrisokane (1900–50), Birr (1838–57), Athy (1852–1954) and Newtownforbes (1869–1950). In addition, the archives of thirty-two industrial schools, orphanages and residential homes run by the order are held here, but these are not open to third parties under the hundred year rule. Similar material relating to St Joseph's Reformatory School and St George's Industrial School run by the Good Shepherd Sisters is held in the archives of the Good Shepherd order in Limerick.

Archives of the Sisters of the Holy Faith including those of their schools are deposited in the Holy Faith Convent, Glasnevin, Dublin. Those of the Loreto Sisters are in the order's central archive at 55, St Stephen's Green, Dublin 2. Records of the Dominican sisters are held in the order's archive at Harold's Cross, Dublin and their school record are stored in their convents in Cabra and Griffith Avenue, Dublin. The Ursuline Convent archives are in Cork as are the records of St Angela's College, Cork.[93]

The Jesuit archives in Lower Leeson Street, Dublin 2 include records of the order at home and abroad, the papers of Fr Peter Kenny S.J., founder of the Jesuit college, Clongowes Wood (1814) and of Fr William Delany S.J., rector of University College, Dublin (1883–1909). The records of Clongowes Wood College are held in the college itself. The archives of the Holy Ghost Congregation, including those relating to Blackrock College, Rockwell College and St Mary's College, Rathmines, are in the provincial archives in South Richmond Avenue, Dublin 6. Records of the Irish Christian Brothers are held for St Mary's Provincialate in the North Circular Road, Dublin 1 and those for the St Helen's Provincialate are in Dun Laoghaire, Co. Dublin. The Allen Library in North Richmond Street, Dublin 1 has records relating to the history of the CBS O'Connell's school and the work of the order, much of which was collected by Brother W.P. Allen in the twentieth century. Other individual schools and colleges have their own archives, which may be consulted by appointment. See Helferty and Refaussé (eds), *Directory of Irish archives.*

(OPW 4973/61): see R. Lohan, *Guide to the archives of the Office of Public works* (Dublin, 1994), pp 70–1.   **92** See *The Dublin Builder*, 1 (1859), p. 60. The building still stands along Lower Gardiner's Street in Dublin and is used by the Department of Education and Science.   **93** See Raftery & Parkes, *Female education in Ireland*; Judith Harford, *The opening of higher education to women in Ireland* (Dublin, 2008).

Erasmus Smith Trust, Zion Road, Rathgar, Dublin 6

The archives of the Erasmus Smith Trust are held at The High School (est. 1870), Rathgar, Dublin 6, which is the only surviving school owned by the Trust. The administrative material includes minutes of governors' meetings, records of the four original Erasmus Smith grammar schools (Galway, Ennis, Tipperary and Drogheda) and those relating to 200 so-called 'English schools' located in parishes across Ireland. The collection also includes estate maps and architectural plans of schools. The records are extensive and relate in particular to areas where the Trust held land such as in Limerick and Tipperary. Records of The High School are also held in the archive.

Records of older private schools such as The King's Hospital, Dublin (est. 1670), Wilson's Hospital, Multyfarnham (est. 1761),[94] Alexandra College, Dublin (est. 1866), Clongowes Wood College (est. 1814), St Columba's College, Rathfarnham (1843), and Victoria College, Belfast (est. 1859), are held in the schools. Those of two old endowed schools – Morgan's School and Mercer's School, both in Castleknock, Dublin 15 – are held in The King's Hospital archives. Records of the Masonic Boys' School (est. 1867) and of the Masonic Girls' School (est. 1792) are stored in the Freemasons' Hall, Molesworth Street, Dublin 2.

INTO head office, Parnell Square, Dublin 1

This office holds the records of the Irish National Teachers' Organization (est. 1868).

Irish Labour History Society Museum, Beggar's Bush, Haddington Road, Dublin, 4

Among the museum's most important collections are the records of the Association of Secondary Teachers of Ireland (est. 1909).

III. OFFICAL PAPERS

Journal of the Irish House of Commons

The Irish House of Commons demonstrated an active concern for the care of destitute children. In the eighteenth century this care was undertaken by voluntary charitable institutions. The Foundling Hospital (est. 1730) in Dublin, the Cork Foundling Hospital (est. 1735) and the 'Charter schools' of the Incorporated Society were the most active. Material relating to the Foundling Hospital can be found in the Journal of the Irish House of Commons. Reports were undertaken in 1791–2 (*Two reports on the state of the Foundling Hospital, March 1791* (*Commons' Jn. Ireland*, xiv (432)) and *Report of committee of enquiry into the state and management*

---

94 There are also records of Wilson Hospital's in the National Archives (NAI, BR WM1).

of the Foundling Hospital, April, 1792 (*Commons' Jn. Ireland*, xvii (pt. 2) (332)). Due to the political unrest of the 1790s nothing further was done to reform the hospital and in 1797 the Irish parliament set up another committee of enquiry which produced the *Report of committee of enquiry into the state of the Foundling Hospital, May 1797* (*Commons' Jn. Ireland*, xvii (pt. 2) (432)). The 1797 report eventually did bring about an improvement in conditions within the institution. Conditions in the Charter schools were no less harsh and inhumane, and in response to the critical report by John Howard, a Quaker reformer, a parliamentary inquiry was established in 1788.[95] However, despite its critical findings, no further action was taken. See *Report on the state of the Protestant Charter schools, April 1788* (*Commons' Jn. Ireland*, xii (454)).

British Parliament Papers, 1800–1922

The British parliamentary papers are the main official source for the history of Irish education in the nineteenth century. It is essential before consulting these papers to study the standard finding aids. Complete sets of parliamentary papers are available on microfiche in Trinity College Library and in the National Library and there now exists an online database (HCCP) of digital copies of the papers.[96] Cockton's *Subject catalogue of the House of Commons parliamentary papers, 1801–1900* lists all papers relevant to Ireland. Under the heading 'education', the relevant papers are listed with full references featuring the session number, paper number, volume, page number and the file number of the Chadwyck-Healey microfiche edition of the papers. Researchers may also find it useful to consult Cockton's *House of Commons parliamentary papers, 1801–1900: guide to the Chadwick-Healey microfiche edition* and Parkes's *Guide to Irish education in the British parliamentary papers, in the nineteenth century and after, 1801–1920.* There are printed general indexes to the parliamentary papers covering each decade and the relevant papers are listed under the heading 'Education (Ireland)'. This general index is comprised of six volumes (see above p.88). Within each volume relevant material is also listed under other headings such as 'agriculture', 'universities (Ireland)', 'endowed schools (Ireland)', 'science and art (Ireland)', 'reformatory and Industrial schools (Ireland)' and 'population (Ireland)'.[97]

These parliamentary papers consist of bills, reports, and accounts and papers presented to the House of Commons in each session. There are two types of

---

95 Robins, *The lost children*, pp 82–4. **96** http: www.eppi.ac.uk. **97** See *General index to accounts and papers printed by order of the House of Commons and to the papers presented by command, 1801–1852* (Shannon, 1968).

reports – those generated by select committees, which consisted of members of parliament, and those compiled by royal commissions which were officially set up by the Crown and manned by experts from outside parliament. Guidelines on citation of parliamentary papers may be found in 'Irish Historical Studies, rules for contributors' in *Irish Historical Studies*, 33:131 (May 2003), 355–6. It is important when consulting a parliamentary report to consider why it was commissioned as this had an influence on its findings. For instance, the royal commission on primary education (Ireland) was established in 1868[98] in response to a demand for recognition of the rights of denominational schooling, and its final recommendations reflected this. Among the report's major suggestions were the introduction of denominational colleges for training national teachers and closure of the system of non-denominational model schools.

Since it became policy from early in the nineteenth century for centralized government to assume increased responsibility for education, the parliamentary papers contain not only reports of successive select committees and commissions set up to review Irish education, but also the annual reports of the various government boards established to provide education. The reports of the commissioners of education in Ireland date from 1814, those of the commissioners of national education from 1834, and those of the Queen's colleges and the Queen's University from 1849 and 1852 respectively. The annual reports of the reformatory and industrial schools date from 1862, those of the commissioners of intermediate education begin in 1879, while the reports of the royal university of Ireland commenced in 1881 and those of the Department of Agriculture and Technical instruction date from 1900. These reports continued to be presented to the British parliament until the establishment of the Irish Free State and Northern Ireland in 1922.

It is proposed to give here only details of the most important bills, reports and accounts and papers for Irish education, particularly those relevant to local history. The general indexes should be consulted for the full lists.

(a) Irish education bills

Bills dealing with Irish primary education in the nineteenth century were few. As explained in chapter one, the most important initiative, namely the establishing of the national school system in 1831, was achieved not by a bill but by a formal letter written by the chief secretary, Lord Stanley, to the chairman of the new board of commissioners of national education in Ireland.[99] This action enabled the

---

98 *Royal commission of inquiry into primary education (Ireland)* [Powis commission] i, *Report of the commissioners* [C 6], H.C. 1870, xxviii, 1.   99 *Letter from the secretary for Ireland to his grace the duke of Leinster, on the formation of a Board of Education*, H.C. 1831 (196), xxix, 757. The letter was reprinted in H.C. 1837 (485), ix, 585. There were two versions of the Stanley

Whig government to avoid a long hostile debate in parliament about the provision of funds for Catholic schools. (All bills had to be read three times in parliament before being passed into law and the procedure allowed much time for debate. If a bill was radically amended at committee stage in parliament, a new amended bill was published.) Other attempts to introduce education bills failed. Thomas Wyse, MP for Waterford, presented a bill in 1831 to 'advance the education of the people' but withdrew it when Stanley put forward his plan for the national system.[1] Four years later, in an attempt to place the new national system on a full legal basis, Wyse introduced another bill, which was not passed.

In the 1870s there were a number of bills for national education which aimed to improve the working conditions of national teachers by supplementing their salaries from local sources, providing loans for the construction of teachers' residences, and introducing retirement pensions.[2] Another bill in 1884 made provision for public loans to be obtained for the building and extension of non-vested schools and denominational training colleges. Thus professional initial training of national teachers began to develop.[3]

The most important education bill was introduced in 1892 to provide free and compulsory education.[4] However, the effect of the 1892 Irish Education Act (55 & 56 Vict. c. 42) was limited as it applied in the first instance to towns and cities only and in rural areas compulsion was optional. The act made education free and compulsory but opt out clauses for seasonal labour and the permitted employment of children over eleven (provided they had a certificate of minimum proficiency in the fourth standard school subjects) meant that the impact of the act on school attendance was limited. By 1920 the average attendance rate for national schools was still only 69.7%.[5]

Letter and both are to be found in the report of the Powis Commission in 1870; see *Royal commission of inquiry into primary education (Ireland)* [Powis commission], i, *Report of the commissioners* [C 6], H.C. 1870, xxviii, pt 1, 22–6. **1** *Bill for the establishment and maintenance of parochial schools and the advancement of the education of the people*, H.C. 1831 (286), i, 491; *Bill for the establishment of national education and the advancement of elementary education in Ireland*, H.C. 1835 (285), i, 443. **2** *Bill to provide for additional payments to teachers in national schools in Ireland*, H.C. 1875 (233), iv, 407. This National school teachers' Act, 1875 (38 & 39 Vict. c. 96) gave optional powers to Poor Law unions to levy a local rate to augment teachers' salaries. It had little success as less than half the unions contributed; see *Bill to afford facilities for the erection, enlargement and improvement and purchase of dwelling-houses for residences for teachers of certain national schools in Ireland*, H.C. 1875 (279), iv, 415; *Bill for improving the position of teachers in national schools in Ireland*, H.C. 1878–9 (246), iv, 555. **3** *Bill to amend the law relating to the building of national schools, industrial schools and training colleges in Ireland*, H.C. 1884 (45), vii, 55; amended in Commons, H.C. 1884 (224), vii, 59. **4** *Bill to improve national education in Ireland*, H.C. 1892 (240), iv, 645; amended in Commons (420) iv, 645. The bill was amended eight more times between 1893 and 1908. The act applied to towns and cities only and school attendance committees were to be set up by these local authorities. With the establishment of county councils in 1898, these local councils were empowered to levy a local rate and to set up school attendance committees to enforce the act. **5** *Eighty-sixth report of the commissioners of national education in Ireland for the school year 1919–20* [Cmd 1476], H.C. 1921, xi, 447.

There were two important education bills in the first decade of the twentieth century, both of which aimed at the structural reform of Irish education: neither passed into law. The Irish Council bill of 1907, introduced by the chief secretary, Augustine Birrell, attempted to devolve certain powers including control of education to a Dublin-based council.[6] The bill was strongly opposed by the Catholic Church as it proposed to increase the State management of education and it was also opposed by the nationalist party who viewed it as a 'halfway house' to home rule.[7] In 1919 the McPherson education bill, which proposed to establish a single centralized government department to co-ordinate the provision of education at primary, secondary and technical level, was also defeated by the strong opposition of the Catholic Church and the Irish nationalist party.[8]

At secondary level the most important bill was that of 1878 which set up the intermediate education system of examinations for schools.[9] The bill laid down the structure of the Intermediate Board, comprised of seven members appointed by the lord lieutenant, plus two paid assistant commissioners to act as secretaries. The funds, derived from the disestablishment of the Church of Ireland under the Irish Church Act of 1869, were up to and not exceeding one million pounds. The Board was required to present an annual report to parliament and its rules required the sanction of the lord lieutenant. The duties of the Board were listed as 'instituting and carrying on a system of public examinations', 'providing for the payment of prizes and exhibitions' and 'providing for the payment to mangers of schools complying with the prescribed conditions of fees dependent on the results of public examinations of students'. The Board was prohibited from holding any examination in religious instruction or paying any school for teaching it; the State funding was for secular instruction only and religious education remained the responsibility of individual schools. The conscious clause protected the religious rights of pupils by stating that 'no pupil attending such school is permitted to remain in attendance during the time of religious instruction which the parents and guardians of such pupil shall not have sanctioned'. Section 6 of the bill defined the powers of the Board to organize and maintain the system of examinations while clause 6.4, which was added as the bill was passing through parliament, permitted the 'benefits of this Act' to be applied to the education of girls. The bill itself was very prescriptive and both the programme of subjects to be examined and the scale of result fees to be paid were stated. Therefore the subsequent rules

6 Leon Ó Broin, *The chief secretary: Augustine Birrell in Ireland* (Hamdeon, CT & London, 1970). 7 *Bill to provide for the establishment and function of an administrative council in Ireland and for other purposes connected therewith*, H.C. 1907 (182), ii, 481. 8 *Bill to make further provision with respect to education in Ireland and for other purposes connected therewith*, H.C. 1919 (214), i, 407. An earlier bill relating to setting up a local education authority in Belfast, which was in great need of improved educational provision, was introduced (*Bill to make better provision for primary education in the city of Belfast*, H.C. 1919 (240), ii, 665) and another bill in 1920 tried to recover the aborted McPherson bill, H.C. 1920 (35), I, 563. However, both were unsuccessful. 9 *Bill, intituled, An Act to promote intermediate education in Ireland,*

of the Board had to be closely based on the act and, unlike the more loosely drawn up Stanley Letter which established the national school system, the act allowed for little change or development.

In 1890 the finances of the Board were increased by an allocation of the so-called 'whiskey money' raised from local taxation from customs and excise duties.[10] The Irish share of the fund was paid to both national and intermediate education and provided a welcome source of extra finance for the increased number of results fees and prizes required as more school entered for the examinations. In 1900, following the recommendations of the Palles Commission, a bill was passed under which the Intermediate Board was empowered to change its rules and it was no longer bound by the schedule of 1878 act. It was given the power to appoint an inspectorate subject to the sanction of the lord lieutenant and the treasury in London. The new rules introduced in 1902 brought many changes to the examination programme. The subjects were grouped under two headings, the grammar school course and the modern course, and the Board adopted 'joint' courses in science and drawing with the new Department of Agriculture and Technical Instruction. The Board continued to be short of money despite receiving the additional source of income. This income varied from year to year so from 1911 it was fixed at £46,566.[11]

In 1914, in an effort to raise the standard of secondary teachers' qualifications and improve their working conditions, the Secondary Teachers' Registration Council bill was introduced by Chief Secretary Birrell. The Council was to consist of representatives of the teaching profession, the Intermediate Board, the Department of Agriculture and Technical Instruction and the universities and it was to lay down minimum qualifications for secondary teachers and produce a register of teachers. The bill also proposed to provide a teachers' salaries grant of £40,000 to be paid to schools where the manager employed at least one lay teacher (as opposed to a clerical teacher) at a ratio of 1:40. The first register of intermediate school teachers (male and female) was introduced in 1918.[12] Many teachers had no university degree and fewer still had, as yet, a professional teaching qualification. A number of the female convent teachers had taken the University of Cambridge teachers' training syndicate certificate while some graduates had taken

H.C. 1878 (249), iii, 533; amended in Commons, H.C. 1878 (275), iii, 543.   **10** *Bill for the distribution and application of certain duties of customs and excise; and for other purposes connected therewith,* H.C. 1890 (244), v, 425; amended in Commons, H.C. 1890 (404), vi, 437.   **11** A number of later bills were relevant to intermediate education, including *Bill to amend the law relating to intermediate education in Ireland,* H.C. 1900 (210), ii, 511; amended in Commons, H.C. 1900 (315), ii. 515. In 1913 a bill enabled the Board to pay grants to schools on a basis other than examination fees. See *Bill to amend the law relating to intermediate education in Ireland* (no.2), H.C. 1912–13 (351), ii, 885 and a similar bill (H.C. 1913 (157), iii, 201 which was amended in Lords, H.C. 1913 (322), iii, 205).   **12** *Bill to amend the law relating to secondary education in Ireland* (219), H.C. 1912–13 (219), ii, 879; H.C. 1914 (161), iii, 477. The first teachers' register lists all the secondary teachers employed, both religious and lay, with the name of their schools.

the National University of Ireland or the University of Dublin diploma in education.[13]

Other bills related to endowed schools and to the establishment of reformatories and industrial schools. The most important was the educational endowments bill of 1885 which set up the educational endowments commissioners empowered to reform existing school endowments.[14] Under the 1857–8 bill relating to reformatory schools, voluntary schools could apply to be certified and receive grants and were to be inspected annually by the inspector of reformatory schools.[15] The industrial schools' bill of 1867, which was a extension of the English Industrial Schools' Act of 1857, similarly empowered voluntary schools to receive grants to care for and maintain children in danger of neglect and crime.[16] These industrial schools were mostly to be run by religious orders and financed by the State.

Three important bills related to the development of university education, namely the colleges bill of 1845 which established the three Queen's colleges, the university bill of 1879 which founded the Royal University of Ireland, and the Irish universities bill of 1908 which established the National University of Ireland. For the purposes of a local study, it can be illuminating to examine the impact of the presence of a university such Queen's College Cork on a provincial city since the institution brought increased educational opportunities for the neighbouring population and provided a stimulus for the growth of second-level education in the city and its environs. The university also brought to the city an increased number of academics, together with their families, and this contributed to the intellectual and social life of the city.

The 1845 colleges bill[17] outlined the structure and organization of the three Queen's colleges. It was passed in parliament only after bitter debate and

---

13 *Register of the intermediate schoolteachers in Ireland* (Dublin, 1919).   **14** *Bill, intituled, An Act to reorganize the educational endowments of Ireland*, H.C. 1884–5 (176), i, 445.   **15** *Bill to promote and regulate reformatory schools for juvenile offenders in Ireland*, H.C. 1857–8 (50), iv, 237; amended in Commons, 1857–8 (140), iv, 245, amended in Lords, 1857–8 (244), iv, 255. The 1858 act was amended in 1868 (*Bill to amend the law relating to reformatory schools*, H.C. 1867–8 (65), iv, 375) and under an act of 1881 (*Bill to amend the Industrial schools Act, and the law relating to reformatories (Ireland), and to enlarge and extend the powers of the Poor Law authorities in respect thereto*, H.C. 1881 (4), ii, 365) Grand Juries and certain town councils were empowered to contribute to the building of reformatory schools.   **16** *Bill to extend the Industrial schools Act to Ireland*, H.C. 1867 (17) iii, 215; amended in Commons, H.C. 1867 (102), iii, 229, H.C. 1867–8 (6), ii, 523.   **17** *Bill to enable her majesty to endow new colleges for the advancement of learning in Ireland*, H.C. 1845 (299) (400), i, 357, 365. For details of the passing of the bill, see Moody & Beckett, *Queen's, Belfast*, i, 8–32. The bill, which was put forward by the prime minister, Sir Robert Peel, and home secretary, James Graham, was opposed by the Catholic Church, Daniel O'Connell, and the Protestant right-wing in parliament. It was part of the conciliation policy of Peel's conservative government and was preceded by the Maynooth College grant in 1844 and the setting up of the Board of Charitable Bequests, which had Catholic representatives on it. See R.B. McDowell, *Public opinion and government policy in Ireland, 1800–46* (London, 1955); D. Kerr, *Peel, priest and politics: Sir Robert Peel's administration and the Roman Catholic Church in Ireland, 1841–1846* (Oxford, 1982); Susan M. Parkes, 'Higher education, 1793–1908' in W.E. Vaughan (ed.), *A*

opposition from those who objected to the non-denominational, public funded and secular nature of these institutions. The bill was an example of pioneer education legislation as it was the first time there had been an attempt to establish a university which was financed by public funds so as to create access for the middle classes to third level education. The Queen's University, consisting of the three Queen's colleges, was incorporated in 1850.[18]

The 1879 Royal University bill established a new examining and degree-awarding university and at the same time abolished the Queen's University. Graduates from the Queen's colleges henceforth were awarded degrees from the Royal University of Ireland as were students from the Catholic University College. The bill made provision for teaching fellowships, scholarships and prizes and specifically included women: 'The senate shall institute and make provision for carrying on such examinations for candidates of matriculation and degrees, and such other University examinations in secular subjects, including examinations for women for degrees ...' The bill was a compromise measure aimed at finding an acceptable solution to the 'university question' after the failure of Gladstone's university bill of 1873.[19]

The Irish Universities bill of 1908 was a further compromise measure. The acceptable solution to the 'university question' was eventually provided, largely by the work of Chief Secretary Birrell and Dr William Joseph Walsh, Catholic archbishop of Dublin.[20] Two new non-denominational universities were established – the National University of Ireland and Queen's University, Belfast. The National University, consisting of three constituent university colleges in Dublin, Cork and Galway, was seen as a 'university for Catholics' while Queen's College, Belfast, now elevated to university status, maintained a strong Protestant tradition.

new history of Ireland, v: *Ireland under the union, part ii, 1870–1921* (Oxford, 1996), pp 539–70. **18** The founding of the Queen's colleges had a considerable effect on the development of other universities in the British Empire. The foundations of universities in Sydney (1850), Melbourne (1853) and in Calcutta (1855) were all directly connected with the experience gained in Ireland during the 1840s: see Eric Ashby, *Universities: British, Indian and African; a study in the ecology of higher education* (London, 1966). **19** *Bill, intituled, an Act to promote the advance of learning and to extend the benefits connected with university education in Ireland*, H.C. 1878–9 (250), vii, 591; amended in Committee, H.C. 1878–9 (283), vii, 599. A number of other education bills relating to university education were introduced in the 1870s. In 1873 Gladstone's abortive university bill (*Bill for the extension of university education in Ireland*, H.C. 1873 (55), vi, 329) aimed to create a single university of Dublin, which would include Trinity College, the Queen's colleges and the Catholic University. This bill which pleased none of the parties was defeated in parliament by three votes only. Under the pressure of Gladstone's bill, Trinity College moved to make itself a non-denominational university. Arising from this initiative led by Henry Fawcett, MP for Brighton, a bill was introduced which abolished all religious tests, with the exception of those in the divinity school (see *Bill to abolish tests in Trinity College Dublin, and the University of Dublin*, H.C. 1873 (no. 3) (124), vi, 375). **20** *Bill to make further provision with respect to university education in Ireland*, H.C. (1908), 184 ii, 1057; *Irish universities bill as amended by standing committee*, H.C. 1908 (306), ii, 1075; *Lords amendment to the Irish universities bill*, H.C. 1908 (358), ii, 1097); see Thomas J. Morrissey, *William J. Walsh, archbishop of Dublin, 1841–1921* (London, 2000), pp 210–37.

For technical education there were two important bills – the 1889 bill which empowered local authorities to levy a rate for technical education and the 1899 bill which established the Department of Agriculture and Technical Instruction. The 1889 Technical Instruction Act had little effect in Ireland in the absence of a county council structure, although some of the larger cities, notably Belfast, Dublin and Cork, were able to use the act to support technical schools. As well as setting up a central authority to support technical education, the 1899 act also invested power in the newly established county councils to establish technical instruction committees and to open schools.[21]

(b) Reports

(i) Reports of royal commissions and parliamentary committees relating to all levels of schooling in Ireland

There are a large number of parliamentary reports relating to education at all levels and these provide a wealth of detail for research in a wide variety of aspects of Irish education and policy. Each report usually consists of the following components – an agreed final report which summarises the findings of the commission or committee and lists its recommendations; minutes of evidence which record verbatim interviews with witnesses called to the commission or committee, and appendices and returns of relevant further written information submitted to the commission. Therefore most reports run to two or three volumes and the reference number of each is required to locate the particular volume.[22]

For the specific purposes of a local study, five of these education reports are especially pertinent. The first, compiled by the commissioners of Irish education inquiry in 1825, surveyed existing schools prior to the introduction of the national school system in 1831.[23] The second notable report was written by the commissioners of public instruction public who, in 1835, examined religious instruction in

---

21 *Bill to enable councils of counties and municipal boroughs to provide technical schools and classes,* H.C. 1889 (211), vii, 350; *A bill for the establishing of a Department of Agriculture and other industries and technical instruction in Ireland, and for other purposes connected therewith,* H.C. 1899 (180), i, 55; *Lords amendment to the Agriculture and Technical Instruction (Ireland) bill,* H.C. 1899 (300), i, 93.   **22** For example, the *Report of her majesty's commissioners appointed to inquire into the endowments* [Kildare commission] of 1857–8 was published in four parts, each in a separate volume, and referenced as H.C. 1857–8 (2336–I–IV), xxii, pts i–iv. Part i is the final report, parts ii and iii contain the minutes of evidence with documents and index, and part iv contains the tables of schools and endowments. A minority report by Archibald John Stephens, one of the commissioners who refused to sign the report, was published separately in another volume (*Separate report by Archibald John Stephens, Esq.,* H.C. 1857–8 (2345), xliv, 409).   **23** The commissioners published nine reports: *First report,* H.C. 1825 (400), xii, 1; *Second report,* H.C. 1826–7 (12), xii, 1; *Third report,* H.C. 1826–7 (13), xiii, 1; *Fourth report,* 1826–7 (89), xiii, 157; *Fifth report,* 1826–7 (441), xiii, 359; *Sixth report,* H.C. 1926–7 (442), xiii, 385; *Seventh report,* H.C. 1826–7 (443), xiii, 501; *Eighth report,* H.C. 1826–7 (509), xiii, 537 and *Ninth report,* H.C. 1826–7 (516), xiii, 999.

existing schools in each benefice and diocese.[24] The third is that of the endowed schools' commission of 1857–8 which listed the origins and endowments of the schools in each parish[25] while the fourth is the report published by the 1870 royal commission on primary education, which undertook a survey of all existing primary schools. The last report was compiled by the endowed school commission of 1881 which undertook yet another survey of school endowments. A comparative longitudinal study of educational provision in a local area can be undertaken using these five reports.

The reports of the 1825 Irish education inquiry provide the most detail on educational provision in Ireland in the 1820s, on the eve of the introduction of the national school system. A nationwide parochial school survey were carried out in 1824 by both the Catholic and Protestant parish clergy who recorded the number of parish and pay schools along with their teachers' names, pupil numbers and attendance, and sources of finance. The report also contains details on the workings of education societies and schools that were in receipt of parliamentary grants, including the Kildare Place Society and the charter schools, as well as the Hibernian Society's schools for the children of soldiers and sailors, Belfast Academical Institution and St Patrick's College, Maynooth. Ten years later the reports of the commissioners of public instruction in Ireland presented another parochial survey, making it possible to track the growth of schooling in a locality over this ten-year period.

For example, in 1824 in the parish of Rosenallis in Queen's County (Laois), there were five Catholic pay schools with thatched roofs and mud walls at Mullyhanna, Gurteen, Corbally, Nyra and Mountmellick, where the average teacher's salary was £8 per annum. In Mountmellick there were four schools run by individual masters. John Donohue had a school, which was a lime and stone thatched house worth £10 and the teachers' salary was £12. There were forty-one pupils on roll, twenty-five boys and sixteen girls, of whom forty were Catholic. Another school was run by John and Susanna Dawson, both Protestants. The teachers' salaries amounted to £55 18s. 6d. and the school-house was 'built with lime and stone and slated, and would cost £200'. There were ninety-six pupils on roll, thirty-one Protestants and sixty-five Catholics, of whom forty-two were boys and fifty-five were girls. The school was supported by a grant from the Kildare Place Society and 'is conducted under the management of a numerous committee of ladies and gentlemen, who subscribe to its supports'. There was also a school run by William Mullen, a Quaker, in a slated house. The master's salary was £40 per annum and there were thirty pupils on roll. A fifth school was run by Valentine and Maria Dunne, both Catholics, in a slated house. The teacher's salary was £80 per annum and there were thirty-five pupils on roll, of whom sixteen were

24 *First report of the commissioners of public instruction (Ireland), with an appendix,* H.C. 1835 (45) (46) xxxiii, 1, 829; *Second report of the commissioners on public instruction (Ireland),* H.C. 1835 (47), xxxiv, 1. **25** *Report of her majesty's commissioners appointed to inquire into the endowments* [Kildare commission], iii: *Papers accompanying the report (tables of schools and endowments),*

Catholic and nineteen were Protestants. The largest school in Mountmellick was the Leinster Provincial School run by the Society of Friends (Quakers), which was a boarding school. The master was Henry Ferris and the mistress was Jane Shannon. The master's salary was £80 per annum as compared with the mistress's income of £15 per annum. The boarders paid fees of £24 per annum, '[al]though for children unable to pay, £10 per annum, only is required'. There were fifty-five dissenters on roll and thirty-seven Catholics.[26] These 1824 returns show the state of small schools in Ireland. Some were well housed, others not, and the salaries of the teachers range from £8 to £80 per annum. The figures also show the prevalence of 'mixed education' of Protestant and Catholic children in these schools and the extent of co-education.[27]

Twenty years later, in 1856, the Kildare Endowed schools commission was established to examine the existing provision of secondary education and the work of endowed schools.[28] A survey of endowed schools in each county and the nature of the endowments was undertaken, and this is especially useful to local historians as it records details concerning the foundation and purpose of these schools. The tables featured in the survey list the name and locality of the school, its foundation and original endowment and land grant (usually from the local landlord), the acreage of the site in acres, roods and perches (a. r. p.) and details of the value of the endowment including the estimated annual value of the school, the income from the land and from local funds. The school's aim and its course of instruction is described. Details of the master's appointment, his annual salary, the party by whom he is paid, and any additional income from school fees and other benefits such apartments, land and fuel are included. So too is data relating to the capacity of the school building, the numbers of pupils on roll and their religious denomination, average daily attendance and annual charges. For example, in the parish of Rosenallis in Queen's County (Laois) a school was founded on 16 August 1822 thanks to a grant of £73 16s. 11d. from the lord lieutenant's fund, subscriptions of £36 18s. 5½d. and a land grant from the marquis of Drogheda. The school site consisted of one rood valued at £3 11s. 6d. The object of the

H.C. 1857–8 (2336–IV), xii, pt iv, 1.   **26** *Second report of commissioners of Irish education inquiry, abstract of returns in 1824, from the Protestant and Catholic clergy in Ireland, of the state of education in their respective parishes*, H.C. 1826–7 (12), xii, 768–70.   **27** Returns made for schools by the Catholic and Protestant clergy often differed. Those made by the Protestant clergy have been used here. Two examples demonstrate the conflicting figures: in the case of Mountmellick, the Catholic cleric's return for the Dawsons' school cited thirty-four Protestants and twenty-six Catholics and his return for the Dunnes' school cited twenty-four Catholics and seventeen Protestants on roll. Fortunately the commissioners published both sets of returns.   **28** *Report of her majesty's commissioners appointed to inquire into the endowments* [Kildare commission], H.C. 1857–8 (2336–i–IV), xii, pts i–iv. Two of the commissioners, Archibald John Stephens, a Protestant and H.G. Hughes, a Catholic, refused to sign the final report as in their opinion it failed to take account of the rights of denominational education. As a result, Stephens published a minority report (*Separate report*

school was 'for the resident master to teach children, selected by the minister of the parish or master, English, and arithmetic under the regulation of the minister' and the course of instruction consisted of 'reading, writing, English grammar, geography, arithmetic, and needlework'. The teacher was appointed by the minister and was paid an annual salary of £12 by the rector. He had no other income. The school's capacity was eighty-one children, although only twenty-two were on roll and the average daily attendance was sixteen. Of those on roll, twenty were United Church (Church of Ireland) pupils and two were Roman Catholics. The school was free.[29] In his report on the school, written on 9 May 1856, the assistant commissioner, George Whitley Abraham, was very critical of what he witnessed during his visit, complaining that 'the girls in this school seem to receive very little instruction. Their reading is a mere attempt and they are not expected to parse. The arithmetical text-book (Thompson) is never used, and the school is altogether in a state of very imperfect efficiency'.[30]

On the other hand, at Rathdowney, in the same county, Erill had been founded in 1823 with a grant of £92 6s. 2d., subscriptions of £92 6s. 2d. and a grant of land from the Ladies Fitzpatrick. There, English grammar, writing, reading, geography and arithmetic were taught as well as the Roman Catholic catechism to Roman Catholic pupils. The school was connected with the National Board and so the master was paid a higher salary of £26 by the National Board and was in receipt of an additional £7 from the landlord, Mr Fitzpatrick. The master also had free apartments, land worth £5 and school fees amounting to £5. The school had an assistant teacher who was paid £22 by the National Board and £6 by Mr Fitzpatrick. The building had capacity for 100 pupils but there were 151 on roll, of whom 147 were Roman Catholics and four were United Church. However, the average daily attendance was only sixty. Whitley Abraham also reported on some of the larger endowed schools in Queen's County including the provincial school of the Society of Friends in Mountmellick (deemed 'most satisfactory'), Preston's School at Ballyroan ('very unsatisfactory'), and the Incorporated Society's Day School at Strabally ('unsatisfactory').

The Kildare commissioners took evidence from witnesses in towns around the country and cross-references to individual evidence regarding the state of a school are noted in the tables featured in the report. For instance, evidence concerning Preston's School at Ballyroan was given in Maryborough by the Revd John Lyon, who had been appointed school master in 1838 and who, in the 1850s, had only four pupils. Loftus Bland, MP for King's County, also gave evidence and stressed the need for a good classical school in the county.[31] Evidence was also taken in

by Archibald John Stephens, Esq., H.C. 1857–8 (2345), xlvi, 409). **29** *Report of her majesty's commissioners appointed to inquire into the endowments* [Kildare commission], iii, *Papers accompanying the report (tables of schools and endowments)*, H.C. 1857–8 (2336– IV), xxii, pt iv, 1. **30** Ibid., 206, 212. The commission appointed six assistant commissioners to visit and report on the schools. **31** *Report of her majesty's commissioners appointed to inquire into the endowments* [Kildare commission], i, *Evidence taken before her majesty's commissioners of inquiry*

1857–8 from the major educational endowments such as the Erasmus Smith Trust, the Incorporated Society for Promoting in English Protestant Schools in Ireland, the Royal Free Schools, as well as from smaller private trusts such the Colonel Roberston schools in Donegal,[32] the schools of the Society of Friends, the Christian Brothers and the Claremont Institution for the Education of the Deaf and Dumb.[33]

Overall, the report of the Kildare commission showed how many local school endowments were under-utilized and the report recommended a more strict system of supervision by inspection and a central registry. However, the report failed to be implemented due to strong opposition from both the Church of Ireland and the Catholic hierarchy to the proposed system of 'mixed', non-denominational intermediate schools. At this time the Catholic Church strongly resisted the notion of so-called 'mixed education' (whereby Catholics and Protestants were educated together in the same school). The publication in 1859 of James Kavanagh's polemic work entitled *The Catholic case stated* played a significant part in steering Catholic opinion against 'mixed education'.[34]

Although the report of the Kildare commission had little result, later attempts were made to reform the endowed schools and to make more equitable and effective use of their resources. In 1881 the Rosse commission on educational endowments[35] surveyed the endowments, property, and curriculum of the endowed schools. Commissioners conducted interviews with principals and carried out school visitations. Their report is indexed both by school and by name of witnesses so it is easily accessible. For example, in Belfast, witnesses included the Revd Henry Parker, headmaster of the Methodist College and the Revd John Conway from St Malachy's College while in Cork the Revd Thomas Moore, principal of

into the state of the endowed schools in Ireland, H.C. 1857–8 (2336–II), xxii, pt ii, 229–43. A full list of the towns visited and the name of witnesses called is included in this volume. A further volume of evidence, with documents and an index, is contained in vol. ii, H.C. 1857–8 (2336–II), xxii, pt iii, 1.   **32** For details see *Report of her majesty's commissioners appointed to inquire into the endowments* [Kildare commission], iii, *Papers accompanying the report (tables of schools and endowments),* H.C. 1857–8 (2336–IV), xxii, pt iv, 524–5.   **33** Rachel Pollard, *The Avenue.* For a full list of schools reported on by the commission, see table of contents in *Report of her majesty's commissioners appointed to inquire into the endowments* [Kildare commission], H.C. 1857–8 (2336–I), xxii, pt i, ii–iv.   **34** Norman, *Catholic Church in the age of rebellion,* pp 53–85; James Kavanagh, *The Catholic case stated – mixed education* (Dublin, 1859). The report of the Kildare commission encouraged the Catholic Church to expand its own provision of secondary education and by 1870 there were forty-seven Catholic intermediate schools, twenty-three of which were diocesan colleges and twenty-four were under the control of religious orders or congregations of priests, such as the Carmelites, the Holy Ghost Fathers, the Marist Fathers, the Jesuits and Dominicans. **35** See *Report of the commissioners appointed by the lord lieutenant of Ireland* [Rosse commission] [C 2831], H.C. 1881, xxxv, 1. Questionnaires submitted by the schools to the commission are in the National Archives.

Midleton College and the Revd James Burke, director of the Christian Brothers' school, were interviewed. The report also includes a list of existing endowed schools in each county. It is therefore possible to conduct a comparative study of the condition of endowed schools in a locality as reported by the Kildare commission in 1857 and then twenty years later by the Rosse commission. The tables record the date of foundation of each school, the acreage of site, the names of trustees, the appointment of master/mistress and his or her salary, the course of instruction, the size of the school building, the number of pupils on roll and their religious denomination. Cross-references to the evidence given by witnesses are also listed in these tables.

An example of a wealthy endowment was Morgan's School in Castleknock, Co. Dublin. It was founded in 1784 with an endowment of 2,269 acres in the city and county of Dublin, in County Leitrim, in Drogheda and in County Limerick. The annual income from the land was £543 12s. 9d. The trustees included the lord primate, the lord chancellor and the chief justice of the queen's bench. The school was established 'for the clothing, lodging, dieting and educating children of reduced Protestant parents, and for the apprenticing them to Protestant masters'. In 1857 the curriculum included reading, writing, grammar, geography, arithmetic, English, Grecian and Roman history, Euclid, algebra, mensuration, book-keeping, vocal music, drawing, scriptures and catechetical instruction. The master's salary was £92 per annum with apartments, and an additional sum of £15 from the endowment, along with fuel and candles. The school had room for 160 boys with twenty-one boarders; the average attendance was forty pupils, all members of the established Church of Ireland. Twenty-one pupils paid fees of £12 per annum and the rest attended for free. The assistant commissioner, Mr F.W. McBlain, wrote of his visit the school:

> The school is well conducted and the enrolment on the whole in a satis-
> factory condition. I examined the boys in English history and geography, the
> answering in which was of a creditable character. I also examined their copy
> books and found the writing decidedly good. The schoolhouse does not
> contain the conveniences, which such an establishment should possess. It has
> neither baths nor water closets, and the lavatory accommodation is miserable.[36]

By 1881 the master and matron were paid £100 per year and had apartments, with fuel, light and vegetables free of charge. By then there was a schoolroom, two dormitories, and teacher apartments 'in good repair'. Thirty pupils were on roll, all of them Church of Ireland. The annual charge was £18 per year and twenty free places were provided.[37]

36 *Report of the commissioners appointed by the lord lieutenant of Ireland* [Rosse commission] [C 2831], H.C. 1881, xxxv; *Report of her majesty's commissioners appointed to inquire into the endowments* [Kildare commission], iii, *Papers accompanying the report (tables of schools and endowments)*, H.C. 1857–8 (2336–IV), xxii, pt iv, 16–17, 40–1. **37** *Report of the commissioners*

The Rosse commissioners also invited five educationalists to visit and report on different groups of schools. For example, Revd J.P. Mahaffy of Trinity College, Dublin was invited to submit a report on grammar and boarding schools while Revd T.T. Gray of Trinity College reported on the royal schools.[38]

(ii) Reports of commissions and select committees on educational provision in specific sectors / levels

Primary education The four major commissions which are useful for studying the national school system in the nineteenth century are the Powis royal commission (1870), the Belmore commission (1898), the Dill vice-regal committee (1913) and lastly, the Killanin vice-regal committee (1919).

The Powis report consists of eight volumes, printed in five parts, which detail the history and workings of the national system since its establishment in 1831. The commission took two years (1868–70) to complete its work.[39] Its report included an examination of the National Board and its activities in the management and building of schools, the rate of school attendance, the publication of school books, the inspectorate and teacher training. Among the wide range of witnesses interviewed were Archbishop Paul Cullen of Dublin, Alexander Mac Donnell, the resident commissioner of the National Board, and Patrick Keenan, the chief of inspection of the National Board, as well Thomas Allies of the Catholic Poor School Committee in England.[40] Witnesses were called from other educational bodies such as the Church Education Society, the Erasmus Smith Trust and the Christian Brothers. A special report was undertaken by two of her majesty's inspectors in England, Revd B. Cowie and S.N. Stokes, into the National Board's Marlborough Street Training College along with the Board's network of model schools.[41] Therefore, the Powis commission is a useful staring

---

appointed by the lord lieutenant of Ireland [Rosse commission] [C 2831], H.C. 1881, xxxv; *Report of her majesty's commissioners appointed to inquire into the endowments* [Kildare commission], iii, *Papers accompanying the report (tables of schools and endowments),* H.C. 1857–8 (2336–IV), xxii, pt iv, pp 348–9. Arthur Murphy, headmaster of Morgan's School and Mr J.P. Hamilton, land agent for the governors, were called as witnesses: see ibid., 781–5, 779–827.   **38** *Report of the commissioners appointed by the lord lieutenant of Ireland* [Rosse commission] [C 2831], H.C. 1881, xxxv, *Appendix to the report,* 233–61, 223–9. Another report, completed by Mr H.K. Moore of Trinity College, focussed on primary schools, including national schools, Christian Brothers schools and the schools run by the Erasmus Smith Trust.   **39** *Royal commission of inquiry into primary education (Ireland)* [Powis commission] [C 6], H.C. 1870, xxviii, 1.   **40** Richard Aldrich & Peter Gordon, *Dictionary of British educationalists* (London, 1989), p. 7.   **41** *Royal commission of inquiry into primary education (Ireland)* [Powis commission], i, pt ii: *appendix to the report; also special reports on the model schools (district and minor), and the central training institution, etc., Dublin, and on agricultural schools* [C 6a], H.C. 1870, xxviii, pt ii, 1 (minor model schools were smaller and non-residential, for example, Parsonstown, Omagh). See *Royal commission of inquiry into primary education (Ireland)* [Powis commission], vii: *returns from the National Board* [C 6–VII], H.C.

point for a study of all aspects of primary education and the workings of the National Board in its first forty years. One of the total 129 recommendations of the Powis report was the introduction of a system of payment by results, which aimed to increase teachers' salaries, improve attendance, and provide an examined core curriculum.[42] The report also recommended reform of teacher training, recognition of denominational training colleges, closure of the Board's model schools and an end to the Board's publication of schoolbooks. The report accepted that the national system, although in law remained denominational, was in practice non-denominational, and that the rights of the Churches to manage their own schools and to provide teacher training should be recognized.

The 1898 Belmore royal commission was concerned with the national school curriculum and the introduction of more practical subjects.[43] Evidence was gathered from a wide range of witnesses from England, Scotland, Scandinavia and the Continent with particular reference to the educational ideas of the kinder-garten methods of Friedrich Froebel.[44] Among those interviewed were two leading educationalists in England, Sir Joshua Fitch and Sir Philip Magnus.[45] Other English witnesses included A.W. Bevis of the Birmingham School Board who came to Ireland in 1900 to organize courses for teachers in manual instruction, and W.H. Heller of the London School Board who came to organize elementary science course for teachers.[46] The commissioners also went to Sweden to interview Herr Otto Sälmon, director of the Slöyd seminarum at Näas as Sälmon was an expert on the teaching of educational woodwork.[47] The Slöyd

1870, xxiii, pt v, 361) for details of the origin of each model school with the names of those who signed the initial application. The minute books of the Powis commission are in the National Archives.   **42** Payment by results was introduced by the National Board in 1872. **43** *Royal commission on manual and practical instruction in primary schools under the Board of National Education in Ireland, First report of the commissioners and minutes of evidence* [C 8383], H.C. 1897, xliii, 1; *Second report of the commissioners* [C 8531], H.C. 1897, xliii, 109; *Third report of the commissioners* [C 8618], H.C. 1897, xliii, 401; *Final report of the commissioners* [C 8932], H.C. 1898, xliv, 1.   **44** Joachim Liebschner, *Foundations of progressive education: the foundation of the National Froebel Society* (Cambridge, 1991); Joachim Liebschner, *A child's work: freedom and guidance in Froebel's educational theory and practice* (Cambridge, 1992). **45** Aldrich & Gordon, *Dictionary of British educationalists*, pp 85, 161–2. Fitch was chief inspector of teacher training colleges in England and an expert in primary teaching training. He was author of *Lectures on teaching* (London, 1881) and *Educational aims and methods* (Cambridge, 1900). Magnus was a leading pioneer of technical education. He had been director of the City and Guilds of London Institute (1880–8), superintendent and secretary of the Institute's department of Technology (1888–1913), a fellow of London University and a member of the senate (1898–1931).   **46** *Royal commission on manual and practical instruction in primary schools under the Board of National Education in Ireland* [Belmore commission], *Second report of evidence, comprising that taken in England between March 18th and April 9, 1897, being the supplement to the second report of the commissioners* [C 8532], H.C. 1897, xliii, 113.   **47** *Royal commission on manual and practical instruction in primary schools under the Board of National Education in Ireland* [Belmore commission], *Third volume of minutes of evidence, comprising that taken between April 29 and July 21, 1897, being a supplement to the third report of the commissioners* [C 8619], H.C. 1897, xliii, 405.

system emphasized the educational value of handcraft and woodwork as an essential part of a general education and these had become part of the elementary curriculum in England.[48] The recommendations of the Belmore commission included the abolition of payment by results in national schools and the intro- duction of practical subjects into the curriculum such as kindergarten methods, educational handwork and woodwork, drawing, elementary science, cookery and laundry work for girls and agriculture for boys. The revised programme of primary instruction (1900) was largely based upon these recommendations.[49]

The third important report on the national system was generated by the Vice- regal committee of inquiry into primary education (Ireland) 1913, chaired by Sir Samuel Dill,[50] which was concerned with the salaries and promotion of teachers and the increasing friction between the National Board and the national teachers. Since the abolition of payment by results in 1900, graded salaries for teachers had been introduced. Assessment was by inspection, and this system led to bitter disagreements between the resident commissioner, Dr William Starkie, the inspectorate and teachers. The Dill committee attempted to tackle the problems, drawing evidence from a large number of witnesses including officials of the National Board, the inspectorate, and teachers. However, despite it recom- mendations to reform the inspection system and the administration of the Board, the issue of teachers' salaries continued to dominate the education scene.[51]

The fourth major report on the national system was that of the vice-regal committee of inquiry into primary education (Ireland) 1918, chaired by Lord Killanin, himself a member of the National Board.[52] Its brief was to report on

---

48 Evelyn Chapman, *Slöyd; or hand-work as a factor in education* (London, 1888); S. Barter, *Manual instruction. Woodwork, The English Slöyd* (4th ed., revised, London & New York, 1905). Barter was organizer and instructor in woodwork for the London County Council Education Committee. The teaching of elementary science was greatly influenced by the work of H.E. Armstrong (1848–1937) of the City and Guilds Technical College, London. He was author of *Essays in the teaching of scientific methods* (London, 2nd ed., 1925); see G.Van Praagh, *H.E. Armstrong and science education* (London, 1973). **49** *Royal commission on manual and practical instruction in primary schools under the Board of National Education in Ireland* [Belmore commission], *Final report of the commissioners* [C 8923], H.C. 1898, xliv, 1. **50** *Vice-regal committee of inquiry into primary education (Ireland)* [Dill commission], *First report of the committee* [C 6828], H.C. 1913, xxii, 231; *Appendix to the first report of the committee, minutes of evidence 13th February–12 March, 1913* [C 6829], H.C. 1913, xxii, 235; *Second report of the committee* [C 7228], H.C. 1914, xxvii, 1; *Appendix to the second report of the committee, minutes of evidence, 13th March–25th June, 1913* [C 7229], H.C. 1914, xxviii, 5; *Third report of the committee* [C 7479], H.C. 1914, xxviii, 533; *Appendix to the third report of the committee, minutes of evidence, 26th June–17th September, 1913* [C 7480], H.C. 1914, xxviii, 587; *Final report of the committee* [C 7235], H.C. 1914, xxviii, 1081. **51** The committee was chaired by Sir Samuel Dill, Queen's University, Belfast and other members included Professor Jeremiah Henly of the Church of Ireland Training College and Thomas Kettle, professor of economics at University College, Dublin. Witnesses included Starkie and the chief of inspection, Alfred Purser. The president of the INTO, Catherine Mahon, was one of the most important witnesses; see O'Connell, *A hundred years of progress*, pp 406–9; Síle Chuinneagáin, *Catherine Mahon, first woman president of INTO* (Dublin, 1998). **52** *Vice regal*

possible improvements in the position, conditions of service, promotion and remuneration of teachers in Irish national schools, and on the distribution of grants from public funds for primary education in Ireland, with a view to recommending suitable scales of salaries and pensions for different classes of teachers, having regard to the character, length of training necessary, the special qualifications obtained, the nature of duties to be performed and other relevant considerations. The committee's chief concern was with the salaries of teachers which had been a continuous cause of difficulty between the INTO and the government.[53] However, its recommendations ranged wider as the committee foresaw that increased salaries could not be borne by the central exchequer only but would require a local education rate to be levied by newly established local county education authorities. The government's decision to introduce the McPherson education bill in 1919 was influenced by the findings of the Killanin committee.

For a study of the curriculum and daily life of a national school researchers will find another set of parliamentary reports especially useful. The early working of the National Board, the problems of proselytism and the strict separation of secular from religious instruction were investigated by two parliamentary reports during the 1830s. As early as 1837 a select committee of the House of Lords was established to review the plan for education in Ireland and a number of witnesses were interviewed including members of the National Board and clergy of different denominations.[54] The backdrop to this initiative had been a highly publicised incident which occurred on Achill Island, Co. Mayo in 1835 in which Revd Edward Nangle of the Protestant mission quarrelled with the local national school teacher and the priest.[55] The report also reviewed the work of the first four National Board inspectors and highlighted varying levels and forms of opposition to the national system expressed by the Churches.[56] Another report, compiled by a select committee of the House of Commons and presented to parliament in 1837, also examined the working of the national system. Like the House of Lords

committee of inquiry into primary education (Ireland), 1918 [Killanin committee], *Final report of the committee*, i, *Report* [Cmd 60], H.C. 1919, xxi, 791; *Report of the committee*, ii, *Summaries of evidence, memoranda and returns* [Cmd 178], H.C. 1919, xxi, 789. A vice-regal committee was one appointed by the lord lieutenant of Ireland rather than by the Crown. Other members included representative of the INTO, the Churches and the National Board. Two government appointments were A.N.B. Bonaparte-Wyse, secretary to the National Board and Maurice Headlam, treasury remembrancer; see Maurice Headlam, *Irish reminiscences* (London, 1947). **53** See O'Connell, *A hundred years of progress*, pp 180–3. **54** *Report of the select committee of the House of Lords on the plan of education in Ireland, with minutes of evidence*, H.C. 1837 (543–I), viii, pt i; *Minutes of evidence taken before the select committee of the House of Lords on the plan of education in Ireland*, H.C. 1837 (543–II), viii, pt ii, I. (The select committee consisted of members of the House of Lords itself.) A cross-section of witnesses, both clergy and laity, showed different opinions on the national system in various localities. **55** See *Third report of the commissioners of national education in Ireland for the year 1836*, pp 52–3, H.C. 1836 (44), xxxvi, 90–91. **56** Eustás Ó hEideáin, *National school inspection in Ireland: the beginnings* (Dublin, 1967), pp 29–49.

committee, this group interviewed members of the National Board, 'those who objected to the principles of the National Board, and those who accepted the principles but disliked the practice.[57] Evidence was taken from the first resident commissioner, Revd James Carlile, from A.R. Blake, a Catholic founder member of the Board, and from Dr McArthur, the first head of the Board's Marlborough Street Central Training Institution and model schools. Two of the first inspectors, Robert Sullivan and J.F. Murray, gave evidence as did Revd Henry Cooke of the Presbyterian Church, who with his fellow churchmen, strongly opposed the rules regarding the separation of religious instruction in national schools.[58] Twenty years later, in 1854, another select committee of the House of Lords report was presented to parliament: this one focused mainly on religious education and use of the Board's own school books.[59] The context for this report was as follows. The Board published two scriptural reading books for use in combined hours of secular instruction.[60] In 1853 the Church of Ireland Archbishop Richard Whately of Dublin, himself a member of the National Board, visited Clonmel District Model School where he discovered to his chagrin that these scriptural books were not being used in any of the schools under the Board's management. A major row developed on the question of whether use of these religious books was in fact compulsory. When the Board eventually conceded that it was not mandatory, the archbishop resigned from the Board. The select committee interviewed Whately, together with other members of the National Board, inspectors and clergy, but the rule on the optional use of these scriptural books was unchanged and Whately's influence was fatally undermined as a Board member.[61]

The Dale report of 1904 is very useful for assessing the implementation of the revised programme of 1900.[62] F.H. Dale, who was invited by the government to undertake the survey, travelled around Ireland, visiting in all eighty ordinary national schools and eight large convent national schools. His terms of reference were

---

57 *Report of the select committee appointed to inquire into the progress and operation of the plan of education in Ireland*, H.C. 1837 (485), ix, 1; see Akenson, *Irish education experiment*, pp 157–87. The evidence of Revd James Carlile, first resident commissioner of national education, is printed in the appendix to *Third report of the commissioners of national education in Ireland for the year ending 31st March 1836*, pp 63–9, H.C. 1836 (44), xxxvi, 81; that of A.R. Blake, one of the first commissioners, appears on pp 69–107. **58** Ó Heideáin, *National school inspection in Ireland*, pp 35–75. **59** *Report from the select committee of the House of Lords appointed to inquire into the practical workings of the system of national education, with minutes of evidence*, H.C. 1854 (525), xv, pts i & ii, 1. **60** These were *Scriptures lessons* and *Lessons on the truth of Christianity*. **61** See Akenson, *Irish education experiment*, pp 258–74. He argues that Whately's belief in the value of 'mixed' education had been very important and that after his resignation, the denominational nature of the national system became amplified. D.H. Akenson, *A Protestant in purgatory: Richard Whately, archbishop of Dublin* (Hamden, CT, 1981). **62** *Report of Mr F.H. Dale, his majesty's inspector of schools, Board of Education, on primary education in Ireland* [Cd 1981], H.C. 1904, xx, 947. Dale was in Ireland from April to June 1903.

to inquire and report how typical Irish elementary day schools compare with similarly circumstanced public elementary schools in England as regards premises, equipment, staffing and instruction; and to what causes differences in economy and efficiency appear to be chiefly due.

Dale presented his report under these four headings and found that in the case of school situated in towns, the premises were markedly inferior to those of their English counterparts but in rural school premises compared favourably. He recommended that new schools should be built and the existing schools should be cleaner and more effectively heated. New desks and writing material were required (Dale found slates still in use). He advised that teachers' salaries be improved, and that reliance on untrained monitors to teach classes ought to be reduced. Dale was also critical of the lack of training and guidance for teachers in implementing the new revised programme. Indeed, he considered the proposed curriculum too ambitious and counselled that it be curtailed. Finally, he recommended that in order to provide the funding necessary for improving the national system, a structure of local education authorities should be set up, which could raise a local education rate and supervise schools as was the practice in England. When Dale's report was published in 1904 it was interpreted as both a criticism of the existing system of local clerical management and a threat to the Church's role in education.[63] In addition, the impact of the report was weakened by its having been written by 'an outsider' who had only visited the country for three months. Therefore, despite being practical and farsighted, the report's recommendations were not, on the whole, implemented, although the National Board did reduce the requirements of the revised programme.[64] Nonetheless, for historians of Irish education the Dale report presents a valuable survey of the state of the country's national schools at the beginning of the twentieth century.

Secondary/intermediate education and endowed schools For secondary/intermediate education there are only two major parliamentary reports, firstly, that of the Palles vice-regal commission (1898), which during its twenty years in operation examined the system of payment of results on which the intermediate examinations were based, and secondly, that of the Molony vice-regal committee on teachers' salaries (1919).[65] The Palles commission was chaired by Chief Baron Christopher Palles, chairman of the Intermediate Education Board. When the Board requested the government to set up an enquiry to examine the workings of

---

63 See Miller, *Church, State & nation*, pp 118–38; Titley, *Church, State & the control of schooling*, pp 17–25. **64** Courses in elementary science and in manual instruction were curtailed. **65** *First report of the commissioners on intermediate education (Ireland), with appendix* [Palles report] [C 9116, 9117], H.C. 1899, xxii; *Final report* [C 9511], H.C. 1899, xxii; *Evidence* [C 9512], H.C. 1899, xiii; *Part II of Appendix to final report* [C 9513], H.C. 1899, xxiv; *Report of the Vice-regal committee on the condition of service and remuneration of teachers in intermediate schools* [Molony committee] [Cmd 66], H.C. 1919, xxi, 645.

the intermediate system the government agreed, provided the commission was made up of Board members. The report, therefore, had a narrow focus and although a substantial body of evidence was collected, little changed in the system. The main issue was whether the system of payment by results should be continued, given the narrow examination syllabus and the burden these examinations placed on both staff and pupils in schools. The commission took evidence from a large number of witnesses from schools where pupils were sitting the examinations, and written submissions were also received from many others. As a result, historians can consult returns from individual schools throughout the country.[66] The commission recommended the retention of payment by results, declaring that an alternative system of capitation school grants could not be implemented until there an efficient school inspectorate was put in place.[67] Some curricular reform did take place as the examinations were divided into distinct courses (classical course, modern literary course, mathematical course, experimental science course) and this encouraged pupils to study more science, mathematics and modern languages.[68]

Partly because of the failure of the Palles commission to recommend any radical change and partly to encourage the structural reform of education, the government invited F.H. Dale, the English Board of Education inspector, to return to Ireland. This time, his task was to carry out a survey of secondary education and he was accompanied by a colleague, T.A. Stephens.[69] Their report was to be more farsighted and more influential than that produced by Dale in 1904. The terms of reference were in set out in four parts – the co-ordination of intermediate education with other grades of education, the premise and staffing of intermediate schools, the allocation of Intermediate Board funds, and the conditions of teachers working in intermediate schools. The inspectors, who visited nearly eighty intermediate schools in all, 'had the advantage of learning the views of a large number of ladies and gentlemen whose position and knowledge rendered them able to speak with special authority upon the subjects of our inquiry'. The report, which examined the four specific areas, made realistic recommendations. The

---

66 See *Report of the commissioners on intermediate education (Ireland), with appendix* [Palles report], *Part II of Appendix to final report* [C 9513], H.C. 1899, xxiv, 1. Query sheets were sent out to all the schools and submissions returned; see *Minutes of evidence* [C 9512], H.C. 1899, xxiii, 1, 472–81; Raftery & Parkes, *Female education in Ireland*, pp 87–94. **67** The 1900 Intermediate education (Ireland) Act gave the Board the right to change its own rules and to hire inspectors. A temporary inspectorate was introduced in 1901 but it was not until 1909 that a permanent inspectorate was established; see Hyland & Milne (eds), *Irish educational documents*, i, 217–18, 226–9. **68** *Rules of examinations – programme of examinations for Board of Intermediate Education for 1902*, H.C. 1901 (199), lvii, 13. **69** *Report of Messrs. F.H. Dale and T.A. Stephens, his majesty's inspectors of schools, Board of Education, on intermediate education in Ireland* [Dale and Stephens report] [Cd 2546], H.C. 1905, xxviii, 709.

system of payment by results should be abolished and a permanent inspectorate appointed. The number of intermediate examinations should be reduced from four (preparatory, junior, middle and senior grades) to two (intermediate and leaving certificates). Intermediate teachers' salaries should be increased and teacher training and professional register introduced. Much greater co-ordination was required between intermediate education and primary and technical education and in order to achieve this goal, it was recommended that a single central education authority be established.[70] The report was not well received by the Catholic Church authorities as it criticized the system of local clerical management and supported the introduction of a State inspectorate and a central board of control. However, the report was partially successful in that it did persuade the government to continue with its endeavours to reform Irish education administration.[71]

The on-going issue of secondary teachers' salaries eventually led to the setting up of another vice-regal committee in 1918, chaired by Lord Chief Justice Thomas Molony.[72] This committee was concurrent with the Killanin committee on primary salaries and both reported in March 1919. The Molony committee met with twenty witnesses, including managers, principals and teachers and its report offers revealing insights into the workings of the system at school level. It made recommendations supporting the abolition of payment by results, the introduction of a minimum incremental salary for secondary teachers and a pension scheme. It also pressed for the introduction of a scheme of local education rating and for the establishment of a single central authority to finance and administer education at all levels.

Acting on the advice of these two vice-regal committees, the government was persuaded to introduce the ill-fated Macpherson education bill, which eventually was defeated by the combined forces of the Catholic Church and the nationalists. The main clauses of the bill provided for the establishment of local education committees for each county and county borough. It was envisaged that these would have elected members and exercise authority to provide books for schools, transport to schools, special education for '"afflicted" children', scholarships for

---

70 Ibid., 84–7; Miller, *Church, State & nation*, pp 22–5. The two inspectors were referred as the 'English tourists' by the Irish press.   **71** In 1924 under the Free State government the public examinations were reduced to intermediate and leaving certificates and a compulsory professional qualification, the higher diploma in education, was required of all registered secondary teachers.   **72** *Report of the Vice-regal committee on the condition of service and remuneration of teachers in intermediate schools* [Molony committee] [Cmd 66], H.C. 1919, xxi, 645. For the first time women were appointed to sit on a government education committee, namely Henrietta White, principal of Alexandra College, Dublin, and Mary Ryan, professor of romance languages at University College, Cork and two union representatives of the association of secondary teachers, Annie McHugh, St Brigid's High School, St Stephen's Green, Dublin and Elizabeth Steele, Victoria College, Belfast; see Raftery & Parkes, *Female education in Ireland*, pp 94–101.

secondary education and to initiate the establishment and maintenance of evening continuation schools.[73]

Technical and scientific education For the historical development of technical and scientific institutions there are a number of valuable reports. Of these, the most important are the report on a proposed Science and Art Department for Ireland (1868)[74] and that of the royal commission on technical instruction, chaired by Lord Samuelson (1884).[75] Since its foundation in 1853, the Science and Art Department, South Kensington, had supplied grants for the teaching of science and art in Ireland.[76] By the 1860s demand was growing for Ireland to have its own department which would serve and support the distinct needs of Irish industry. The 1868–9 commission was invited to examine how this could be best achieved. However, the commission succeeded in having its original brief changed – it would now examine the issue of whether Ireland should or should not have its own department – it produced a report which examined the major institutions in receipt of grants, including the Royal Dublin Society, the College of Science, and the Royal Irish Academy. Among those interviewed were Sir Robert Kane, dean of the College of Science,[77] Patrick Keenan, chief of inspection at the National Board,[78] and A.B. Corlett of the Queen's Institute.[79] Despite the evidence presented by the witnesses in favour of a separate department, the commission advised against it, much to the disappointment of the Irish lobby. Consequently, the Irish scientific institutions continued to be supported by the South Kensington

73 Miller, *Church, State & nation*, pp 436–41; Titley, *Church, State & control of schooling*, pp 54–70; *Bill to make provision with respect to education in Ireland, and for other purposes connected therewith* [Cmd 214], H.C. 1919, i, 407. **74** *Report of the commission on the Science and Art Department in Ireland*, i, *Report*, H.C. 1868–9 (4103), xxiv, 1; ii, *Minutes of evidence, appendix, and index*, H.C. 1868–9 (4103–1), xxiv, 43. **75** *First report of the royal commission on technical instruction* [Samuelson commission] [C 3171], H.C. 1881, xxvii, 153; *Further reports with evidence and appendix* [C 3981], H.C. 1884, xxix, xxx, xxxi xxxi, pt.1. Samuelson was an iron master in Yorkshire, a MP and a strong supporter of technical education; see Aldrich & Gordon, *Dictionary of British educationalists*, p. 217; Michael Argles, *South Kensington to Robins, 1851–1963* (London, 1964). **76** For lists of schools in receipt of Science and Art Department grants together with examinations results see annual reports of the Science and Art Department, South Kensington: first report for 1853, H.C. 1854 (1783), xxviii, 269; forty-sixth report for 1899 [C 9191, C 9192], H.C. 1899, xxvii, 245, xxviii, 1. Other institutions which received grants were the Science and Art Museum, Dublin, the Metropolitan School of Art, Dublin, Botanic Gardens, Glasnevin, the National Library, the Royal Hibernian Academy of Arts, and Royal Zoological Gardens. **77** *Report of the commission on the Science and Art Department in Ireland*, i, *Report*, H.C. 1868–9 (4103), xxiv, 1; ii, *Minutes and evidence, appendix and index*, H.C. 1868–9 (41103–I), xxiv, 43; evidence Kane, 415–55. **78** Ibid., 515–48. **79** Ibid., 389–402. Corlett along with Anne Jelliicoe founded the Queen's Institute in Molesworth Street in 1861 to offer technical training for the daughters of gentlemen who needed to earn their own living. The courses offered included law writing, telegraphy, sewing (machine), and porcelain painting. See *Report of the Science and Art Commission*, ii, 21–3; Patricia Phillips, 'The Queen's Institute, Dublin (1861–81)' in McMillan (ed.), *Prometheus's fire*, pp 446–63.

department until the establishment of the Department of Agriculture and Technical instruction in 1899.[80] By the 1880s Britain was facing strong competition from Europe in her manufacturing industries. As a result, in 1881 the Samuelson royal commission on technical education was established to carry out a comparative study of technical education in Britain and selected countries across Europe, and to consider the effectiveness of technical education in relation to industry. Ireland was included in this examination. The Samuelson second report (volume one) contains a special section on Ireland and volume four is comprised solely of evidence gathered in Ireland.[81] Sir Patrick Keenan, resident commissioner of national education, gave an historical outline of the attempts of the national school system to encourage agricultural education,[82] and Br Dominic Burke, a pioneer of science teaching in North Monastery School, Cork discussed the practical approaches to science teaching adopted by his school.[83] Professor W.K. Sullivan, president of Queen's College, Cork presented a detailed plan entitled 'Scheme for technical education for Ireland', which was a master plan for development.[84]

During the nineteenth century the British parliament's response to the intense rivalry between the Royal Dublin Society (RDS, est. 1731), Ireland's leading scientific institution, and the new college of science (est. 1867) was to instigate a series of inquiries into the relationship between the RDS and various other institutions. Their reports offer useful insights into the provision of science education in early and mid-nineteenth-century Ireland.[85] For instance, the report

---

80 This 1868 report provides useful detail on the state of Irish scientific and technical education in the mid-nineteenth century. See Phillips, 'Queen's Institute' in McMillan (ed.), *Prometheus's fire*; J.J. Cooke, 'The movement for a separate department of technical instruction in Ireland, with particular reference to the Dublin Corporation' (unpublished MLitt thesis, TCD, 1984); Kieran Byrne, 'Approaches to technical education in nineteenth-century Ireland' in *Technical education: essays dedicated to the memory of Michael Clune*, pp 5–25; 'Science teaching and technical instruction' in Coyne (ed.), *Ireland industrial and agricultural* (Dublin, 1902), pp 155–74; see extract from the report of the commission on the Science and Art Department in Ireland, 186–89 in Hyland & Milne (eds), *Irish education documents*, i, 263–66; Mary Mulvihill, *Ingenious Ireland* (Dublin, 2002). **81** *Royal commission on technical instruction* [Samuelson commission], *Second report*, ii [C 3981], H.C. 1884, xxx; iv [C 3981], H.C. 1884, xxxi, pt 1. **82** Ibid., *Second Report*, ii [C 3981–I], H.C. 1884, xxx, 271–81. This article was reprinted in Coyne (ed.), *Ireland: industrial and agicultural*, pp 137–45. **83** Kelleher, *James Dominic Burke*, pp 108–11. **84** *Royal commission on technical instruction* [Samuelson commission], iii [C 3981–II], H.C. 1884, xxxi; Hyland & Milne (eds), *Irish educational documents*, i, 267–72. For details of Sullivan's career, see Murphy, *The college: a history of Queen's / University College, Cork*, pp 97–138. **85** *Report of the select committee appointed to inquire into the administration of the Royal Dublin Society with a view to the wider extension of the advantages of the annual parliamentary grant to that institution and to whom the return of the charter, rules and regulations of the Dublin Society was referred*, H.C. 1836 (445), xii, 335. This government inquiry into the RDS arose because Dr Daniel Murray, Catholic archbishop of Dublin, was 'blackballed' at a membership election in 1835. The report recommended changes to the constitution of the Society. It also advised that the Society's museum, library and botanic gardens should be opened to a wider public. See also *Report of select committee on the Royal Dublin Society and scientific instruction in Ireland*, H.C. 1863 (3180),

of the 1864 select committee on scientific institutions (Dublin) recommended that the Museum of Irish Industry (est. 1845) be upgraded to a college of science. In 1867, following yet another report,[86] the college was founded to provide 'a complete course of instruction in science applicable to the industrial arts ... and to aid in the instruction of teachers for local schools of science'.[87]

Reformatory and industrial schools Several other commissions which dealt with specialist areas of education in both Britain and Ireland produced reports which feature valuable material for conducting comparative studies of the treatment afforded young offenders and educational provision for them. For instance, the Aberdare commission on reformatory and industrial school (1884) examined Irish reformatories and industrial schools as part of its brief. It made a separate set of recommendations for Ireland since there were marked differences in its legislation and administration of the system as compared to the rest of Britain. Among those called to give evidence was Sir John Lentaigne, government inspector of reformatory and industrial schools.[88] Also relevant to Ireland is the British report on the education, condition, and employment of blind, deaf and dumb persons in 1889[89] which likewise includes a section on provision in Ireland together with a set of separate recommendations.[90] In this instance, Sir Patrick Keenan, resident commissioner of national education, was among those interviewed while Archbishop William Joseph Walsh of Dublin submitted a detailed paper on the work of Catholic institutions.

xvii, pt 1. This report recommended that the Museum of Irish Industry should be taken over by the RDS. However, the proposal stirred such strong objections from the country's other scientific institutions that a second inquiry was set up in 1864 and this recommended that the Museum remain autonomous and become a college of science (see *Report of select committee on scientific institutions (Dublin)*, H.C. 1864 (495), xiii, 1). **86** *Report of the commission on the College of Science, Dublin*, H.C. 1867 (219), lv, 771. **87** The new college offered a three-year course for associateship and women were admitted from the outset. By the end of the century the college had outgrown its premises at 45, St Stephen's Green and new buildings were opened on Merrion Street in 1911. The college, which came under the control of the DATI in 1900, became part of University College, Dublin in 1926. Reports on the work of the Royal College of Science are to found in the annual reports of the Science and Art Department, South Kensington to 1899, and in the reports of the DATI from 1900. The college records are in the Archives Department of University College, Dublin. See also Simon Lincoln, *Mansion, museum and commissioners: a history of the OPW in St Stephen's Green* (Dublin, 2002). **88** *Report of the reformatories and industrial schools commissioners* [C 3876], H.C. 1884, xlv, 1. The report was chaired by Lord Aberdare, a Scottish statesman, who also chaired the departmental committee appointed to inquire into higher and intermediate education in Wales in 1880. That report led to the Welsh Intermediate Act of 1889; see J. Gwynn Williams, *The university movement in Wales* (Cardiff, 1993), pp 63–88. **89** *Report of the royal commission on the blind, deaf and dumb in the united Kingdom, with evidence and appendix* [C 5781], H.C. 1889, xix, 1, xx, 1; see also K. Ellis, 'The development of the education of the blind in Ireland, from 1898' (unpublished MEd. thesis, TCD, 1974). **90** *Report of the royal commission on the blind, deaf and dumb, etc. of the United Kingdom with evidence and appendix* [C 5781], H.C. 1889, xix, 114–23, Keenan's

(iii) Annual reports

Reports by educational institutions and agencies The British parliamentary papers contain the annual reports of all major educational institutions in receipt of parliamentary grants. These include the commissioners of education from 1813, the commissioners of national education from 1831, the Board of Intermediate Education from 1878, the educational endowments commissioners from 1885, the Department of Agriculture and Technical Instruction from 1900, the inspector of reformatory schools from 1862, the Queen's colleges from 1845, and the Royal University from 1879.

The most useful annual reports on educational institutions for local history scholars are those generated by the commissioners of national education (CNEI) that contain details of individual national schools from the 1830s. The reports grew in size and content as the system developed and by the 1850s had extensive appendices and reports on the workings of the National Board. For instance, the nineteenth report for the year 1852 contains lists of all national schools, together with roll numbers, average attendance, gender of the pupils, the number of teachers and monitors, details of the amounts paid out in gratuities and premiums to teachers, in school requisites and free stock of school books, and in local contributions.[91] A short general report for the year gives the numbers of schools in operation, the number of pupils on roll, the religious denomination of pupils, the number of teachers trained, the salaries of the teachers and monitors and so on. The appendices contain a copy of the Stanley Letter of 1831, the rules and regulations of the commissioners, the annual expenditure of the Board, and the form of leases for national schools. In addition, there are lists of school books, which could be bought from the Board at cost prices, and copies of application forms and instructions for aid applications for building a school house or for a teacher's salary and books. The twelve practical rules for teachers are also featured. These highlight the qualities which a national teacher was expected to possess. She or he was 'to promote by precept and example, CLEANLINESS, NEATNESS and DECENCY'. Furthermore the teacher was

evidence, i [C 5781], H.C. 1889, xix, 778–85, ii [C 5781], H.C. 1889, xx, 221–7. The institutions visited in Ireland were the Merrion Female Institution, Claremont Institution for the Deaf and Dumb in Glasnevin, St Mary's School for the Deaf and Dumb in Cabra, St Joseph's School for the Deaf and Dumb in Drumcondra, St Joseph's Asylum and School for Male Blind, Drumcondra, the Molyneux Asylum in Lesson Park and the Association for Improving the condition of the Blind: see vol. ii, 221–7. **91** *Nineteenth report of the commissioners of national education in Ireland, for the year 1852*, H.C. 1852–3 (1688), xliii, pt ii, 1. In 1852 there were 4, 875 national schools in operation with 544, 604 pupils on roll. Of these schools 1,892 were in Ulster, 1,167 were in Munster, 1,176 were in Leinster, and 640 were in Connacht. In addition to the lesson books, the Board published a range of other textbooks, for example, *Epitome of geographical knowledge*, *First book of arithmetic* and *Sacred poetry*. The Board also sanctioned other books published by commercial publishers, such as Thomson's *Treatise on arithmetic*, Hullah's *Manual of Wilhem's vocal music* and Dawes's *Suggestive hints towards improved secular education*. School requisites included slates, large and

1. TWELVE PRACTICAL RULES for the TEACHERS of NATIONAL SCHOOLS.

1. The Teachers of National Schools are required—To keep at least one copy of the GENERAL LESSON suspended conspicuously in the School-room, and to inculcate the principles contained in it on the minds of their Pupils.

2. To exclude from the School, except at the hours set apart for Religious Instruction, all Catechisms and Books inculcating peculiar religious opinions.

3. To avoid fairs, markets, and meetings—but above all, POLITICAL meetings of every kind ; to abstain from controversy ; and to do nothing either in or out of School which might have a tendency to confine it to any one denomination of Children.

4. To keep the Register, Report Book, and Class Lists accurately and neatly, and according to the precise form prescribed by the Board.

5. To classify the Children according to the National School Books; to study those Books themselves; and to teach according to the improved method, as pointed out in their several prefaces.

6. To observe themselves, and to impress upon the minds of their Pupils, the great rule of regularity and order—A TIME AND A PLACE FOR EVERY THING, AND EVERY THING IN ITS PROPER TIME AND PLACE.

7. To promote, both by precept and example, CLEANLINESS, NEATNESS, and DECENCY. To effect this the Teachers should set an example of cleanliness and neatness in their own person, and in the state and general appearance of their Schools. They should also satisfy themselves, by personal inspection every morning, that the Children have had their hands and faces washed, their hair combed, and clothes cleaned, and, when necessary, mended. The School apartments, too, should be swept and dusted every *evening,* and white-washed at least once a year.

8. To pay the strictest attention to the morals and general conduct of their Pupils and to omit no opportunity of inculcating the principles of TRUTH and HONESTY : the duties of respect to superiors and obedience to all persons placed in authority over them.

9. To evince a regard for the improvement and general welfare of their Pupils, to treat them with kindness, combined with firmness, and to aim at governing them by their affections and reason, rather than by harshness and severity.

10. To cultivate kindly and affectionate feelings among their Pupils ; to discountenance quarrelling, cruelty to animals, and every approach to vice.

11. To record in the School Report Book the amount of all grants made by the Board, and the purposes for which they were made.

12. To take strict care of the FREE STOCK of Books granted by the Board ; and to endeavour to keep the School constantly supplied with National School Books and requisites, for sale to the Children, at the reduced prices charged by the Commissioners.

MAURICE CROSS, ⎱ Secretaries.
JAMES KELLY, ⎰

5 'Twelve practical rules for teachers'. These rules, which dated from the 1840s, show the high ideals and the social and moral behaviour required of national school teachers. The main principle of school order was 'A TIME AND PLACE FOR EVERYTHING, AND EVERYTHING IN ITS PROPER TIME AND PLACE' (*Appendix to the nineteenth report of the commissioners for national education in Ireland for the year 1852*).

to avoid fairs, markets and meetings – but above all political meetings, ... to pay strict attention to the morals and general conduct of their pupils and to omit no opportunity in inculcating the principles of TRUTH and HONESTY; the duties of respect to superiors and obedience to all persons placed in authority over them.[92]

The programme of study or the classification examinations for teachers are included along with copies of examination papers. Teachers were divided into three main classes and promotion depended on passing the examinations for each class. The programme for study for a second class teacher featured grammar, spelling, geography history, natural philosophy, geometry, mensuration and algebra. The list of set books include the *Fifth book of lessons, Introduction to the art of reading, Geography generalized, Epitome of geography*, Thomson's *Treatise on arithmetic*, Thomson's *Euclid*, Thomson's *Algebra lessons on reasoning*, the Board's book on mensuration and Professor McGauley's *Lectures on natural philosophy*. (Female teachers could take mental arithmetic instead of the courses in higher mathematics.)

The 1852 report also contains particular details of the religious denomination of the pupils and teachers in the national system. This return was designed to examine whether mixed education of Protestant and Catholic children was taking place. The return gives the number of pupils of each denomination in each school as well as the name and religious denomination of the patron. The district inspectors were asked to submit a return on this subject.[93] The report also contains a useful list of the schools in which paid monitors were employed, recording the names and classification of the monitors.[94] The course for monitors covered three years in reading, etymology, spelling, arithmetic, grammar, geography, the art of teaching and needlework. The report also contains a list of schools where premiums were paid to named teachers who were most distinguished 'by the order, neatness, and cleanliness observable in themselves, their pupils and in the schoolhouses'. A similar list was compiled for teachers in workhouse schools.[95]

Later CNEI reports were more detailed. For example, the 1857 report contains informative accounts of the country's thirteen new district model schools which were regarded as the 'flagships' of the national system. Each district inspector

small, quills, copybooks, ink stands and ink powder. The Board's books sold widely in the prisons, army barracks, and lighthouses as well as in India, Canada and Australia where readers in the English language were required. See ibid., 631–7. **92** *Nineteenth report of the commissioners of national education in Ireland, for the year 1852*, H.C. 1852–3 (1688), xliii, pt ii, 109. **93** Ibid., 71–278, inspectors' reports and returns, 335–404. The names of the inspectorate with their districts are listed on 699–705. In 1852 there were 498,018 pupils on roll, of whom 24,684 were members of the Established Church, 424,717 were Roman Catholic, 40,618 were Presbyterians, 1,908 were classed as other Protestant dissenters and the denomination of 1,091 was not stated, 333–4. **94** Ibid., 617–34. **95** Ibid., 579–96, workhouse schools, 653–9. The last section of the report has a list of national schools in workhouses and gaols, agricultural schools and industrial schools. The winners of the Lord Morpeth's (earl of Carlisle) premium for outstanding teachers in 1852 are also listed.

reported on the model schools in his jurisdiction, praising its spacious buildings and schoolrooms. In the late 1850s these schools were still recruiting pupils and confidence in the influence of the schools was still at a high level. The inspectors' reports describe the activities in each school and outline the curriculum followed by junior and senior classes who used the Board's textbooks. Teachers' names are listed as are those of the resident male pupil teachers and the female monitresses. Details of the educational and parental background of pupil teachers are included and this gives an insight into the social background of aspiring teachers. For example, Galway Model School (est. 1852), trained twenty-seven pupil teachers in the five years, of which four were members of the established Church of Ireland, two were Presbyterians, one was a dissenter, and the remainder were Catholic. Pupil-teachers' parents included a postmaster, farmer, coachman, dealer, teacher, shopkeeper, ship-carpenter, constable and revenue officer and three pupil-teachers were styled orphans. Their course of training lasted up to a year, but the majority stayed for only eight months. Most subsequently become national school teachers but some used their education to enter other positions – two had become clerks in Liverpool, one emigrated to Australia and another to America, another was working in a draper's shop, another become assistant to the professor of chemistry at Queen's College, Galway and two went on to train for the priesthood, one in Cork and the other in Belgium. In this way, it is possible to see how the model school served as a ladder by which young men and women gained access to further education and alternative careers.[96] However, six years later, in 1863, the inspector reported that the school's numbers were declining, and 'owing to the denunciation of the Roman Catholic Bishop of Galway', 199 Roman Catholic pupils were said to have been withdrawn, and the Catholic monitresses had been directed to resign. He continued 'I regret to be compelled to report that the opposition which was then commenced has been continued, and that consequently a considerable number have felt themselves compelled to forgo advantages which were calculated and designed to promote their elevation in the social scale'.[97]

The Belfast Model School on the Falls Road was opened in 1857 as one of the largest and best-equipped schools in the country. P.J. Keenan, head inspector of national schools, reported on the opening of the school and used the occasion to publicize and praise the work of model schools in general. In his public address at the inauguration of the school he spoke about the value of such an institution as a model of good practice:

> ... a district model school ... is a school established on such principles, organised on such plans, regulated by such a course of discipline, and con-ducted on such as a method of instruction, as to be a model or pattern for

96 *Appendix to the twenty-fourth report of the commissioners of national education in Ireland for the year 1857*, H.C. 1859 (2456–I), vii, 57–61. 97 *Appendices to the thirtieth report of the commissioners of national education in Ireland for the year 1863*, pp 109–11, H.C. 1864 (3351),

MR KEENAN'S REPORT UPON THE BELFAST DISTRICT MODEL SCHOOL.
Appendix C. Plate VI. View of Girls' School-room.

6 Drawing of the girls' schoolroom in the Belfast Model School (1857) showing desks and seats for writing, circles for the reading drafts and visual aids including a set of globes for geography. (Head Inspector P.J. Keenan's report on the opening of the Belfast model schools, *Appendix to the twenty-fourth report of the commissioners of national education in Ireland for the year 1857*).

teachers, or school managers, or school committees to copy or imitate. The model, or pattern, may refer to the various very different phases of a school; sometimes the architecture or construction of the building; sometimes to the arrangement of the furniture; sometimes to the regulations in respect of religious instruction; it may refer to all, or any of these, as far as they can be copied or imitated by others; and, in this regard, every well-conducted school, may, in some measure, be said to be a model; but in the strict sense of the word, as educationists define it, a model school is one in which there is reasonable excellence in all these respects, and which, in addition is either attached to an institution for the training of teachers, or is in itself, along with an elementary school, a seminary for the same purpose.[98]

xix, pt ii, 149–54.　**98** *Twenty-fourth report of the commissioners of national education in Ireland for the year 1857*, pp 82–76, H.C. 1859 (2456–I), vii, 138–52. The architectural plans for the Belfast Model School are in this report. They show the ground plans of the schools and details of three schoolrooms for boys, girls and infants. The school was designed by

In addition to comments on the model schools the head inspectors reports summarised progress that took place in the districts under their supervision over the course of the year. These head inspectors' reports may include short accounts of particular schools visited by inspectors and these contain a substantial amount of detail. In 1857 Inspector Keenan reported on schools in Donegal including those in the Inishowen peninsula[99] while Head Inspector W.A. Hunter did so for Clare, Limerick, Tipperary, Kerry and Cork. For example, having visited Kilmurry school in County Clare he wrote

> Kilmurry, Mixed – 1. Schoolroom unsuitable, but the best that can be obtained; it is attached to the chapel, a portion of which has been partitioned off for the school; furniture tolerable, no reading tablets; a large map of the world. 2. Teacher lately appointed; not trained; not yet examined for classification; previously a paid monitor. He manifests considerable skill in his profession, and with application and care he will become a useful teacher. 3. Attendance accurately recorded, but some irregularities in the register. 4. Reading indifferent throughout; pronunciation bad; answering on subject of lessons intelligent, arithmetic fair; geography deficient. Inscription not up; general lesson not suspended. The boys are in the habit of wearing their caps in the school, a remnant of the hedge system.[1]

This report reveals some of the difficulties associated with implementing the national system at local level, including the lack of a suitable school building, untrained young teachers, poor reading skills, and yet the inspector shows a realistic and encouraging approach to the school in his overall assessment.

Reports on implementation of the new curriculum nationwide following its introduction in 1900 feature in the annual reports of the CNEI and provide a useful contextual background for any study of schools in a specific locality. For example, the report for 1907 carried comments made by Mr W.M. Heller, the organiser for elementary science, on the lack of practical work being undertaken:

> Considering how small a part manual and practical instruction yet plays in the curriculum of National schools, increased attention is necessary to the individual practical work of the pupils. There are many schools where the Commissioners' suggestions as regards the organisation of individual practical work have been most successfully carried into effect, and the pupils exhibit interest in and an understanding of their work. But in the majority

Frederick Darley, architect of the National Board (see 96–7). **99** Ibid., 225–35. **1** Ibid., 259–70. The inspectors' reports were made under the following five headings: 1. House furniture 2. Teacher 3. School accounts 4. Pupils 5. Miscellaneous. The inscription was the name and date of the national school which should have been placed on the outside of the building. The general lesson was comprised of a collection of scriptural extracts which encouraged goodwill and harmony, and it was required to be displayed in all national

of schools the practical work is shirked, although a little thought and system would enable much valuable training to be given without interruption of other lessons. The co-ordinated training of hand, eye, and brain is still, in my opinion, the greatest need in the schools; the natural principle in education of 'learning by doing' is far too little appreciated.[2]

The annual reports compiled by other educational institutions are smaller and are of less use to researchers with an interest in local studies. The reports of the Intermediate Education Board for Ireland contain lists of the examination results and subjects taken by both boys and girls along with their programme of study. The finances of the Board and the schools which are in receipt of results payments from the Board are also recorded.[3] In 1900 there were a total of 363 schools in receipt of Board grants, of which 149 were exclusively for girls.[4] For example, in 1900 in Kerry, five boys' schools were receiving grants (Christian schools in Dingle, St Brendan's Seminary in Killarney, St Michael's College in Listowel, Christian Schools in Tralee and Intermediate and University School, Tralee). Two girls' schools, namely the Loreto Convent in Killarney and the Presentation Convent in Tralee, also received grants. In Donegal three boys' schools earned results fees (St Eunan's Seminary in Letterkenny, the Prior endowed school in Lifford and Mrs Holtan's private school in Newtowncunningham) as did four girls' schools (the Convent of Mercy, Ballyshannon, Loreto Convent in Letterkenny, the Ladies' School in Newtowncunningham, and the Royal School, Raphoe). The Intermediate Education Board reports also feature lists of examiners and extracts from their reports making it possible for the progress of a particular school subject to be gauged. Boys and girls sat the same papers and were examined by the same examiners, which was important in ensuring that the academic achievements of female students received appropriate recognition. For instance, Patrick J. Hogan, MA, who examined the boys' senior grade first English paper observed:

> The answering of the candidates was, on the whole, highly satisfactory. The essays in this grade may be regarded as the test of the influence of the intermediate system on the mental development of the students who have passed through all the grades. Many of the essays, especially those com-

schools.   **2** W.M. Heller, 'General report on science instruction' in *Appendix to the seventy-third report of the commissioners of national education in Ireland for 1906*, [Cd 3861], H.C. 1908, xxvii, 525–30. He was one of the most active organisers. He continued to work for the National Board until its closure in 1924. He subsequently transferred to the technical branch of the new Department of Education.   **3** *Report of the Intermediate Education Board for Ireland for 1879* [C 2600], H.C. 1880, xxiii, 31 down to *Report of the Intermediate Education Board for Ireland for 1920* [Cmd 1398], H.C. 1921, xxi, 397.   **4** *Report of the Intermediate Education Board for Ireland for the year 1900*, xi, 73–95 [Cmd 588], H.C. 1901, xxi, 369. The 'Christian schools' were run by the Irish Christian Brothers, who entered large numbers of pupils for the examinations. A number of private schools were opened to prepare pupils for the Intermediate examinations.

JUNIOR GRADE.

GREEK.*—*Maximum of marks,* 1,200.

Marks

1. **XENOPHON**; Anabasis, Book III.   200 ⎫
   LUCIAN; Walker's Selections; 1, 2, 6, 7, 8, 11, 13, 14,   ⎬ 400
16, 19.   200 ⎭
   2. Grammar.   230 ⎫
   3. Short sentences for translation into Greek, the more   ⎬ 460
difficult words being supplied.   230 ⎭
   4. A passage or passages from some other Greek work
or works for translation at sight; aid to be given by a vocabulary
of unusual words.   220
   5. Grecian History from B.C. 479 to B.C. 404.   120
                                                          ――――
                                                          1200

LATIN.*—*Maximum of marks,* 1,200.

1. **CAESAR**, de Bello Gallico; Books II. and III.   200 ⎫
   VIRGIL, Æneid, Book III.; questions on scansion may   ⎬ 400
be asked.   200 ⎭
   2. Grammar.   230 ⎫
   3. Short sentences for translation into Latin; the more   ⎬ 460
difficult words being supplied.   230 ⎭
   4. A passage or passages from some other Latin work
or works for translation at sight.   220
   5. Outlines of Roman History from B.C. 264 to B.C. 133. 120
                                                          ――――
                                                          1200

ENGLISH.†—*Maximum of marks,* 1,200.

1. **SCOTT**, Lay of the Last Minstrel; Cantos IV., V., VI. 175 ⎫
   LAMB; Adventures of Ulysses.   Andrew Lang's text   ⎬ 350
(E. Arnold), or John Cooke's text (Browne & Nolan).   175 ⎭
   2. Grammar, including Orthography, Punctuation, Parsing,
and Analysis of simple sentences.   200
   3. Composition.   200
   4. Geography; Distribution of Land and Water and their ⎫
relative position and Areas; Mountain Chains and Systems; ⎪
Seas and Oceans; Rivers and Lakes.   ⎬ 200
   Physical and Political Geography of Great Britain and ⎪
Ireland, and the Outlines of our Colonial Empire.   ⎭
   5. Outlines of the History of England and Ireland from
A.D. 1399 to 1603.   250
                                                          ――――
                                                          1200

* See Notes 2, 3, 4, 5, on the Programme, page 51.
† See Note 2 on the Programme, page 51.

7 Intermediate Education Board junior grade examination syllabus in Classics and English, with marking scheme (*Rules and programme of the Intermediate Education Board, 1894*).

ENGLISH.

Second Paper.

WEDNESDAY, 15th JUNE—AFTERNOON, 3 to 6 P.M.

Examiners
{
JOHN D. COLCLOUGH.
Rev. JAMES DONNELLAN.
WILLIAM GRAHAM, M.A.
Rev. J. EDGAR HENRY, D.D.
JAMES J. MACKEN, B.A.

MITFORD: Essays from "*Our Village.*"

1. (a.) "God made the country and man made the town." What reflections are introduced (in "*A visit to Richmond*") by this quotation?
(b.) Why is it suggested that Richmond Hill has been over-rated?

2. State the reasons which Miss Mitford assigns for her strong partiality towards country boys.

3. By what epithets or phrases does the authoress characterize—
The cuckoo,
The glowworm,
The greyhound,
The beech,
The birch?

4. (a.) Explain the following allusions:—
"My luck exceeded even hers of the Glass Slipper."
"A terrible solecism in political economy."
"Sent to Coventry."
(b.) What is the meaning of the following words which occur in these essays?
Lissomer,
Macadamise,
Deedily,
Drouthy,
Sabaean.

5. (a.) From a perusal of "Our Village," what writers appear to have been among Miss Mitford's favourite poets and novelists?
(b.) "Your good cricketer is commonly the most industrious man in the parish." Why?

THE HISTORY OF ENGLAND AND IRELAND FROM
A.D. 1399 to 1603.

6. What were the chief provisions of 'Poynings' Law'? When and where was it passed?

7. When, between whom, and with what result were the following battles fought?—Verneuil, Knockdoe, Northampton, Pass of the Plumes, Homildon Hill.

8. What were the claims to the throne of the House of York and the House of Lancaster respectively, as based *on descent?*

9. For what are the following personages noteworthy in English or Irish history?
Sir Henry Bagenall,
Lord Lovel,
O'Sullivan Beare,
Lady Catherine Gordon.

10. (a.) What attempt was made in the reign of Henry V. to dethrone the reigning dynasty? What was the issue of the attempt, and what its date?
(b.) Under what pretext did Henry V. renew the Hundred Years' War with France? What sieges and what battle took place in the war during his lifetime? Give dates.

GEOGRAPHY.

11. (a.) Name the principal rivers which flow into the Irish Sea.
(b.) Name the five most populous cities of Great Britain, giving, approximately, the population of each.

12. Define "volcano." Name four volcanos in Europe, and the situation of each.

13. Briefly contrast the Atlantic Ocean with the Pacific in respect of (a) area, (b) number and character of islands.

14. (a.) Name the situation and the capital of each of the following British possessions:—
British Columbia,
British Guiana,
British Honduras.
(b.) Where are Penang, Gozo, St. Helena, Chitral, Mauritius, Vancouver I.?

15. A vessel trading between Belfast and Waterford calls at the chief seaport town of each intervening county. Name these towns with their counties.

8 Extract from an Intermediate Education Board junior grade examination in English, 1898 (*Intermediate Education Board Examination papers, 1898*). The paper included questions on the history and geography of England and Ireland.

mended for composition prizes, bore evidence of the great culture and wide reading on the part of the writers, and, considering the limited time in which they were written, showed a more finished style than might be anticipated. This applies more particularly to the essays written on the 'The use and abuse of prose fiction', several of which exhibited an extensive acquaintance with modern literature. Essays on 'Patriotism' displayed a keen interest in the Boer War and a healthy impartiality as to the patriotic virtues of both belligerents ... The grammar questions were well answered, and the analysis was correctly given in nearly all instances. The candidates seemed to have devoted most attention to the historical grammar, and to have relied upon their memory for the ordinary grammar ...[5]

Commenting on the girls' performance in the senior grade paper he wrote:

Remarks in connection with the senior grade (boys) examination apply also in great part to the answering of the girls. The composition reached a good standard of average merit, and were, in many cases, excellent in style and treatment of subject. In fact it was difficult to make a selection for the composition prizes, as the superior merit of more than a dozen essays deserved recognition ... Current events in South Africa prevented the compositions on 'Patriotism' from exhibiting a comprehensive view of the subject ... The answering on the 'Tempest' was the result of careful study of the prescribed edition of the play. Most candidates, however, failed to distinguish the services upon which Ariel was employed in act IV from his other services in the course of the play.[6]

The annual reports of the commissioners of education in Ireland date from 1814 to 1920.[7] They were concerned with the administration of the royal school endowment, the Preston Endowed Schools at Navan and Ballyroan in Abbeyleix, the Carysfort endowment in County Wicklow, the Leamy endowments in Limerick, the Viscount Limerick endowment, Dundalk as well as other small funds. In addition there were the annual reports generated by the educational endowments commissioners: they are comprised of proceedings, evidence taken from the educational institutions under reform and information on the new endowments

---

5 *Report of the Intermediate Education Board for Ireland for the year 1900*, p. 23 [Cmd 588], H.C. 1901, xxi, 369. **6** Ibid., 24–5. Copies of the examination papers of the Intermediate Board are in the NLI. Textbooks for the set courses of the intermediate examinations were published by the Irish educational publishers. These books contained detailed notes on the texts for use of teacher and pupils alike. For example, Fallon & Co. Limited, School and College series, *Intermediate examinations, 1909, Thackeray, Addison, Steele and Goldsmith*; William Cowper, *The Task (Book I)* (Dublin & Belfast), Fallon's *New intermediate series* (general editor Revd T. Corcoran), Helena Concannon, *Irish history for junior grade classes: the defence of our Gaelic civilisation, 1460–1660* (Fallon Brothers, Dublin & Belfast). **7** See from *Annual report of the commissioners of education in Ireland*, H.C. 1814–5 (29), vi, 1753 to *Annual report*

9 Photograph of the 'Nine Graces' – the first women graduates of the Royal University of Ireland in 1884. Among the group were Alice Oldham: *third, centre row, l to r*, who became secretary of CAISM, and Isabella Mulvany: *third, back row, l to r*, who became headmistress of Alexandra School, Dublin.

schemes drawn up by the commissioners.[8] Also informative are the annual reports of the inspector of reformatory and industrial schools which date from 1862.[9]

The annual reports of the Queen's colleges and the Queen's University record data on the number of students in each year, along with their religious affiliation, the names of the students graduating with prize winners and publications produced by academic staff.[10] The reports of the Queen's University run from

[Cmd 1507], H.C. 1920 (xi), 381. **8** See from *Report of the educational endowments (Ireland) commissioners for 1885–6* [C 4903], H.C. 1886, xxvi, 89 to *Report ... for 1885–6* [C 5232], H.C. 1894, xxxi, 81. These reports are listed under the heading 'endowed schools' in the index to parliamentary papers. **9** See from *Report of the inspector appointed to visit reformatory and industrial schools in Ireland*, H.C. 1862 (2949), xxvi, 651 to *Fifty-eighth report for 1919* [Cmd 1128], H.C. 1921, xxiv, 623. These reports contain details of the offences committed along with the offenders' age and social condition. The financial costings of the system are presented and after the Industrial school Act, reports on the industrial schools are included (1870 onwards). **10** See from *Report of the president of the Queen's College, Belfast, for the academic year 1849–50*, H.C. 1850 (1272) xxv, 715 to *Report for the academic year 1908–9* [Cd.

1852 to 1882 and include such diverse material as the vice-chancellor's annual address and a list of graduates with their colleges and degrees awarded. Reports of the Royal University date from 1882 and run to 1908: these contain lists of degrees awarded each year, along with numbers of men and women taking the examinations. These data were used during the campaign to gain admission for women to university colleges in an effort to show how successful women graduates were. Between 1883 and 1900 a total of 2,326 women matriculated at the RUI, 521 were awarded BA degrees, forty-three were awarded MA degrees, while thirty-one won scholarships and three became junior fellows.[11]

Researchers interested in technical education will find two sets of annual reports particularly informative, namely the annual reports of the Science and Art Department, South Kensington, from 1854 to 1899, and those of the Department of Agriculture and Technical instruction from 1900 to 1920. The South Kensington reports contain accounts of those institutions which were in receipt of grants from the Science and Art Department, namely the Royal College of Science, Dublin, the Science and Art Museum, Dublin, and the Metropolitan School of Art, Dublin.[12] It also lists the individual schools which entered pupils for the Science and Art Department examination.[13] The annual reports of the Department of Agriculture and Technical Instruction published details of the programme of instruction issued by the Department and recorded the number of schools taking these courses. They also feature reports on institutions run under the auspices of the Department (for example, the Science and Art Museum, the National Library and the Metropolitan School of Art) as well as progress reports on the work of the local technical instruction committees.[14] Also available are annual reports and a number of returns relating to reformatory and industrial schools, which give details of schools, numbers of juvenile offenders and copies of relevant government circulars issued to the schools.[15]

4831], H.C. 1909, xx, 715; also from *Report of the president of Queen's College, Cork, for the academic year 1849–50,* H.C. 1850 (1272), xxv, 717 to *Report for the academic year 1908–9* [Cd 4825], H.C. 1909 xx, 803; from *Report of the president of Queen's College, Galway for the academic year 1849–50,* H.C. 1850 (1272), xxv, 719 to *Report for the academic year 1908–9* [Cd 4883], H.C. 1909, xx, 831. These reports are listed under the heading 'universities (Ireland)' in the index to the parliamentary papers.   **11** See from *First report of the Royal University of Ireland for 1882* [C 3615], H.C. 1883, xxvi, 393 to *Twenty-seventh report for 1908* [Cd 4706], H.C. 1909, xx, 896. The reports contain the vice-chancellor's address at the annual meeting of the RUI. See *Appendix to the first report of the royal commission on university education (Ireland)* [Cd 826], H.C. 1902, xxxi, 389.   **12** John Turpin, *A school of art in Dublin in the eighteenth century: a history of the National College of Art and Design* (Dublin, 1995).   **13** See from *Annual report of the Science and Art Department, South Kensington,* H.C. 1854 (1783), xxviii, 269 to *Forty-sixth annual report* [C 9191, C 9192], H.C. 1899, xxvii, 245, xxviii, 1. **14** See from *Annual report of the Department of Agriculture and Technical Instruction (Ireland) for 1900–01* [Cd 1314], H.C. 1902, xx, 511 to the *Annual report for 1918–19* [Cd 929], H.C. 1920, ix, 171.   **15** For example, *Return of name, locality of every reformatory school in Ireland, religious persuasion, date of certification of each school … etc.* H.C. 1861 (421), lii, 599; *Copy of the circular issued July 1871 by the inspector of reformatory and industrial schools in Ireland, to managers of*

Name of School.	Name and Address of Secretary.
DUBLIN:	
Balbriggan : Loreto Convent, . .	Mrs. M. M'Namara, Loreto Convent, Balbriggan R. S. O.
Blackrock : Dominican Convent, Sion Hill.	Sister M. Bernard, Sion Hill Convent, Blackrock.
Cabra : St. Mary's Dominican Convent, .	Mrs. A. C. Murphy, St. Mary's Dominican Convent, Cabra.
Dalkey : Art School, Bay View, . .	Mrs. M. Murphy, Loreto Abbey, Dalkey S. O.
Dalkey : Loreto Abbey, . . .	Mrs. J. Ryan, Loreto Abbey, Dalkey S. O.
Dublin : Alexandra College, . .	Rev. T. R. S. Collins, B.D., 65, Pembroke-road, Dublin.
Dublin : Belvedere College, . . .	Rev. N. J. Tomkin, S.J., Belvedere College, Great Denmark-street, Dublin.
Dublin : Christian Brothers' Novitiate, Marino.	Rev. Br. J. C Whitty, Christian Brothers' Novitiate, Marino.
Dublin : City of Dublin Technical Schools,	Arnold Graves, Esq., City of Dublin Technical Schools, Lower Kevin-street, Dublin.
Dublin : Dominican Convent, Eccles-street.	Miss T. O'Sullivan, 19, Eccles-street.
Dublin : Loreto Convent, North Great George's-street.	Mrs. Mary Corcoran, Loreto Convent, 43, North Great George's-street.
Dublin : Loreto Convent, St. Stephen's-green.	Mrs. M. G. Reddin, Loreto Convent, 53, Stephen's-green, E.
Dublin : Mechanic's Institute, . .	M. Dobbin, Esq., Mechanic's Institute, Lower Abbey-street.
Dublin : Railway Institute, . .	G. D. M. Beard, Esq., 3, St. Michael's-terrace, South Circular-road, Dublin.
Dublin : St. Margaret's Hall, Mespil-road,	Mr. French, 9, Dartmouth-square, Dublin.
Dublin : St. Mary's University College, .	Sister M. J. Keighron, St. Mary's University College, Muckross Park, Donnybrook.
Dublin : University College, St. Stephen's-green.	Henry C. M'Weeney, Esq., F.R.U.I., University College, St. Stephen's-green.
Kingstown : St. Mary's Dominican Convent.	Rev. E. D. Byrne, St. Mary's Convent, Kingstown.
Rathfarnham : Loreto Abbey, . .	Mrs. M. O'Reilly, Loreto Abbey, Rathfarnham.
Rathmines : Hibernian Marine School, .	C. Dickinson, Esq., Grove House, Rathmines.
Rathmines : Loreto Convent, Charleville-road.	Mrs. M. Boylan, Loreto Convent, Charleville-road, Rathmines.
Ringsend : Pembroke Technical Schools,	Arnold Graves, Esq., Cambridge-road, Ringsend.
Sandymount : Academical Institution, .	C. E. M'Gillivray, Esq., 61, Park-avenue, Sandymount.
Terenure : Carmelite College. . .	Rev. J. L. M'Cabe, Carmelite College, Terenure.
GALWAY:	
Galway : City of Galway Technical Institute.	Very Rev. P. J. Lally, St. Joseph's, Galway.
Galway : City of Galway Technical School.	Very Rev. P. J. Lally, St. Joseph's Galway.
Galway : Dominican Convent, Taylor's-hill.	Sister M. Michael Morris, Dominican Convent, Taylor's Hill, Galway.
Gort : Convent of Mercy, . . .	Patrick F. Nilan, Esq., J.P., Lavally, Gort, Co. Galway.
KERRY :	
Kenmare : Convent of Poor Clares, .	Mrs. A. M'Carthy, Convent of Poor Clares Kenmare, Co. Kerry.
Killarney : Loreto Convent, . .	Mrs. M. Peart, Loreto Convent, Killarney.
Killarney : Presentation Convent,	Mrs. M. B. Moran, Presentation Convent, Killarney.
Listowel : St. Michael's College, . .	D. Nolan, Esq., William-street, Listowel, Co. Kerry.
Tralee : Presentation Convent, .	Sister Mary Counihan, Presentation Convent, Tralee.
KILKENNY :	
Kilkenny : Christian Brothers' Schools, .	J. Brennan, Esq., Court House, Kilkenny.
Kilkenny : Pococke College, . .	Rev. F. J. Hartley, A.B., William-street House, Kilkenny.
LIMERICK :	
Hospital : Presentation Convent, .	Mrs. M. de P. Gubbins, Presentation Convent, Hospital, Knocklong R. S. O., Limerick.
Kilfinane Classical and Civil Service School.	Rev. J. Carrick, Kilfinane, Co. Limerick.
Limerick : Municipal School of Science and Art.	W. M. Nolan, Esq., Town Clerk, Limerick.

10 Schools in Dublin, Galway, Kerry, Kilkenny and Limerick that offered South Kensington Science and Art classes in 1900 (*First general report of the Department of Agriculture and Technical Instruction for the year 1900–1*). The administration of the grants for these classes was transferred to the new Department of Agriculture and Technical Instruction in 1901.

Census of population returns and reports The reports of the decennial census of population in the parliamentary papers contain details of age, education and literacy levels through the nineteenth century. During that period, the growth of literacy was very marked as mass schooling grew. Whereas in 1841 the illiteracy rate was 53%, by 1870 it had fallen to 33% and by 1901 it was down to 14%. It was, of course, literacy in English that was acquired. Meanwhile, the number of Irish speakers was steadily declining from mid-century: in 1851 the Irish-speaking population was 23% of the island's total; by 1871 that proportion had dropped to 15.5% and by 1901 it fell further still to 14.4%. Based on the census data it can be concluded that the illiteracy rate for men was higher than for women and that by 1901 the male illiteracy rate was down to 13.2 % while for women it had dropped to 10.7%. The original street and house returns for the 1901 census and the 1911 census may be consulted by researchers in the National Archives, Bishop Street, Dublin and the 1911 returns are now available on line at census.nationalarchives.ie. Copies of returns relating to individual counties are also held in many county libraries throughout Ireland. The house returns include the details of whether or not the person could read and write or not and thus the literacy rates of a family, or household or street can be ascertained.[16]

(c) Accounts and papers (including returns on educational institutions)

In parliamentary accounts and papers, there are a large collection of short accounts and papers, which deal with specific subjects as requested by the House of Commons. These include a number of returns of schools which contain details of all the national schools in Ireland and which therefore represent an important body of material for scholars researching the history of one or more schools in a specific locality. Also useful are the short reports, copies of correspondence, memorials and copies of minutes within this category of parliamentary material. Helpfully for researchers, the papers are listed under subject headings such as 'convent schools', 'teacher training and model schools', 'schoolbooks', 'the Irish language', 'educational statistics expenditure and the parliamentary vote'. A full list of the accounts and papers may be found in the general indexes (together with reference numbers) to the parliamentary papers under the headings of 'education', 'universities', 'endowed schools', and so on and these lists should be consulted. The following is only a selection from the wide range of material available.

Roman Catholic industrial schools, correspondence ... etc., H.C. 1872 (153), i, 863, H.C. 1872 (152–I), i, 869; *Return giving the text of all circulars issued by the lord lieutenant of Ireland in connection with the administration of the industrial Schools (Ireland) Act*, H.C. 1899 (114), lxxvi, 99. **16** See *Population censuses of Ireland*: for 1821, see H.C. 1824 (577), xxii, 411; for 1831, see H.C. 1833 (634), xxxix, 59; for 1841, H.C. 1843 (504), xxiv, 1; for 1851, see pt iv, *Report on ages and education*, H.C. 1856 (2053), xxix, 1; see pt vi, *General report*, H.C. 1856 (2134), xxxi, 1; for 1861, see pt ii, *Report and tables on ages and education*, i, H.C. 1863 (3204–I), lvi, 1

Four returns relate to the state of education in the whole country. The first is a return relative to schools and education in 1824. It features lists of diocesan and royal schools, charter schools, charitable schools, schools funded by the lord lieutenant's fund, and those in receipt of grants from the Kildare Place Society along with details on parish schools returned by the Church of Ireland clergy.[17] The archdeacons of each diocese were asked to make a return of the schools in each parish; some gave good detail, others did not. For example, the return for the parish of Rathfarnham, Co. Dublin reads as follows:

> There are two schools in this parish and a Sunday school. The former is supported by 40s. per annum from the rector and a small weekly stipend from each of the children. The latter is supported by an annual salary of £6 10s. from a private individual, and one penny a week from each of the children, which at the end of the year, is disposed of to their advantage. The attendance in both are (sic), in general, thirty, including Protestants and Catholics.[18]

The next useful return is of all national schools in 1862 (published in 1864), which gives the name, profession and religion of the school patron, along with the name, religion, class and year of training of head and assistant teachers, work mistresses and paid monitors.[19] In addition, it lists the name and profession of the head inspector, the numbers on roll, the average daily attendance and the number of pupils classified by creed. The main concern behind the compilation of this return was to monitor adherence to the National Board's rules concerning separation of religious and secular instruction hours. Details of each school, therefore, included the timetable for religious instruction, the name and creed of the teacher, the number of pupils who attend religious instruction with their parents' consent and the number of those who do not. For example, in the parish of Rosenallis in Mountmellick, the two national schools had now grown in size. In the early 1860s the boys' national school (roll no. 922) had five teachers – a head, assistant and three monitors. There were 225 pupils on roll, all Catholics, save one who did not attend religious instruction. The timetable for religious instruction included one class per day on five days. At the girls' convent national school (roll no. 7183) the teachers included the nuns and six female monitors. There were 286 pupils on roll, all of them Catholic. Religious instruction

and ii, H.C. 1863 (3204–I), lvii, 1, also pt iv, *Report and tables relating to religious profession, education and occupation of the people*, i, H.C. 1863 (3204–III), lix, 1 and ii, H.C. 1863 (3204–III), lx, 1.   **17** *Accounts and papers relative to schools and education*, H.C. 1824 (179) (286) (350) (403) (461), xxi, 383, 471, 545, 601, 619. This return was printed before the publication of the 1825 Irish education inquiry.   **18** Ibid., *Parish school returns*, H.C. 1824 (286), xxi, 15. **19** *Return, by counties and parishes, of all schools in connections with the Board of National Education in Ireland in operation on 31st December 1862; religious denomination of the patron; name and religion of head and assistant literary teachers, work mistresses, and paid monitors; numbers of pupils in 1862, classified by creeds, etc.; nature of religious instruction given, etc., Part I, province of Ulster*, H.C. 1864 (481), xlvii, 1; *Part II, province of Munster*, H.C. 1864 (481–I), xlvii, 269; *Part III, province of Leinster*, H.C. 1864 (481–II), xlvii, 461; *Part IV, province of Connaught*, H.C.

was held on five days a week.[20] This 1862 return shows not only the steady growth of the national system but also the more pronounced denominational structure of schools as 'mixed' education of Catholic and Protestant children diminished. It shows the lack of trained teachers and the extensive use of young pupil monitors to teach the large numbers of children. In 1866 it was estimated that 55% of national teachers were untrained. This grave situation arose partly due to the continuing impasse between the Catholic Church and the National Board regarding the Church's demand for denominational teacher training.[21]

In 1879–80 another detailed return of all national schools was made, this time to gauge how effectively the new payment by results system was working since its introduction in 1872.[22] The number of pupils examined in each school is listed along with the amount of money paid out in results fees. The fees for first class were 2s. for a pass in reading and 1s. for a pass in spelling, writing and arithmetic. Therefore, if there were six successful pupils in all subjects, the amount paid to the teachers was a bonus of £30. In fifth class, for instance, 2s. 6d. was paid for a pass in reading and arithmetic, 1s. for spelling, and 1s. 6d. for writing, grammar and geography. If ten pupils were successful in all subjects the maximum bonus paid would be 25s. for reading and arithmetic, 15s. each for writing, grammar, and

1864 (481–III), xlvii, 603. **20** Ibid., *Part IV, province of Connaught*, H.C. 1864 (481–III), xlvii, 614. The names of the teachers and the monitors are listed in this return but have not been included here as personal details need to be used with discretion in a local area. **21** *Correspondence between the government and the commissioners of national education, on the subject of the organisation and government of model schools*, H.C. 1866 (456), lv, 213–5; *Correspondence between the government and the commissioners of national education upon the proposals with respect to the training and model schools contained in the letter of the Rt. Hon. C.P. Fortescue, M.P., to the commissioners, dated 19th June 1866; minutes and memorandum upon the subject*, H.C. 1867 (225), lv, 747. In 1863 the Catholic Church had placed a 'ban' on attendance at the Board's model schools and the Central Training Institution. As a compromise measure the government suggested that locally managed superior 'model' schools could be recognised as centres for teacher training and that denominational lodging houses should be attached to the Central Training Institution. Although these co-called Fortescue proposals were not implemented, they represented an important step towards the recognition of denominational teacher training colleges. Also in 1863 the Board agreed to recognize some 'superior schools', among them large convent schools, as training schools where so-called female monitresses could be more highly paid. There was strong opposition from the Presbyterian Church in particular, as this new rule was seen to be directing more money towards convent schools. See *Royal commission of inquiry into primary education (Ireland)* [Powis commission] i, *report of the commissioners* [C 6], H.C. 1870, xxviii, 178–85; Akenson, *Irish education experiment*, pp 305–10; Paul Cullen, *Pastoral letters and writings of Cardinal Cullen*, ed. P.G. Moran (3 vols, Dublin, 1882); anon., *Convent versus model schools – a pamphlet* (Belfast, 1864). **22** *Returns of numbers of pupils examined for results fees in each school in Ireland under the Board of National Education in 1877–8 and 1878–9*, H.C. 1880 (33), lv, 13. This volume also contains a return for model schools, giving the social background of parents of pupils attending the schools. The largest number were children of traders (2,429), labourers (1,287), and farmers (1,324). These figures show that model schools were not just schools that catered predominantly for the children of the middle class as their critics claimed, and that they were, in fact, attended by children from towns and surrounding rural areas.

geography and 10s. for spelling. However, in many schools the success rate was limited due to poor regular attendance by senior pupils. The inspectors used to write a short report in the 'Observation and suggestions book of the district inspector' which was kept in the school, commenting on pupils' performance in different classes. For instance, when an inspector named W.M. Bole visited a national school in the Inishowen peninsula in Donegal on 15 January 1883 from 10.15a.m. to 3.15p.m. he remarked that 'the junior classes have been successfully taught and their general progress is respectable. The higher class are weak but the numbers in attendance have been larger than usual, at the same time their attendance has been irregular.'[23] He noted that whereas in first class, nine out of ten pupils passed and in second class eight out of eight were successful, in third class, only two out of a total of five passed, in fourth class only two out of six passed and in fifth, only one of two pupils passed. These figures illustrate the problems associated with poor attendance and testify to teachers' difficulties in retaining senior pupils in school and in securing a full bonus payment. (A pupil had to have attended for a minimum of one hundred days to be eligible to earn a result fee.)

In 1891 a further return of all national schools was made.[24] On this occasion the details recorded included the total numbers on roll, the average attendance, the number, religious denomination and classification of the teachers. Data was also collected on teachers' incomes, the amount received by the school in capitation grants, result fees and local aid, and the total amount paid to each school from fees, parliamentary funds and from rates. The schools were listed by inspectorial district (not by county) and in order of roll number. This return, undertaken in 1891, was contemporary with the decision to introduce compulsory and free education under the 1892 Irish Education Act.

---

23 Inspector's observation and suggestion book, 1883 (in private collection).   **24** *Return from schools in Ireland, showing the names of those receiving grants from the national education commissioners, distinguishing the mixed from the unmixed, giving the number on roll and average attendance; the number, religion, and classification of teachers; amounts received by teachers from the national education commissioners; and received by the school from subscriptions, fees, parliamentary funds and rates,* H.C. 1892 (23–I), lx, 427. Another return including the monastic and convent schools in receipt of grants, the Board's model schools and the training colleges, was undertaken in 1890: Returns made by the Irish National Education commissioners: (A) showing for 1890, for each ordinary school (exclusive of monastery, workhouse, and other model schools), its denomination, and whether the management is clerical or lay, whether there is a local committee recognised by the National Education commissioner, the number on the rolls, the attendance, the teachers' emoluments, and the income from various sources, with summaries showing the average cost per pupil, etc.; (B) return similar to (A) relating to convent and monastic schools; (C) return for ordinary national schools in 1860, 1870, 1880, and 1890, showing the number of schools, the number on the rolls, the attendance, the grants for various purposes, and the local aid, also the average cost per pupil; (D) and (E) returns similar to (C) for convent and monastic schools, and for Board model schools; (F) to (H) returns relating to training colleges; H.C. 1892 (260–I), xi, 1. For use of this material see the example of the study of Wicklow schools, pp 186–9.

Finally, in the *Appendix to the seventy-second report of the commissioners of national education for the year 1905–6*, there is a full list of national schools in operation at that time. This records the number of schools in each county along with details of the rural district, roll numbers, post town, religious denomination of the teacher, average on roll, average daily attendance, accommodation per square foot per pupil, and the income from parliamentary funds and local sources.[25] This return was linked to a campaign by the commissioners of national education to obtain building grants for new schools since many of the older ones were in poor condition and the new 1900 revised programme of curriculum required more space for practical subjects. The government had refused to release the building grants in an effort to encourage the introduction of local education rating. However, the following year (1906) the grants were released. The seventy-third report of the commissioners of national education stated that their aim now was to provide a classroom for every teacher, each with a separate entrance, along with dual desks for the pupils (to replace the long traditional bench desks), a cloakroom and a lavatory. It was also stated that schools needed rooms for the new subjects such as cookery and elementary science.[26]

Other parliamentary papers that relate to the national system include the charter of incorporation (1845) which legally empowered the Board to hold property and build its own schools;[27] memorials from the Catholic hierarchy demanding greater recognition of denominational rights in education, particularly in the area of teacher training,[28] and papers dealing with negotiations between the Board and the Catholic hierarchy regarding recognition of denominational teacher training colleges for national teachers, for which a scheme was finally agreed in 1883.[29] Regarding schools books, the Board published its own textbooks and until the 1850s these were highly successful, selling to other schools at home and abroad. However, commercial educational publishers objected to these low

25 *Appendix IV to the seventy-second report of the commissioners of national education in Ireland for the school year 1905–6* [Cd 3725], H.C. 1907, xxii, 637. This volume of parliamentary papers is devoted to Irish education and includes the annual reports generated by the commissioners of national education, the Royal University, the Intermediate Board and the three Queen's colleges. **26** *Seventy-third report of the commissioners of national education in Ireland for the year 1906–07* [Cd 3699], H.C. 1907, xxii, 1075; see Hyland, 'Educational innovation: a case study'; Miller, *Church, State & nation*, pp 118–38. **27** *Charter of incorporation lately granted by her majesty to the Board of National Education in Ireland*, H.C. 1846 (193), xlii, 191. **28** *Memorial of Roman Catholic prelates relative to national education in Ireland, and reply of the chief secretary for Ireland*, H.C. 1860 (26), liii, 659; *Memorials by the Roman Catholic prelates in Ireland on the subject of university and national education in Ireland, and correspondence relating thereto*, H.C. 1866 (84), lv, 243; *Papers relating to the letter of the Roman Catholic bishops, demanding the introduction of the denominational system into certain schools, and the destruction of the model schools*, H.C. 1867 (473), lv, 731; *supplemental return*, H.C. 1867 (473–I), lv, 737. **29** *Correspondence between the government and the commissioners of national education on the subject of the organization and government of training and model schools*, H.C. 1866 (456), lv, 213; *Correspondence between the Irish government and the commissioners of national education on the subject of training schools in Ireland*, H.C. 1883 (144), liii, 471.

priced books undercutting their place in the market.[30] In 1852 the treasury declared that in future the National Board was to distribute its books to it own schools only and not to sell copies to other schools.[31] It was also in 1852, following the controversy over use of the Board's scriptural books in model schools (and the resignation of Archbishop Richard Whately), that the Board's rules were changed in order to make use of these scriptural books optional.[32]

Another set of returns relate to the teaching of Irish in national schools. In the early years this was of little concern to the National Board as its function was to promote literacy in English. However, by the 1870s elements within the Gaelic revival movement began lobbying the Board to include the Irish language in the school curriculum. One such lobby group was the Society for the Preservation of the Irish Language and it was due to its pressure that Irish was introduced first as an extra subject to be taught outside of school hours for a result fee of ten shillings.[33] After 1900 Irish could be taught either within school hours or as an extra subject outside of school hours for a special result fee. The teaching of Irish in schools became more widespread with the growth of the Gaelic League and nationalism, and the National Board had to respond to that demand. It was in this context that a bilingual programme became available in 1904.[34]

Although fewer accounts and papers exist for intermediate education since the Board was mainly concerned with examinations and results payments, these are nonetheless useful as sources of information on the workings of the intermediate system. The receipts and accounts of the Intermediate Board were published annually from 1880 to 1921[35] as were the rules of programmes and examinations.

30 *Correspondence with Messrs Longman & Co. and John Murray on the publication of school-books by the commissioners of national education in Ireland*, H.C. 1851 (in 1405), xxiv, 101. **31** *Treasury minutes and correspondence relating to Irish national school-books, etc.*, H.C. 1852–3 (961), xciv, 485. **32** *Copy of the resolution adopted by the Board of National Education in Ireland, excluding the use of certain books in schools under their management*, H.C. 1852–3 (826), xciv, 479. The Powis commission in 1870 recommended that the National Board should cease to publish its own schools books, and that a wider range of books should be used, subject to the sanction of the Board. A list of books sanctioned for use in national schools in the 1890s features in *Return relating to school-books, applied for other than those published by the commissioners of national education in Ireland, showing the titles and authors, applicants' names, designation and address and the result in each case*, H.C. 1894 (137), lxvii, 1. **33** *Memorial of the Council of the Society for the Preservation of the Irish Language and others, in favour of placing the teaching of the Irish language on the results programme of the national schools*, H.C. 1878 (342), ix, 495; *Correspondence between the Irish executive and the commissioners of national education in Ireland, with respect to the teaching of Irish, in national schools*, H.C. 1884 (81), lxi, 617. **34** *Return showing the number of national schools in each county in Ireland in which Irish is taught as an extra subject ... and in which it is taught as an ordinary subject; and the number of intermediate schools ... in which Irish is taught, etc.*, H.C. 1906 (115), xci, 1; *Return showing how many national schools there are in each junior inspector's district in the counties of Waterford, Cork, Kerry, Clare, Galway, Mayo, Sligo, Donegal, in which the pupils can speak Irish*, H.C. 1912–13 (253), lxvi, 61; see Thomas O'Donoghue, *Bilingual education in Ireland, 1904–1922* (Perth, 2000). **35** See *Accounts and receipts and expenditure of the Intermediate Education Board for Ireland ... 1880*, H.C. 1881 (418), lxxiii, 225; *Accounts and receipts ... 1921*, H.C. 1922 (sess II)

The Board was required to submit any changes in its rules to the lord lieutenant and parliament for approval. In 1902 major changes were made to the rules whereby subjects for examination were grouped in two distinct courses, classical and modern. Equal marks were allocated to all subjects and the dominance of the classics was reduced. In 1906 a controversy arose when the House of Commons refused to sanction a change in the rules proposed for 1907 relating to the Irish language. (Rules were made for the following year's examination.) The subsequent debate raised a fundamental question about the Board's legal rights to manage its own affairs.[36] In 1913 the proposed teachers' salaries grant was being debated and the Catholic Headmasters' Association objected to the scheme on the grounds that it required schools to employ lay teachers in proportion to clerical teachers. After lengthy correspondence, in which Chief Secretary Augustine Birrell held his ground, a compromise was reached whereby the required ratio of lay to clerical teachers was applied to the Catholic and Protestant schools as a group rather than at individual school level. In 1914, in another measure to improve the secondary teaching profession, the Registration Council was established to oversee teachers' qualifications.[37]

In the case of endowed schools, a large number of returns for royal and endowed schools were made under the supervision of the 1813 commissioners of education, only a sample of which are mentioned hereafter.[38] For technical education, the accounts and papers contain data on the numbers attending the Royal College of Science, on expenditure of the Science and Art Department, South Kensington in Ireland and on the administration and staffing of the Department of Agriculture and Technical Instruction, with particular reference to the local authorities' technical education schemes.[39]

(12), iii, 281.   **36** See *Rules of examinations – programme of examinations … 1902,* H.C. 1901 (199), lvii, 13 to *Rules of examinations … 1922,* H.C. 1921 (184), xxvii, 339; *Correspondence between the Irish government and the commissioners of intermediate education in Ireland on the subject of the resolution of the House of Commons of 21st May 1906, with reference to the rules and programme of examination for 1907* [Cd 3213], H.C. 1906, xci, 531.   **37** *Correspondence between the chief secretary for Ireland and Catholic Headmasters' Association in reference to the proposed grant for £40,000 per annum for the improvement of the position of secondary teachers in Ireland* [Cd 6924], H.C. 1913, l, 771; *Proposed scheme for the application of the teachers' salaries grant* [Cd 7368], H.C. 1914, lxiv, 72; *Rules as to the constitution and procedures of the Registration Council,* H.C. 1914–16 (201), lii, 71; *Regulations for the registration of intermediate school teachers in Ireland* [Cd 9015], H.C. 1918, xix, 453 and [Cmd 122], H.C. 1919, xxxix, 385.   **38** For example, *Returns from the diocesan and other endowed schools,* H.C. 1831 (106), xv, 501; *Administration and course of instruction in royal, diocesan and private schools in Ireland,* H.C. 1836 (in 630), xiii, 565.   **39** *Return of the number of students of the Royal College of Science of Ireland, who entered and paid fees for the full course of the first second and third years, … etc.,* H.C. 1873 (67), lii, 609; *Return showing the amount expended in Ireland by the Science and Art Department on technical education,* H.C. 1893–5 (198), lxxvii, 631; *Officials employed … by county and urban councils … in carrying out the provisions of the Technical instruction (Ireland) Act,* H.C. 1905 (48), lx, 513; *Return showing schemes adopted by local authorities,* H.C. 1905 (70), lxviii, 689; *Return showing how much the Department of Agriculture (Ireland) cost for administrative purposes in the past year, distinguishing that cost into expenditure on educational administration, expenditure on non-*

A large number of accounts and papers relating to universities are available and are listed in the indexes to the British parliamentary papers under 'universities'. These include papers relating to university education at a general level, especially the demand for recognition of the Catholic University.[40] They also relate to various matters concerning the Queen's University and the Queen's colleges, ranging from students numbers (notably Catholics) to the occurrence of a fire at Queen's College, Cork, and the position of the president's residence in the three Queen's colleges.[41] Returns for the Royal University relate to staffing and finance issues while those for Trinity College, Dublin concentrate largely on student numbers and revenue.[42]

(d) Hansard's parliamentary debates

Hansard's multi-volume edition of parliamentary debates contains an invaluable verbatim record of debates in the British parliament at Westminster. These provide vital insights into contemporary opinion regarding education. Especially interesting are the debates which occurred in October 1831 when the Irish chief secretary, Lord Edward Stanley, introduced the new scheme of 'national education' for Ireland. The proposal was put forward during a debate on the finance vote for Ireland in a deliberate ploy to avoid attention being drawn to this radical proposal. Stanley suggested that the annual vote (or sum) of £30,000 should be taken away

educational administration, and administration expenditure common to both, H.C. 1913 (49), liii, 1. In the general indexes to the parliamentary papers these accounts are listed under 'Royal College of Science', 'Science and Art Department' and 'Agriculture' respectively. **40** *Memorials by the Roman Catholic prelates in Ireland on the subject of university and national education and correspondence relating thereto; and memorials on the subject of university education in Ireland,* H.C. 1866 (84), lv, 242; *Correspondence relative to the proposed charter to a Roman Catholic university in Ireland,* H.C. 1867–8 (288, 380), liii, 779; *Declaration of the Catholic laity of Ireland on the subject of university education in that country,* H.C. 1870 (140), liv, 645. The Catholic laity claimed to have the right to choose whatever system of education they wished and demanded 'equality in all educational advantages afforded by the State'. **41** *Return of the names of the matriculated students who entered the Queen's colleges in Ireland in 1849, showing the date of matriculation, religious profession, and faculty and department,* H.C. 1860 (554), liii, 695; *Return of the name, date of appointment, and salary of the presidents, vice-presidents, fellows and professors of Queen's colleges, etc.,* H.C. 1857 (129–I), xv, 401; *Correspondence of the Queen's colleges in Ireland in reference to the residence of the presidents in their respective colleges,* H.C. 1859 (197–I), xxi, pt ii, 411; *Copy of depositions taken before the justices of the peace in the case of the burning of Queen's College, Cork,* H.C. 1864 (194), xlvi, 437: *Return of the number of Roman Catholic students on the books of the Queen's colleges … etc.,* H.C. 1877 (450), lxvii, 757. The return showed that there were 255 Catholic students attending, the largest number being in Cork.   **42** *Copy of warrant authorising an inquiry by the solicitor-general for Ireland and Mr Strange, MP into the recent riots at Trinity College, Dublin,* H.C. 1857–8 (188), xlvi, 505. At a public parade to mark the return of the viceroy, several TCD students were injured in a clash with police and troops. See also *Return of the revenue enjoyed by Trinity College, Dublin, of the value of each living in gift of the college, perpetuities purchased, etc.; number of Protestant and*

from the Kildare Place Society and given to a new State education board. The result was a short debate.[43]

Also of interest is the long and controversial parliamentary debate which took place when the Irish chief secretary, James Graham, introduced the colleges bill in May–July 1845.[44] The bill was opposed by conservative Tories and High Anglicans, who objected to State-funded secular universities. One MP, Sir Robert Inglis who represented Oxford, denounced it as 'a gigantic scheme of godless education'.[45] The debate in 1878 on the intermediate education bill was also lengthy and much discussion focused on whether girls' school should be included in the payment by results scheme.[46] This bill was first introduced into the House of Lords to try to speed up its passing and when Lord O'Hagan spoke, he praised the bill in the following terms:

> It respected the rights of the conscience; it did not interfere with religious susceptibilities; it encouraged individual effort and rewarded it; it absolutely and impartially dispensed the bounty of the State; it aided and improved and consolidated the efforts of scholastic institutions; and it did all this without vexatious interference with the internal management of these institutions.[47]

Researchers who wish to search for material relating to education in Hansard's parliamentary debates should first consult the indexes to Hansard under the heading 'education'.[48]

III. OTHER CONTEMPORARY PRINTED SOURCES

Commercial directories such as the *Dublin Almanac*, the *Dublin Post Office Directory* and *Thom's Official Directories* are valuable sources for the history of education as they contain details of government departments, schools and colleges, educational and charitable societies based in the capital. In the case of directories relating to Dublin, under the heading 'trades directory' typically one finds a list of 'seminaries for young gentlemen' and 'seminaries for young ladies' which highlights the number of private schools in the capital. The annual *Irish Catholic Directory* carried advertisements for Catholic schools and convents both in Ireland and England and these revealed details of the attributes of individual schools, including location and curriculum offered. For instance, the following advertisement for St Joseph's

---

Catholic undergraduates registered on the 1st January 1868, H.C. 1867–8 (301), liii, 805. There was a total of 1,392 students on the books, of whom seventy-six were Catholic. **43** *Hansard, 3*, vi, 1249–1305 (9 Sept. 1831). **44** Ibid., lxxx, 346–64 (9 May 1845). **45** Ibid., 377–80; see Moody & Beckett, *Queen's Belfast*, i, 10. The colleges became commonly known as the 'godless colleges'. **46** *Hansard, 3*, ccxli, 7–19 (21 June 1878); McElligott, *Secondary education*, pp 30–40; Raftery & Parkes, *Female education in Ireland*, pp 76–9. **47** *Hansard, 3*, ccxli, 423 (28 June 1878). **48** *Hansard's Catalogue and breviate of parliamentary papers, 1696–1834 with introduction by P. Ford, professor emeritus and G. Ford,*

Ursuline convent in Sligo (under the patronage of the most Revd Dr Clancy, bishop of Elphin), published in 1900, read thus:

> This convent is beautifully situated, possessing all the advantages of a country residence while in sufficient proximity to the town of Sligo. The grounds are extensive, and afford every facility for the enjoyment of healthful exercises, with a charming view of the sea, mountains, and surrounding country. The buildings comprise spacious dormitories and bathrooms, study and classrooms, library and chapel, an extensive recreation hall, with a suite of music rooms attached, all carefully designed and suitably furnished, with a view to the comfort and good order of the pupils.
>
> The academic course comprehends all those attainments which are necessary, useful and ornamental in society and unites every advantage which can contribute to a refined education. For some years now many pupils of this convent, in compliance with the wishes of their parents, have been permitted to present themselves for the intermediate and South Kensington science and art examinations, and in every case with the most satisfactory outcome.[49]

Lists of these commercial and professional directories, many of which contain information on towns and villages throughout the whole of Ireland, may be found in John Grenham's *Tracing your Irish ancestors* (Dublin, 1992) and also in James G. Ryan's *Irish records: sources for family and local history* (Dublin, 1997 ed.).

Samuel Lewis's *Topographical dictionary of Ireland* (1837) features details of schools in the entry for each town or village throughout the country, and is, therefore, a particularly useful source for researchers investigating the history of specific schools at local level. For example, the entry for Armagh City reads as follows:

> The free grammar-school, to the south of the observatory, is endowed with seven townlands in the parish of Loughgilly, comprising 1514 acres, and producing a clear rental of £1377, granted in trust to the primate and his successors in 1627, for the support of a grammar school at Mountnorris: part of the income is applied to the maintenance of several exhibitions at Trinity College, Dublin. The buildings occupy the four sides of a quadrangle, the front of which is formed by a covered passage communicating on each side with the apartments of the headmaster and pupils; on the fourth side is the schoolroom 56ft long by 28 broad, behind which is a large area enclosed by a wall and serving as a playground. They were completed in 1774, at the expense of £5000, defrayed by Primate Robinson, and are capable of conveniently accommodating 100 resident pupils. A school for the instruction of

University of Southampton (Shannon, 1968).   **49** *Catholic Directory, 1900*, p. 4.

the choir boys has been established by the present primate, the master of which receives a stipend of £78 per annum, and is allowed to take private pupils ...[50]

Also useful are the statistical accounts of Ireland such as Edward Wakefield's *An account of Ireland, statistical and political* (London, 1812). A limited number of contemporary statistical county surveys were also published, among them Hely Dutton's *A statistical survey of the county of Clare* (Dublin, 1808) and his *A statistical and agricultural survey of the county of Galway* (Dublin, 1824).[51] In his book *Tracing the past*, William Nolan provides a list of these early nineteenth-century statistical accounts. Narratives written and published by visitors and travellers are often a rich source for social history and occasionally feature commentaries on education and descriptions of individual schools. Such works include Richard Twiss's *A tour through Ireland in 1775* (Dublin, 1776), Sir John Carr's *The stranger in Ireland* (New York, 1807) and James Glassford's *Notes on three tours of Ireland, made in 1776, 1777, and 1778* (Bristol, 1832). In his account of the condition of the Irish peasantry, published in 1804, Robert Bell referred to the 'poor scholars':

> ... (the reader) will hardly believe that some ... sons of most indigent and obscure peasants in Ireland were able to study and become acquainted with the best Greek and Roman authors; that they had taste to discriminate the beauties contained in them; and frequently conversed with each other in the Latin language; which (bye and bye) they spoke more correctly than English. It was no common thing to see poor lads who left their homes without shoes or stockings, or perhaps the smallest money in their pockets, wandering through the country in search of scholastic instruction, and living on the bounty of those they had applied to for relief, which was hardly ever refused them ...[52]

On the other hand, in one of the best-known of these works, entitled *Ireland: its scenery, character etc.* (London, 1841), Mr and Mrs S.C. Hall entertained high hopes for the new national schools:

> Another subject of importance, too, must claim our attention – the national schools, and their system of education. It is, we know, to be approached with extreme caution; for it, unhappily, furnishes, at the present moment, an arena for contending parties in politics. We shall endeavour, nevertheless, to

50 Lewis, *Topographical dictionary of Ireland*, i, 73. **51** See William Nolan, *Tracing the past: sources for local studies in the Republic of Ireland* (Dublin, 1982), pp 95–8 for list of surveys. **52** Robert Bell, *Description of the conditions and manners as well as the moral, political character, education, etc., of the peasantry of Ireland, such as they were between the years of 1780 and 1790 when Ireland was supposed to have arrived at the highest degree of prosperity and happiness* (London, 1804), pp 41–3, quoted in Hyland & Milne, *Irish educational documents*, i, 72–3.

consider it apart from the interests of any party – protesting on the one hand against the unwise and unchristian course adopted by the Roman Catholic archbishop of Tuam; and on the other against the wholesale sentence of condemnation, pronounced upon it by the High Church party in the State. With one observation, we shall now content ourselves. After visiting very many of the schools and inspecting them closely – we may, perhaps, add with suspicion – it was impossible for us to arrive at any other conclusion, than that the present generation of boys and girls – aided by the uncompromising foe of idleness, prejudice, insubordination and bigotry – EDUCATION – must be a race far superior to their parents, who were reared in ignorance and kept in ignorance …[53]

John McVeagh, in his *Irish travel writing: a bibliography* (Dublin, 1996) provides a useful list of these narratives.

Contemporary journals like that of Elizabeth Smith of Baltiboys near Blessington, Co. Wicklow are also worth consulting as they sometimes contain information relating to schools in a locality. In her journal, Smith recounted the difficulties which she and her husband encountered in dealings with their estate school and described local opposition to the national school system in the 1840s.[54]

Journals and newspapers can also contain relevant material. The *Irish Times* and the *Freeman's Journal* are two important sources for information on the political background to and contemporary discussions of educational issues during much of the nineteenth and twentieth centuries. Also useful are the newspaper-cutting books, 1854–1922 (ED/7 files in the National Archives) and the Larcom papers in the National Library of Ireland (see above). Among the most relevant education publications are the journals of the Irish National Teachers' Organization – *The Irish Teachers' Journal* (1868–1904); the *Irish School Weekly* (1904–56); the *Irish Education Review*, a journal for secondary education (1908–14), edited by Fr Andrew Murphy S.J., and the journal of the Association of Secondary Teachers of Ireland entitled *The Irish Journal of Education* (1910–17), which was edited by P.F. Condon and later by W.J. Williams. Other mainstream journals which contain articles on Irish education include the *Journal of the Statistical and Social Inquiry Society of Ireland, New Ireland Review, Irish Quarterly Review, Irish Ecclesiastical Review, Christian Brothers Educational Review, Irish Monthly* and *Transactions of the National Association for the Promotion of Social Science. History of Education*, the journal of the History of Education Society, published by Taylor & Francis, publishes articles on Irish education[55] while *Irish Educational Studies*, the journal of the Educational Studies Association of Ireland, regularly features articles on aspects of

53 Mr & Mrs S.C. Hall, *Ireland: its scenery, character etc.* (2 vols, London, 1841), i, 157. **54** See *The Irish journals of Elizabeth Smith, 1840–50*, ed. David Thomson & M. McGusty (Oxford, 1980). **55** Farren, 'Irish model schools – models of what?'; Oonagh Walsh's 'The Dublin University Mission Society, 1890–1905' in *History of Education*, 24:1 (Mar. 1995), pp 61–72; Harford, 'The movement for the higher education of women in Ireland; gender

the history of Irish education. Researchers should consult Pádraig Hogan and Donal Herron's bibliography of all articles published in *Irish Educational Studies* during the period 1976–90.[56] It is advisable, too, for researchers to consult relevant local history journals as these often feature articles on education and schools in a local area. For example, the *Dublin Historical Record* has a number of articles on schools, both in the city and the county. As already indicated, Hayes's *Sources for the history of Irish civilization: articles in Irish periodicals* is an essential guide to articles published in journals which are listed under author, place and subjects including 'education', 'schools' and 'universities', although it is important to remember that only articles published prior to 1970 are listed.

In short, there is a great wealth of manuscript and printed primary source material, not to mention secondary sources, available to researchers interested in exploring the history of educational provision in Ireland as a whole as well as at grassroots level. While many of the sources have been used in scholarly publications that have appeared to date, large amounts of material have yet to be uncovered and mined by historians. In the next chapter, some guidance is offered to scholars researching the history of education in Ireland.

equality or denominational rivalry?' **56** Pádraig Hogan and Donal Herron's bibliography of all articles published in *Irish Educational Studies* during the period 1976–90 was published by the ESAI in 1992: see n. 5 above.

CHAPTER 3

Guidelines for researching the history of education in a locality

Studies of educational provision at local level make a valuable contribution to the broader history of education as they examine schooling at the micro level and demonstrate the important place which education and educational institutions have occupied in the social history of every local community. Due to Ireland's political history and the resultant centralized structure of educational provision, official government reports, such as the annual reports of the commissioners of national education, covered the whole country. As a result, it is possible and usually relatively easy for researchers to access material relating to a specific locality. Thanks to the public accountability of most educational institutions which resulted in detailed record keeping by officials operating at local level, we are left with a wealth of school registers, roll books, inspectors reports, attendance books and so on, all of which are essential for local studies.

SOURCE MATERIAL IN THE LOCALITY

When embarking on a study of educational provision at local level it is advisable to select a limited geographical area for study (one or two parishes or alternatively a village, or town). Next, one needs to identify and locate all surviving archival sources and to consult relevant secondary works (both specialist and general studies of the history of education in Ireland) as these often provide leads to other relevant primary and secondary material. Researchers should inquire whether local schools, libraries, museums, newspaper offices or indeed individuals (parish clergy or teachers) have material in their possession. Like all manuscript material, the records of individual schools should to be treated with care as they are unique documents. Researchers also need to exercise due discretion and sensitivity in how they use the personal details of children and local families contained in these archival collections. The same is true in handling particularly sensitive material such as comments and reports on teachers. Clearly the amount and quality of the material that survives will vary enormously. However, if one is fortunate enough to find a substantial collection for an individual school, it is likely to contain some or all of the following. School registers record the names and age of the pupils, the date of their entry and leaving, parents' occupation and details of schools attended previously. School roll books, recording daily attendance, show patterns of absences due to children's illnesses, seasonal labour, fair days or, other exceptional factors such as an epidemic of some infectious disease. Daily report books record attendance class by class, the numbers of pupils listed in the school and the grants paid to the school. The inspectors' observation and suggestion books provide insights into the curriculum and teaching methodology of the classroom as do the organizers' observation books. In particular, the abandonment of the payment by results system and the introduction of the new revised programme of instruction in 1900 brought many changes to national schools.[1] Researchers examining the impact of these changes on schools in a specific locality will find the confidential inspectors' report books, originally held in the schools and in which the progress in the various subjects of the new curriculum were recorded, especially useful. To encourage and assist teachers with the new curriculum, the National Board appointed a group of specialist organizers to run short courses and visit schools.[2] An organizer's observation book was placed in each school for the purposes of recording observations made during these visits and these books are revealing on the difficulties experienced by individual schools in endeavouring to implement the revised programme. These organizers were specially appointed to assist with the implementation of the new revised curriculum of 1900 and worked in areas such as elementary science, manual instruction and woodwork, cookery, laundry and needlework. For example the organizer who visited a national school at Criere in April 1910 wrote the following in that school's organizers' observation book:

> Visited at practical lessons. The girls prepared and cooked very well though the work was rather lacking in order. This was due to too much practical work being attempted. Too many sweet dishes should not be included in the next syllabus.
>
> Suggestions: (1) before practical lesson commences, give an introductory lecture; during the lesson question on all that is being done. (2) Draw up a syllabus of eight demonstration lessons for the next session suitable for first and second year girls.[3]

The punishment book records serious misdemeanours which included 'chatting and sniggering', disobedience, 'general slackness and laziness', 'running thro[ugh] the schoolroom and creating a disturbance' and failure to bring the required two

1. The new 1900 core curriculum consisted of English, arithmetic, kindergarten methods and manual instruction, drawing, object lessons and elementary science, singing, cookery and laundry (later domestic economy); see *Appendix to the sixty-ninth report of the commissioners of national education in Ireland for the year 1902* [Cd 1679], H.C. 1903, xxi. The programme was curtailed in 1905 as it proved too ambitious for small schools. In the case of optional 'extra' subjects included Irish, French, Latin, mathematics and instrumental music, special fees could be earned if they were taught outside school hours.   **2** Organizers were appointed for manual instruction, elementary science and object lessons, needlework, drawing, art, kindergarten, music and cookery and laundry work. The Board also published a series of *Notes for teachers* to provide guidance.   **3** Organizer's observation book, Criere

sods of turf to school each day. As there were instances of excessive use of corporal punishment by a teacher, the National Board required each school to keep a punishment book in which incidences involving the use of the cane were recorded.[4] The 'Instructions to teachers as regard the infliction of corporal punishment in national schools' clearly state that

> Corporal punishment should be administered only for grave transgressions – never for failure in lessons and only a light cane or rod should be used for the purpose of inflicting corporal punishment. The boxing of children's ears, the pulling of their hair, and similar ill-treatment are absolutely forbidden, and will be visited with severe penalties.[5]

Old textbooks, old copybooks and oral interviews are also a valuable source of information concerning daily routine and life in schools. School photographs showing teachers, pupils and the schoolhouse, were often taken at the end of the school year and many survive in the possession of families in a locality.[6] Topics that may be explored in a history of education and schooling in a locality include patterns of attendance and the duration of children's schooling, the school's catchment area, the pupils' and teachers' social background and parents' occupation, textbooks used, the practicalities of implementing the core curriculum and the range of 'extra subjects' taught. Details of the daily life of teachers and pupils are often vividly recalled in oral interviews. In the days before free secondary education, pupils would continue to attend national school up to the school leaving age of fourteen years and the subsequent destination of pupils is often recorded in the school register.

As outlined in chapter two, researchers have access to a wide range of public sources relating to educational provision at various levels. Particularly relevant for local studies are the parliamentary reports, records of the commissioners of national education held in the National Archives of Ireland, and official annual reports. *The second report of the commissioners of Irish education inquiry* (1825–6) serves as a useful starting point for a local survey, as it records details of existing educational provision in each parish, along with the teachers' names and salaries, the number of pupils on the roll and the schools' source(s) of income. Also useful is a

N.S., 1909–10 (private collection).   **4** See Hannigan (ed.), *The national school system, 1831–1924, facsimile documents*, p. 53, for incident concerning the alleged ill-treatment of a child for her failure to bring turf to school.   **5** *Instructions in regard to the infliction of corporal punishment in schools* (Office of National Education, Dublin, c.1910).   **6** Examples of local school studies include Alicia St Leger, *St Luke's School, Douglas, Cork* (Dublin, 2002), David Kerr, *A history of Rathgar National School, 1896–1996* (Dublin, 1996); P.J. Dunne & Eugene Reilly (eds), *Farnham School and its community, 1801–1996* (Cavan, 1996); *Whitechurch parish, old schools 1823 project* (Dublin, 1999); Mary Bowden, *A century of schooling in Rathmullan* (Rathmullen, 2002); Kieran Waldron, *Out of the shadows – emerging secondary schools in the archdiocese of Tuam, 1940–69* (Tuam, 2002); Jimmie Cooke (ed.), *Kilmacow folklore, County Kilkenny, St Senan's Boy's National School, Kilmacow* (Kilkenny, 2008).

contemporaneous return, undertaken in 1824 by the archdeacons of the Church of Ireland, which contains lists of that Church's parish schools throughout the country.[7] A decade later, the *Second report of the commissioners on public instruction* again recorded details of educational provision on a parochial basis and showed the growth of the national school system. Volume III of the endowed schools commission report of 1857–8 features information on the origin, foundation, endowment and attendance of endowed schools in each parish. The educational census conducted by the royal commission on primary education (Ireland) in 1868–70 includes attendance figures for primary schools nationwide, thus making it possible to conduct a study of the growth in educational provision in the fifty years since the 1820s.

In addition to the parliamentary returns of individual national schools,[8] the annual reports of the commissioners of national education in Ireland (CNEI) contain lists of those schools in connection with the National Board, their roll numbers, average daily attendance and so on. Initially the Board listed the schools in numerical order according to their roll number within each county, so it is possible to trace the expansion of schooling in an area over time. However, in the 1860s this method was changed and schools were now grouped according to parishes within each county. Little detail on individual schools features in these reports. However, the general reports compiled by the head inspectors provide valuable insights into the social and economic conditions that prevailed in a particular district. These inspectors' reports are also illuminating in that they offer comments on the problems associated with attempting to implement a core curriculum when grappling with the problems of poverty and low school attendance. During the 1850s they included detailed progress reports on the Board's new district model schools. Particularly useful are the *Appendix to the twenty-fourth report of the commissioners of national education in Ireland for the year 1855*, vol. 11, which has

7 *Accounts and papers relative to schools and education*, H.C. 1824 (179) (286) (350) (403) (461), xxi, 471. The volume also contains lists of the amounts of money paid out to the education societies by the government to date, including all grants paid to schools by the Kildare Place Society, as well as accounts for diocesan schools and the royal school. This return is related to data required by the commissioners of the 1825 education inquiry. See also *Second report of the commissioners on public instruction in Ireland*, H.C. 1835 (47), xxxiv, 1; *Report of the commissioners to inquire into endowments, funds, and condition of schools endowed for the purpose of education in Ireland*, iii, *Papers accompanying the report/tables and endowments*, H.C. 1857–8 (2336–IV), xii, 1; *Royal commission of inquiry into primary education (Ireland)*, vi [C 6–V), H.C. 1870, xxviii, pt v, 1.   8 *Return of all national schools in connection with the Board of National Education, in operation on 31st of December, 1862*, HC 1864 (481) (481–I), (481–II) (481–III), xlvii, 1, 269, 461, 663; *Return of the numbers of pupils examined for results fees in each school in Ireland under the Board of National Education, in 1877–8 and 1878–9*, HC 1880 (33), lv, 13; *Return from schools in Ireland, showing the names of those receiving grants from the national education commissioners, etc.*, H.C. 1892 (23–I), lx, 427; *Appendix to the seventy-second report of the commissioners of national education in Ireland for 1905* [Cd 3725], H.C. 1907, xxii, 637; *Appendix to the seventy-seventh report of the commissioners of national education for 1910–11* [Cd 6043], H.C. 1912–13, xxiv, 277.

a full report on the Marlborough Street Central Training Institution and teacher training, and the *Appendix to the twenty-fifth report of the commissioners of national education in Ireland for the year 1857* which contains a detailed report on the opening of the Belfast Model School, incorporating coloured plans of the design of new school rooms. The study of an individual model school can be undertaken using these reports in conjunction with the special report on model schools featured in the Powis commission report (see vol. I, part II). Further details relating to individual national schools are to be found in the *Appendix to the seventy-second report of the commissioners of national education in Ireland for the year 1905* [C 3725] and in *Appendix to the seventy-seventh report of the commissioners of national education in Ireland for the year 1910–11* [C 6043]. The programme of instruction and the titles of the Board's textbooks are to be found in the annual reports along with programmes for teachers, examination papers and the official rules and regulations of the National Board.

Once an outline of the parameters for the local study have been defined, the education files in the National Archives of Ireland should be consulted. As explained in chapter two, researchers should begin by consulting the consolidated card index to the national school files, which is available in the Reading Room. The (ED/1) applications files contain details of original national schools applications and ED/9 files contain the correspondence between individual schools and central office in Dublin. Material relating to teachers can be found in the salary books (ED/6) while the school registers (ED/2) give a summary of the National Board's communications with each national school.

The locations of schools are marked on the Ordnance Survey 6-inch maps. Each national school had a catchment area of three miles. Therefore, the location of schools depended on the demography of the district and/or the availability of a suitable site, which had to be provided by a local person, often the landlord. Since most children walked to school, the sites were sometimes in central but isolated places within walking distance of several villages. As the majority of children in the nineteenth and early twentieth centuries received a primary education only, secondary schools were usually located only in the towns and children who were privileged to attend either travelled daily by road or rail, or were sent to boarding school. Other useful sources when locating specific schools are the *Ordnance survey memoirs* and *Letter books* of the 1830s and the *General valuation of rateable property in Ireland*, commonly referred to as Griffith's Valuation, of the 1850s.

It is important to place the history of education of a locality within the context of the broader education system and to examine how national education policy worked at ground level. For instance, the implementation of the national school revised programme curriculum in 1900 posed a major challenge to teachers and the difficulties involved in the change from the payment by results system are often revealed in the inspectors' report books and in pupils' records. The importance of the presence of a school within a locality and its influence on the development of a community are key issues in any social history of education. School attendance rates and the number of years spent in school up to seventh and eighth standards can also be traced and, since pupils' progression on to second level remained limited until well into the twentieth century, in cases when it did occur, it tends to be noted in schools' registers.

A SAMPLE STUDY: SCHOOLS IN COUNTY WICKLOW, 1825–1900

Wicklow is a maritime county on the east coast with a high granite mountain range down the centre, dividing the east from the west. In 1841 the county's population was 126,000. It therefore had the second-lowest population density in Ireland (151), County Kerry having the lowest (145). The three small coastal towns of Bray, Wicklow and Arklow had populations of 2,203, 3,141 and 3,254 respectively.[9]

The 1825 education report recorded 258 schools operating in Wicklow and serving 11,817 pupils. Protestant education societies were strong and active in the county. The largest, the Kildare Place Society, supported twenty-six schools,[10] while the Association for Discountenancing Vice, and the Board of Erasmus Smith each gave grants to nine schools. The Incorporated Society had a charter school in Arklow town. However, the majority of the schools were run by individuals and by Catholic parishes: in all there were 181 pay schools and twenty attached to Catholic parishes. Wealthy landlords often provided the initiative and the necessary financial resources to build schools and a large number were of 'mixed' denominations.[11] For instance, in Arklow both Catholic and Protestant pupils attended a school supported by the Kildare Place Society and by the Erasmus Smith Board. It had a 'commodious building'. The master, James Johnson, was a Protestant while the female teacher, Mary Jane Byrne, was a Catholic. Mrs Proby of Glenart paid the mistress £20 per annum and the earl of Carysfort was responsible for building the schoolhouse.[12] At Ballyarthur (Redcross) there was a 'commodious school house', built by Mrs Bayly, and she paid the annual salary of £9 'with board and lodging to the mistress'. In Wicklow town, the parish school had been built of the

9 See Kenneth Hannigan, 'Wicklow before and after the famine' in idem & William Nolan (eds), *Wicklow, history and society* (Dublin, 1994), p. 789; *The Ordnance Survey letters – Wicklow, from the original letters of John O'Donovan, Eugene Curry & Thomas O'Connor, 1838–40*, ed. Christiaan Corlett & John Medlycott (Wicklow, 2005). 10 Further details on schools supported by KPS can be founded in the Society's registers held in the Church of Ireland College of Education archives, Upper Rathmines Road, Dublin 6. 11 William Nolan, 'Land and landscape in Wicklow' in Hannigan & Nolan (eds), *Wicklow, history & society*, pp 649–92. The largest estate in Wicklow was the Fitzwilliam estate of Coolattin, Shilleagh which was comprised of 179,225 acres, the next largest belonged to the See of Dublin (26,469 acres). 12 *Second report of the Irish education inquiry, 1825*, H.C. 1826–7 (12), xii, 836–62. The earls of Carysfort (Probys) owned the estate of Glenart (comprising 16,190 acres) near Arklow. The other landlords in the area were the earl of Wicklow who had 23,081 acres, Bayly of Glenarthur who owned 2,604 acres, Acton of Kilmurragh who had 5,381 acres; Hoey of Dunganstown who had 4,398 acres and Revell of Sea Park, Magheramore, who had 2,769 acres: see Hannigan & Nolan (eds), *Wicklow, history & society*, p. 658.

'best material' at a cost of £160 with a grant of £30 from the Kildare Place Society and a grant of £40 from the lord lieutenant's fund, plus private subscriptions. The earl of Fitzwilliam paid £10 a year. The remainder of the master's salary was made up by subscriptions among the Roman Catholic inhabitants and 'the product of a charity sermon'. Ninety-one Catholics and ten Protestants attended[13] and the schoolhouse had been fitted up by Kildare Place Society. On the other hand many pay schools that had little or no facilities and the teacher was paid a meagre salary. For instance, in the parish of CastleMacAdam, at Coolencarl, a Catholic named Maria Crosbie kept a school in an 'outhouse of mean description granted by a farmer'. Her income was £3 10s. and ten Protestants and fifty Catholic pupils attended, of whom thirty-six were male and twenty-four were female. At Redcross, James Bromie, a Catholic, kept a school 'built of mud, [and] covered with straw'. His income was £10 per annum and he taught twenty pupils, of whom seventeen were boys and eleven were girls. At Cronbawn, Michael Johnson, a Catholic, had a schoolhouse 'built of mud, and thatched' and his income was £20 per year. He had fifty-two pupils, including seventeen Protestants and thirty-five Catholics, of whom twenty-six were boys, and twenty-six were girls. Also at Cronbawn, James Moorhead, a Protestant, kept a 'free' school, which was built of lime and stone. His income was £20 per year but this school received a grant from the Kildare Place Society and the Tygrony Mining Company paid the master £15 per year.[14]

These local returns demonstrate the variations and inequalities that existed in educational provision at local level and highlight the schools' pressing need for additional resources. They also show the extent and importance of local initiative, as demonstrated by landlords and clergy, along with the prevalence of 'mixed' education of Protestants and Catholics and of co-education in schools during the 1820s, on the eve of the introduction of the national system. Factors such as these influenced the original structure of the national school system which was designed to build on local initiative and to encourage joint applications from Protestants and Catholics.

---

13 *Second report of the Irish education inquiry, 1825*, H.C. 1826–7 (12), xii, 840–1. Although the lord lieutenant's fund was intended primarily to support schools for the Catholic poor, a number of grants were given to Protestant schools. Among those in Wicklow who applied for a grant were Thomas Acton, on behalf of Dunganstown School, the Revd Henry Bayly of CastleM'cAdam and Balleese, and the Revd L.W. Hepenstall of Derryalossary. See *Accounts and papers relative to schools and education*, H.C. 1824 (179), xxi, 383–470. **14** The copper mines at Cronebane had been worked since the 1787. By 1835 there were four mines in operation, one of which was leased to a Cornish mining company which employed up to 600 people. The mining company ran a school for the miners' children: see D. Coleman, 'The mining community at Avoca, 1780–1880' in Hannigan & Nolan (eds), *Wicklow, history & society*, pp 761–88. In March 1834 the Associated Irish Mining Company 'resolved that £10 per annum be paid to Mrs Moorehead, the schoolmistress, for the purposes of affording instruction to the children of the miners'. See minutes of the Associated Irish Mining Company, 30 Mar. 1834 (NLI MS 16309, quoted in Coleman, p. 787).

As already highlighted the 1824 parliamentary return contained lists of all Church of Ireland parish schools in the country.[15] These returns, made by Church of Ireland archdeacons, were intended to show the extent of schooling provided by that Church but researchers should be aware that the returns are often lacking in accurate detail. The following is the report on the parish school at Derralossary in Co. Wicklow:

> there is one parish school in the parish, which was erected in 1821. No particular account of the number of children attending has been preserved beyond the year. It generally varies from 15–20. The school is supported by a salary of £12 per annum from the Association for Discountenancing Vice and the stipend from the scholars, which amounted during last year to £2. The incumbent contributes indirectly as a member of the association and of the Wicklow Education Society. There is no fund to keep the house in repair, which of course must fall on him. The number of free scholars is unlimited, it is open to all who come. There are three schools of inferior description assisted occasionally by the Wicklow Education Society. The incumbent is unacquainted with their funds. The number of children at them is about 100; none of them is free. There are likewise three Sunday schools in the parish containing 100 children.[16]

The growth of educational provision in County Wicklow, 1830–60

The growth of educational provision in County Wicklow can be traced by examining the returns featured in the 1835 *Report on public instruction*.[17] These returns were compiled on the basis of dioceses rather than counties and so the statistics are not compatible with those gathered in other surveys and reports. In the archdiocese of Dublin (which included Wicklow) there were 508 schools in operation in 1835, including sixty-two national schools, and Protestant education societies were found to be very active. These returns contain information on subjects taught in the schools (usually reading, writing and arithmetic and needlework for girls). In the parish of Dunganstown there were seven schools, including the Church of Ireland parish school which was still supported by the Association for Discountenancing Vice and Promoting the Knowledge and Practice of the Christian Religion. A Catholic parish school was supported by Colonel Acton and the parishioners. There were two pay schools, one at Ballymoney where the master had 'a house and garden rent free and a ton of coal'. It was supported by Miss Revell. Another school was supported by Mr Revell at Three-Mile-Water. Three hedge schools were also listed. At Glenealy there were three schools, one of which was the first national school in the county (roll no. 984). At Derralossory, the parish school was still in receipt of a grant from the Association for

---

15 *Accounts and papers relating to schools and education in Ireland*, H.C. 1824 (461), xxi, 619–36. **16** Ibid.   **17** *First report of the commissioners on public instruction (Ireland)*, H.C. 1835 (45) (46), xxxiii, 1, 829.

Discountenancing Vice. There were also two private schools, and a national school which, at that moment, was 'discontinued' until such time as a master could be found.

In his *Topographical dictionary of Ireland* (1837) Samuel Lewis described Dunganstown as follows:

> Dunganstown, a parish in the barony of Arklow, County Wicklow and province of Leinster, 4 miles (SW) from Wicklow, on the road to Arklow: containing 3135 in habitants.
>
> ... The soil is fertile, and the system of agriculture in the highest state of improvement; there is an adequate proportion of bog, and a quarry of good slate, which, though bordering on the sea, is not worked for want of a convenient landing place.
>
> The surrounding scenery is pleasingly diversified, embracing extensive mountain and sea views and the neighbourhood is enlivened with several gentlemen's seats and villas of which the principle are West Aston, the residence of Lieut-Col. Acton, Oatlands, of W. Shepherd, Esq., Sheephill, of J. Shepherd, Esq., Sea Park, of J. Revell, esq., Ballymoney, of W. Revell, esq., Ballinclare, of Capt. T. Keoghe; and Springfield, of J. Wright, Esq. Of Dunganstown Castle, the property of the co-heiresses of the late F. Hoey, Esq., ... the only remains are the square tower and an extensive range of domestic buildings, partially covered in ivy ...

On schools in the parish, Lewis commented:

> About 190 children are taught in the public schools, one of which is supported by Lieut. Col. Acton; another for which a building was erected by subscription amounted to £182, aided by a £100 from the parliamentary fund, is supported by subscription. There are three private schools, in which there are about 100 children ...[18]

The next major report featuring material relevant to schools in Wicklow was that of the *Endowed school commissions of 1857–8* which examined educational endowments operating in the county. These included schools funded by the Erasmus Smith Trust at Aghold, Coolkenno, Kilpipe, Kiltegan and Rathdrum as well as the Incorporated Society's charter school at Arklow and the Carysfort Royal School near Aughrim. When one of the assistant commissioners visited the schools he often found unsatisfactory conditions. For instance, in his report on Carysfort Royal School he remarked:

> I examined a mixed class (boys and girls), comprising the most advanced pupils in the school. Their reading (from the third national reading book)

18 Lewis, *Topographical dictionary of Ireland*, i, 577.

was very indifferent. Of geography they scarcely knew anything. None of them could parse a sentence ... There seemed to be very little system in the general conduct of the school, which, considering its large endowments, was in point of efficiency, much below what might have been expected.[19]

It was said that Dunganstown parish school was 'at a low ebb' and at Derralossary parochial school 'the state of instruction in this school was [found to be] indifferent'. The most efficient endowed school the commissioner could find was the Erasmus Smith school at Kiltegan where 'the state of education in the school is satisfactory as far as it goes; but it would be well if the course of instruction were extended so as to embrace some branches of mathematics'.[20]

National school system, 1831

Grappling with the inequalities and inadequate resources identified in these official reports, schools throughout Wicklow and the entire country were in dire need of a better funded, properly managed system of schooling. The process whereby the national school system developed in a local area is a subject for a fascinating and valuable study which can throw into sharp relief the various strengths and weaknesses of the new system. The National Board did not engage in any overall planning in relation to the location of the schools. The first national schools to open were often situated in areas where an enterprising landlord or active parish priest was ready and able to take the initiative in applying to the National Board for a grant in aid. The Board's lengthy application (query sheet) form required detailed information concerning the school, expected attendance, resources available and the location of other schools in the area. If possible, the form was to be signed by both Catholics and Protestants in the district. (The majority of initial applications were for aid for fitting-up at the schoolhouse and for payment of a teacher's salary since the schoolhouse was often already in place.) In Wicklow, among the earliest national schools opened were Baltinglass (male and female) parish schools (roll nos 971 and 972); Ballinure, Grange (roll no. 973);

---

19 *Report of her majesty's commissioners appointed to inquire into the endowments* [Kildare commission], iii, *Papers accompanying the report (tables of schools and endowments)*, H.C. 1857–8 (2336–IV), xxii, pt iv, 251–66. The report includes details of the origins and endowments of the schools as well as the curriculum, the master's salary and pupils' attendance. It is, therefore, a useful source for tracing the history of a school. One finds, for example, that the Preban parochial school received a grant of £78 9s. 3d. from the lord lieutenant's fund, subscriptions of £80 6s. 1d. and grants from George Coates and Earl Fitzwilliam on 7 November 1822. The curriculum taught in the school consisted of the three Rs, along with grammar, geography, plain needlework and scriptures. The master who was resident had free apartments and land in addition to his salary of £5 per annum. In 1856 there were thirty-five pupils on roll, twenty-nine of them Church of Ireland and fifteen Catholic, and the average attendance was twelve.   **20** *Report of her majesty's commissioners appointed to inquire into the endowments* [Kildare commission], iii, *Papers accompanying the report (tables of schools and endowments)*, H.C. 1857–8 (2336–IV), xii, pt iv, 263–5.

Blessington, Baltiboys (roll no. 974); Bray (male and female) (roll nos 975 and 976); Ballyconnell (male and female) (roll nos 977 and 978); CastleMacAdam, Newbridge (male and female) (roll nos 979 and 980); Delgany, Kilmacanogue (roll no. 981); Glendalough, St Kevin's (roll no. 983); Glenelly (*sic*) (Glenealy) (roll no. 984) Kilquiggan (female) (roll no. 663) and Wicklow town (male and female) (roll nos 987 and 988).[21]

Benevolent landlords in the county acted as managers of early national schools for instance Mrs Elizabeth Smith at Baltiboys, Viscount Monck at Calary, Peter la Touche and Robert Pennick at Delgany, Baron de Robeck at Donard and Robert Chaloner at Tinahely. The first of these established a national school on her estate near Blessington in the 1830s. A native of Scotland, Elizabeth was the wife of Colonel Harry Smith who inherited the Baltiboys estate in 1830. She played a leading role in managing the property, trying to improve the life of the tenants, and she kept a journal for most of her life there.[22] Believing that education was a key agent of improvement, Elizabeth applied for aid for a national school at Baltiboys and employed a teacher, Miss Gardiner, to run it. However, she was critical of the organisation of the new system as the following entry in her diary indicates:

> Wrote to the secretaries of the National Board to know what is become of Miss Gardiner's salary, that certainly does seem to be a strangely mismanaged concern. What they do with the immense sum of money voted yearly to them by parliament it is really difficult to make out, they shamefully underpay the teachers and even the pittance they give them is generally due for months, there is no getting any assistance towards improvements or repairs ... One merit they have, and it is a great one, they are most liberal in their supply of school requisites. All their books are admirable, and very cheap, and they give every four years a complete set *to be used in the school*, gratis.[23]

She also encountered opposition from Catholic clergy in the district who discouraged Catholic children from attending the national school. This prompted her to complain to Dr Daniel Murray, Catholic archbishop of Dublin, who was a founder member of the National Board. Furthermore, the local hedge schools continued to attract pupils. Elizabeth's frustration at all of these impediments to the progress of the national school is evident in her diary entry:

21 In the 1830s, when the national schools were first allocated roll numbers, the existing schools were numbered sequentially on a provincial/county basis. The school assigned Roll no. 1 was in Antrim. Wicklow schools were in the 970s. Thereafter all new schools entering the system were allocated roll numbers on a national basis, and when a grant-aided new school building was erected, a new roll number was issued. These roll numbers are a useful guide to the date of opening of a national school. **22** Elizabeth Grant of Rothiemurchus, *The highland lady in Ireland*, ed. Patricia Pelly & Andrew Tod (London, 1991); *Irish journals of Elizabeth Smith*, ed. Thomson & McGusty. **23** See *Irish journals of*

The warfare has been about the schools. Father Germaine did not dare to openly condemn them but he has never publicly shown any interest in them and he must privately have discouraged them or more children would have attended, fewer hedge schools would have been permitted, and they would not have been filled to crowding, seventy to eighty pupils while we had under forty ...[24]

The growth of the national system in County Wicklow, 1850–70

The annual reports of the National Board show steady expansion of the national school system. By 1852 there were 1,176 national schools in Leinster, of which seventy-one were in Wicklow.[25] There were two workhouse schools in the county, one at Shillelagh, the other at Rathdrum. The majority of managers in the county were Catholic clergy who applied for aid. (Protestant clergy were opposed to the system.) One active parish priest in the county was Revd James M'Kenna of Rathdrum who, by 1852, had six national schools operating in his parish, some in the remote mountainous areas of Muckloe, Glenmalure, Macreddin (male and female) and Rathdrum (male and female).[26] By 1863 there were 1,410 national schools in the county, including two convent national schools at Bray and Delgany.[27] The 1864 parliamentary return also gives the names of teachers in these schools along with the times when religious education took place. By this time there were five national schools in the parish of Dunganstown. At Barrendarrig there were two schools, one for males (roll no, 4902) and the other for females (roll no. 4903). William Richley was the master and had seventy Catholic pupils on roll. Catherine Thompson was the mistress and Frances Thompson was workmistress. They had ninety Catholic pupils on roll. In Ballincarrig National School for girls (roll no. 7805), Jane Sherlock was mistress, Elizabeth O'Neill was work mistress and there were ninety-three Catholic pupils on roll. In Newbawn boys' school (roll no. 8181) Patrick Byrne was master, Margaret Byrne was assistant, Bridget Bushe was a senior monitor, and seventy-nine Catholic pupils were on roll.[28] These examples show how schools were increasingly becoming denominational and single sex. The CNEI annual reports also include the names of teachers who were awarded premiums for neatness and order in their schools as well as good service awards. In 1863 seven teachers in Wicklow earned premiums,

Elizabeth Smith, ed. Thomson & McGusty, p. 14.   **24** Grant, *The highland lady in Ireland*, ed. Pelly & Tod, p. 169.   **25** *Appendix to the nineteenth report of the commissioners of national education in Ireland for the year 1852*, i, H.C. 1852–3 (1688), xliii, pt ii, 504–08. The only county in Leinster with fewer national schools was Carlow which had fifty-nine.   **26** Ibid. The Protestant parishes received aid from the Anglican Church Education Society, which was founded in 1839 in opposition to the national system and in support of scriptural education.   **27** *Appendix to the thirtieth report of the commissioners of national education in Ireland for the year 1863*, ii, H.C. 1864 (3351–I), xix, 617–21.   **28** *Returns for national schools*, H.C. 1864 (481), xlvii, 651–61. A monitor was a senior pupil who taught the younger pupils for a small salary. See also Kenneth Hannigan, 'The national schools in Wicklow town, 1832–1919' in *Wicklow Historical Journal*, 1:2 (June 1989), pp 34–45.

one of whom was Catherine Thompson of Barrendarrig girls' school while seven received good service awards, among them Bridget Tyrrell of Baltinglass girls' school, who had taught for seventeen years.[29]

Though in general there are no reports on individual schools in the CNEI annual reports, there are general district inspectors' reports for each area which set the work of individual schools within a local context. Part of County Wicklow was located in District 40, with an inspector based in Wicklow town, and part was in District 44, with an inspector based in Baltinglass. These district reports, compiled by inspectors, covered the state of school buildings, school attendance, proficiency of the pupils, curriculum taught, conditions of the teachers and the attitudes among local residents to religious instruction and the national system in general. In 1863 Mr C. Mahony, inspector for Wicklow, commented on the challenges that marred efforts to encourage regular attendance:

> The cold of January and December keeps the smaller children away, especially where the schoolhouses, instead of being inviting, are as cold and cheerless as the poorest of their homes. A reduction, somewhat less, is continued in March, April, and November by severe weather and in country schools by field labour. Attendance is better in February and October; better still, and above the average in August and September; and best of all in May. June and July ... Employments to be had through visitors along the sea-side prevent town schools from increasing in the same proportion as rural schools in the earlier summer months. Along a coastline, more than fifty miles, attendances are capriciously disturbed, sometimes for several weeks, by the chances of fishing ...[30]

Powis report on primary education, 1870
The education census, compiled by the constabulary on behalf of the Powis commission in June 1868, serves as a useful benchmark for gauging the progress of primary education throughout Ireland. In addition to recording data on all national schools, the constabulary gathered information on privately run schools and on those run by the Church Education Society and by religious orders.[31] In Wicklow county there was still a large number of Protestant parish schools supported by the CES. In the constabulary district of Arklow, there were twenty-five schools; eleven were national schools and five were supported by the Church Education Society. The majority of schools were co-educational, there being four single sex schools in the district. The national schools were in Arklow town, Johnstown Inch, Glenmalure, Brockagh, Seven Churches, Clara, Trooperstown,

---

29 *Appendix to the thirtieth report of the commissioners of national education in Ireland for the year 1863,* ii, H.C. 1866 (3351–I), xix, 711. **30** Ibid., i, 161. **31** *Royal commission of inquiry into primary education (Ireland)* [Powis commission], vi: *educational census: returns showing number of children actually present in each primary school, 25 June 1868, with introductory observations and*

Ballinaclash, Newbridge, Avoca, Rathdrum and Newbawn. There was a national school in the workhouse in Rathdrum and a number of the schools had very a large attendance. At Arklow there were 301 pupils. Brockagh had 141 pupils (seventy boys and sixty-six girls). Rathdrum had 146 on roll (sixty-four girls and eighty-two boys). A total of eighty-two children attended Rathdrum workhouse school, of whom thirty-seven were boys and forty-five were girls.

The five schools supported by the Church Education Society were the remaining parish schools of the Church of Ireland. These were located at Knockanrahan, Arklow, Ballinatone, Laragh, CastleMacAdam and Connary. Of these, Ballintone had thirty pupils (twenty-three boys and nine girls), whereas Laragh had only twelve pupils (nine boys and three girls). In addition, a number of private schools run by individuals were operating at Tinahask, Carrycole, Ferrybank, Shelton in Arklow and at Ballymurtagh. These schools were small with mostly catered for around twenty pupils. The Incorporated Society school in Arklow had twenty-nine boys attending. These 1868 returns show that the national school system was only gradually taking over schooling in the county and that private and parochial schools still operated, albeit on a small scale. Co-education remained prevalent and most of the schools had pupils of one denomination or the other.[32]

Later parliamentary education returns, 1880 & 1892
Subsequent to the 1870 Powis report, there were two parliamentary returns of individual national schools, which are particularly useful for local studies. The first was in 1880 following the introduction of the system of payment by results for teachers in 1872. The 1880 return listed the results fees earned by each national school in the years 1878–8 and 1878–9.[33] One purpose of the payment by results scheme was to increase the daily attendance at schools as well as to offer a bonus incentive to teachers whose pupils did well in the annual examinations by the inspectorate.[34] In Wicklow, for instance, in the parish of Dunganstown the returns for the schools were listed as follows: Barrendarrig boys' school (roll no. 4902) presented thirty-three pupils in 1877–8 and fifty-two in 1878–9. Barrendarrig girls' school (roll no. 4903) presented forty pupils in 1877–8 and fifty-nine in

---

analytical index [C 6–V], H.C. 1870, xxviii, pt v, 1.   **32** Ibid., i, 201.   **33** *Returns of number of pupils examined for results fees in each school in Ireland under the Board of National Education in 1877–78 & 1878–79*, H.C. 1880 (33), lv, 13. This volume of the parliamentary papers comprises education material only, including an annual report on the Royal College of Science, and a return of the occupations of parents of pupils in model schools.   **34** See *Appendix to the fortieth report of the commissioners of national education in Ireland for the year 1873* [C 965], H.C. 1874, xix, 114–27 for details on the programme of instruction and examination for national schools as well as the scale of results fees. The attendance figures can also be ascertained from school roll books. To be eligible to enter for the annual examination and to earn result fees, a pupil had to attend a minimum of ninety days per year. This minimum was subsequently raised to 100 days.

1878–9. Newbawn (roll no. 8181) presented forty-three in 1877–8 and fifty-six in 1878–9. Contrary to this trend, the new school at Brittas (roll no. 11, 372) presented thirty-five pupils in 1877–8 but only twenty-one in 1878–9. From these figures it can be deduced that attendance was still fluctuating, but the pupils were making some progress in the subjects examined and the teachers were receiving bonus payments. In 1873 the Wicklow district inspector, Mr C. Mahony, reported with satisfaction that,

> During the past year the continued working of the results system has most substantially raised the incomes of a large portion of the teachers. A spirit of alacrity and vigour is generally evident, and in many quarters both managers of schools and parents of scholars have been stimulated to interest themselves keenly in the attendance and progress of the children. The clearest evidence has been afforded of the efficacy of the teachers' personal influence, when applied with true earnestness, in improving the amount and character of the attendance.
>
> It has struck me that the female teachers of this district exhibit more hopefulness and energy than the men, and have profited more largely in the results payment, relatively to rates of salary …[35]

In 1892 another parliamentary return provided unit cost details of the amount of money being paid to each school from parliamentary funds. These returns were related to the introduction of free and compulsory primary education by the Irish Education Act (1892). The returns included details of the total number on roll, average daily attendance, the religious denomination and classification of teachers, income of teachers, capitation grants paid, results fees paid, and any additional local

---

35 Ibid., 389–90. The average daily attendance in the national school system was slow to improve. In 1886 it was estimated to be 57.8% and by 1900 this had risen only to 62%: see Akenson, *Irish education experiment*, p. 346. The introduction of compulsory attendance between six and fourteen years by the 1892 Irish Education Act did not greatly improve the situation. Initially the act did not apply to rural areas and there were several periods of peak seasonal labour, such as planting and harvesting potatoes, hay-making and harvesting, during which the act was not enforced. The main enforcement of compulsory education only came with the 1926 School Attendance Act in the Irish Free State and the 1923 Education Act in Northern Ireland. **36** National teachers were classified into three grades – first, second and third class and each class was subdivided into two grades, first and second division, the highest grade being 'first of the first'. Teachers were promoted on the basis of passing a graded set of National Board examinations and receiving favourable inspectors' reports. The salaries of teachers were linked to their classification and were higher for males than for females. By the end of the nineteenth century the male teacher's salary went from £42 for third class up to £84 for the first division of first class. For female teachers it ranged from £33 for third class to £69 12s. for first division of first class. See *Rules and regulations of the commissioners of national education in Ireland, 1898* (Dublin, 1898), pp 64–50. The subjects for which results fees were paid were reading, spelling, writing, arithmetic, grammar, geography, book keeping (optional), needlework for girls, agriculture

aid.[36] For example, in Barrendarrig boys' school where there were eighty-eight pupils on roll, the average daily attendance was forty-two. There was one teacher whose class salary was £41, and in addition he received a bonus of £26 6s. 6d. from results fees. The total amount paid out to the school was £70 6s. per year. At Barrendarrig girls' school there were ninety-one pupils on roll and the average daily attendance was forty-six. There was one teacher with second class classification and a salary of £27 10s. and the bonus from results fees of £26 18s. 6d. The total paid to that school was £54 8s. 6d. At Newbawn there were sixty-eight children on roll, with an average daily attendance of thirty-one. There was one teacher whose third class salary and results fees were £27 10s. and £12 14s. respectively and the school fees of £6 4s. 11d. were collected from the pupils.[37] These sample returns show that the problem of irregular attendance persisted and that there were still a large number of small, one-teacher schools in County Wicklow towards the end of the nineteenth century.

Return of national schools, 1906–7
For a local study, researchers will find another useful return of national schools in the appendix to the seventy-second annual report of the CNEI for 1905–6.[38] This return lists for every national school its rural district, roll number, name, nearest post town, religious denomination of the teacher, average on roll, average daily attendance, accommodation per square foot per pupil, income from the vote, income from local sources and the school's total income. It is, therefore, possible to compare attendance figures and the costs of running an individual school with those featured in the 1892 parliamentary return. In Wicklow, there were 137 national schools in 1906–7 as compared with 128 in 1895. In the rural district of Rathdrum, in the parish of Dunganstown east, three schools – Newbawn (roll no. 8181), Brittas (roll no. 11,372) and Dunganstown Church of Ireland parish school

for boys from fourth class and vocal music. There was also a large number of so-called 'extra subjects' for which extra fees could be paid. These included the classics, French, Irish and German, drawing, higher mathematics and sciences. See *Rules and regulations of the commissioners of national education in Ireland, 1898*, pp 69–70. With this range of subjects the national schools was able to offer a broad curriculum to senior pupils by the end of the nineteenth century.   **37** Returns made by the Irish national education commissioners: (A) showing for 1890, for each ordinary school (exclusive of monastery, workhouse, and other model schools), its denomination and whether the management is clerical or lay, whether there is a local committee recognized by the national education commissioners, the number on the rolls, the attendance, the teachers' emoluments. and the income from various sources, with summaries showing the average cost per pupil, etc; (B) return similar to (A) relating to convent and monastic schools; (C) return for ordinary national schools in 1860,1870, 1880, & 1890, showing the number of schools, the number on the rolls, the attendance grants from various purposes, and the local aid, also the average cost per pupil; (D) and (E) returns similar to (C) for convent & monastic schools; and the Board's model schools; (F) to (H) relating to the training colleges; (c. 260–I), H.C. 1892, lxi, i.   **38** *Appendix to the seventy-second report of the commissioners of national education in Ireland for 1905* [Cd 3725], H.C. 1907, xxii, 637.

(roll no. 15,322) – had recently entered the national system.[39] The average daily attendance at Newbawn was twenty-eight out of forty-eight on roll; at Brittas it was thirty-two out of fifty-five and at Dunganstown it was sixteen out of twenty-one. In Dunganstown south there were now four schools – Barrendarrig boys' school (roll no. 4902) and Barrendarrig girls' school (roll no. 4903), where the average daily attendance was thirty-three and thirty-nine respectively, and two schools in Glenealy (Glenealy no. 1, roll no. 984), and Glenealy no. 2 (roll no. 12,205) the Church of Ireland parish school, where the average daily attendance was thirty-eight and fifteen respectively).[40]

In the early twentieth century the number of small denominational schools continued to increase. By 1914 there were 5,948 national schools attended solely by pupils of one denomination while only 2,273 national schools were attended by pupils of more than one denomination. In Wicklow in 1914, there were eight-six schools attended solely by one denomination compared to thirty-nine attended by pupils of more that one denomination.[41]

Files relating to individual national schools in County Wicklow in the National Archives
In the National Archives there is material to be found relating to County Wicklow in the ED files to which there is an index in the reference section. The ED/1 files of applications for grants for national schools for County Wicklow are ED/1/95–99. Among the ED/2 files which are the official registers of national schools, the registers for County Wicklow are ED/2/146, 147, 148, 150 and 151. The ED/4 files relating to teachers' salaries for the county's schools are in ED/4/55, 73, 76, 79 and 82, while the ED/9 files for individual schools in County Wicklow are listed in the card catalogue of national schools.

ED/17 is an index to the individual registers of national schools, which have been acquired by the archives. For Wicklow, these include the registers of schools

---

39 Following the disestablishment of the Church of Ireland in 1870 the Church of Ireland parish schools gradually entered the national system as they no longer had sufficient finance to run a voluntary parish school.   **40** *Appendix to the seventy-second report of the commissioners of national education in Ireland for 1905* [Cd 3725], H.C. 1907, xxii, 861–3. The existence now of two small denominational national schools in Glenealy is an example of the determination of the Churches to maintain their own school systems.   **41** *Appendix to the eightieth report of the commissioners of national education in Ireland for 1913–14* [Cd 7978], H.C. 1914–16, xx, 626–8. The entry into the national school system of the Protestant parochial schools after 1870 increased the number of small denominational national schools, which were stoutly defended by Church of Ireland: see Parkes, *Kildare Place*, pp 110–14; Kenneth Milne, 'The clergy and the schools' in T.C. Barnard & W.G. Neely (eds), *The clergy of the Church of Ireland 1000–2000: messengers, watchmen and stewards* (Dublin, 2006), pp 213–330; Susan M. Parkes, 'The Reverend Canon Henry Kingsmill-Moore, D.D. Ball. Coll. Oxon, FLS, and Church of Ireland education, 1880–1927' in Sheridan Gilley (ed.), *Victorian churches and churchmen* (London, 2005), pp 279–91. Kingsmill Moore was one of the leaders of the campaign to maintain small schools. The Church of Ireland school in Redcross, Co. Wicklow was a test case in 1900 when its numbers fell to fifteen pupils and the National Board was trying to raise the minimum required to become a recognised national school to twenty-five pupils: see Parkes, *Kildare Place*, p. 110.

such as Conary (ED/17/2004/122/615), Mucklagh, Rathdrum (ED/17/2004/122/619) and Ballyduff, Kiliskey (ED/17/2004/122/613). A number of school registers also have been deposited in the archives by individual schools; for Wicklow these include Glenealy (ED/17/2004/78), Glebe, Wicklow (ED/17/2001/66/7) and St Andrew's, Bray (ED/17/98/45). School registers have been copied on microfiche and can be consulted thus (MFGS 50/1–21).

The first step in the research is to consult the card catalogue of national schools, which are filed under county and by individual school within that county. A reference card for each school lists the relevant ED files available for the school. For example, the card for Glenealy School (roll no. 984) lists the first application for a grant which was made on 2 June 1832 (ED/1/95/no. 8) and a further application on 3 October 1832 (ED/1/95/no. 8). The ED/2 files for Glenealy are ED/2/49/no. 11, 57, 131 and ED/2/56/no. 13. In addition the ED/9 files which relate to Glenealy are numbers 8549, 23425, 25077, 27417 and 20513. These reference numbers can then be followed up to locate the specific files. The ED/2 registers of schools files provide a valuable summary of each school's correspondence with the National Board through the decades. For instance, in the case of Glenealy school (ED/2/49/no. 11) it is recorded that the application for the school was made by Mr John Grant, that it was a joint application, and that it was signed by four Protestants and eleven Catholics. The existing schoolhouse was twenty-two feet by fifteen and there were twenty-two boys and sixty-five girls on roll. The register records that the school was given a grant by the National Board of £12 18s. 0d. for fitting up the school and £4 7s. for requisites. At Newbridge school, CastleMacAdam (roll no. 979) (ED/2/49/ no. 4), the Revd T. Halpin was the applicant and the joint application for the school was signed by nineteen Protestants and nineteen Catholics. The schoolhouse was built in 1821 and it measured thirty-five feet by fourteen. There were sixty-five boys on roll and the master was Thomas Greene. The school was granted £24 13s. 4d. for fitting-up and £9 3s. 5d. for school requisites with a local contribution of £12 15s.

The difficulties of persuading local gentry to support the national system is illustrated by a letter from William Wingfield of Cherry mount, to Revd T. Halpin which was enclosed with the Newbridge, CastleMacAdam application (ED/1/95/no. 3):

> I regret sincerely that I cannot co-operate with you in the instance you require. I am ever ready to promote the interests temporal and eternal of those in this parish, but as I cannot agree in principle and structure of the society from which you purpose to derive aid for your schools, I am obliged, however reluctantly, to decline any interferences, but remain, Rev Sir, your obedient servant, William Wingfield. (I am ready to give my reasons if required).

> To Rev. Thomas Halpin, Ballinapark, 29 March 1832.

The application for Wicklow town boys' school (roll no. 987) (ED/1/95/no. 7) was also made by Mr John Grant and the school was run by a committee. The schoolhouse had been built in 1819 and there were 150 boys on roll. The teacher was Joseph Marney. An application for the Wicklow girls' school was included. It had been established in 1819 and had on roll 157 children. The accompanying letter read:

> We most earnestly, but respectfully, solicit an annual grant of twenty pounds, to aid us to pay the fixed expenses, herein stated, of these schools and also to enable us to purchase a sufficient supply of books and schools requisites at the terms of the Board, to give them gratis or at more reduced prices to the children, many of whom are not able to give one penny, although it should make them accomplished scholars.
>
> We feel ourselves called on, the more earnestly, to press this application on the kind attention of the Commissioners in consequence of the great falling off of late of the annual subscriptions by our small farmers, in so much, that we have to fear the schools will fail, if not aided, so far, by the Board of National Education.
>
> The collection of subscriptions of such farmers, however small from each individual, have been the main support these past twelve years past, of these schools – They now very generally refuse or give with reluctance, – they complain, and in truth, that they have not the means to give their own children a sufficient education.

And we can ever pray,
John Grant, April 25 1831.

Regarding a later application, this time for a school in Glenmalure (roll no. 1993) (ED/1/95/no. 21), made on 8 June 1839, the register of schools (ED/2/49/ no. 29) recorded another difficulty which the schools faced, namely the conduct of the teacher. On 18 August 1842 it was noted that the salary of the teacher at Glenmalure National School had been withdrawn by the national commissioners as and from 1 August 'in consequence of some of the parents of the children having complained to the superintendent that the teacher was in the habit of overcharging for the books, cursing the pupils and using indecent and filthy language'. The manager was requested to appoint another teacher or else the school would be struck off the roll. A subsequent entry for August 29 stated that 'in reply to the fore going, objecting to the report of the superintendent as inaccurate and made upon speculation of parties inimical to the teacher, the superintendent was directed to reconsider his report'. On 4 April 1843 it was noted that the manager of the school was informed that 'the commissioners having carefully examined the report of the superintendent, they are of the opinion that nothing appeared to justify the dismissal of Mr Nolan and therefore have restored him with his salary to this school from the date of his last pay'.

Such details recorded in the register of schools ED/2 files reveal the problems at local level of implementing a national system of education and these details can be found for national schools throughout the country. The wealth of information recorded in the ED/1, ED/2, ED/4 and ED/9 files for each national school provide the basis for a local study and for the history of education in each parish and county.

This short survey of the main sources available for schools in County Wicklow shows the possibilities for conducting an in-depth study of schooling in a specific locality anywhere in Ireland. It also highlights the value of such detailed micro-level studies which trace the gradual development of the national school system at local level and uncover its strengths, weaknesses and challenges. As the above discussion clearly shows, Wicklow was a county with active, resident landlords who were able to take the lead, providing and encouraging education within their immediate locales. It also had a 'mixed' population, which meant that a multi-denominational school system might have been feasible, although as we have seen, the Protestant parishes were able to maintain their distinct parish schools up to the 1880s. It is apparent from the records that the mountainous terrain of central Wicklow negatively impacted attendance rates, making it difficult for pupils and teachers to reach the schoolhouse, especially during winter. It is also clear that the majority of schools in Wicklow remained small in order to be accessible to the children who walking to school, often up to three miles there and back each day.

RESEARCHING A MODEL SCHOOL: CASE STUDY OF
ENNISCORTHY MODEL SCHOOL, 1862

There was no model school in County Wicklow, which left the district without a centre for setting an example of efficient teaching and the training of monitors. The nearest model school was in Enniscorthy, Co. Wexford and it was not a success. One of the last model schools to be opened, Enniscorthy was established in 1862 despite strong opposition from the Dr Nicholas Furlong, Catholic bishop of Ferns.[42] As already noted in chapter two, model schools were built in towns where there appeared to be local support. Leading figures in these towns, both Catholic and Protestant, were encouraged to apply to the Board, making a case for the building of a model school in their locality. A suitable site for the school needed to be offered as part of the application process. In January 1856, the poor law guardians of Wexford wrote to the National Board requesting that a model

42 After Enniscorthy, the National Board opened only three more model schools – in Enniskillen, Cork and Sligo. In 1863 the Catholic Church placed a 'ban' on Catholics attendance at model schools and the National Board decided not to build any more. There were in all twenty-six district model schools. Plans for Enniscorthy Model School may be consulted in the National Archives in the papers of the Office of Public Works (OPW 4973/61).

school be built in the county because they were 'having great difficulty in procuring qualified teachers to conduct the workhouse schools'. The following month, a second letter of support was sent to the Board, this time by the 'clergy, gentry, landholders, merchants and traders of the county of Wexford, including the mayor of Wexford'. The Board replied that there seemed to be adequate educational provision in the area and hence a model school was not needed. In spite of this, the local district inspector found a suitable site in Enniscorthy where the earl of Portsmouth agreed to lease a two-acre site adjoining the town, which the Board's architect, Frederick Darley, visited and approved.

However, warning signals subsequently began to appear. In 1856 the head inspector, J.K. Kavanagh, warned the Board that he was very doubtful that a model school in Enniscorthy would receive sufficient support locally. Two years later, the Church of Ireland rector indicated that while he would not pose any opposition to the establishment of a district model school, he could not yet promise that he would attend the school to give religious instruction to pupils of his persuasion. In December 1859 Dr Nicholas Furlong, Catholic bishop of Ferns, wrote to the Board, condemning the building of a model school in the town:

> I never can approve of an educational establishment whose constitution, rejecting all episcopal control, necessarily endangers the faith of the Catholic children who may resort to it. However high-minded and honourable offi-cials connected with the contemplated model school of Enniscorthy may be, I cannot abandon to their safe-keeping the sacred deposit, for the custody to which I am myself responsible, and which I am bound to guard with the jealous vigilance and watchful care …[43]

He went on to stress that there was a sufficient supply of Catholic education in the town, including three Catholic private schools, three public schools for gratuitous education, two religious communities who educated girls, and the Christian Brothers, who ran a school for boys:

> I object therefore to the establishment of model school in Enniscorthy as a wanton waste of public money – as an act of defiance to the Catholic bishop of the diocese, and the clergy and people who share his sentiments, and a premeditated aggression on the jurisdiction and authority that rightfully belongs to him …[44]

Notwithstanding these remonstrations, the National Board proceeded with the school's construction and in 1860 Bishop Furlong again wrote at length, protesting about the matter. He concluded:

43 *Royal commission of inquiry into primary education (Ireland)* [Powis commission], vii: *Returns from the National Board* [C 6–VI], H.C. 1870, xxviii, pt v, 488–91.   **44** Ibid., 489. The site for the cathedral in Enniscorthy, designed by Augustine Pugin, was also given by the earl of

Let me at parting assure the commissioners that this display of disregard for the just wishes and demands of the Catholic prelates will not in the slightest degree intimidate or disconcert them – that it is unwise and impolitic in a public body, depending for its support on public confidence, ostentatiously to defy those whom the people love and venerate – that I myself and the Catholic clergy of Enniscorthy have had more than one proof of the submission and docility of its faithful people – that the proposed model school, with all its attractions, will not lure them from their fidelity to their pastors – and that with Divine blessing not one Catholic child shall ever cross its threshold …[45]

Enniscorthy model school consisted of three schools, one for infants, another for girls and the third for boys but in 1863 there were only eighty-three children on roll – fifty-eight members of the Established Church, nine Catholics, one Presbyterian and fifteen others. The head inspector, W.A. Hunter, in his report on the school for 1863, wrote of the difficulties faced by the schools:

The opposition, which these schools had to encounter at the opening from the clergy, both of the Established and the Roman Catholic Church, has been in no degree mitigated. So far as the influence of these gentlemen extends, the policy of preventing an attendance at the school has been most strictly adhered to.[46]

Despite this opposition from the clergy, the Enniscorthy school maintained a high standard of work and progress. At the annual examinations, the head inspector wrote of the infant school:

In the infants' school, the children acquitted themselves to our perfect satisfaction; the senior drafts have very correct ideas on grammar and geography, so far as they have been taught. In arithmetic the proficiency was excellent. A sequel class has been prepared by Miss M'Alister, whose answering on all subjects were (sic) most gratifying. The reading and recitation of these children were highly creditable.[47]

The school continued to grow but by 1872 there were 137 on roll, of whom only thirteen were Catholics, so it became *de facto* a Protestant school. By contrast, in the same year the Presentation convent girls' national school in the town had a

Portsmouth. **45** Ibid., 491. **46** *Thirtieth report of the commissioners of national education in Ireland for the year 1863* [C 3351], H.C. 1864, xix, 137–41. **47** Ibid., 141. The sequel book was an additional reader used after the completion of book two of the Boards' national lesson books. Miss M'Allister was appointed in 1862. She later married the headmaster, and when she died 1872 the inspector wrote that she was 'a devoted and skilful teacher' but that 'her subsequent marriage to the headmaster seemed to impair her usefulness as a teacher'. *Appendix to the fortieth report of the commissioners of national education in Ireland for the year 1873* [C 965], H.C. 1874, xix, 192–4.

total of 547 pupils on roll, of whom eighty-eight were young boys in the junior classes.[48]

RESEARCHING AN ENDOWED SCHOOL: OVERVIEW OF SOURCES
AND CASE STUDY OF MERCER'S SCHOOL, CASTLEKNOCK, DUBLIN

When embarking on research into the history of a particular endowed school it is best to begin by consulting the tables of schools and endowments featured in volume III of the Endowed schools commission report (1857–8).[49] These tables list the endowed schools in operation (and those that had lapsed), outlining the origins of the endowment, the property and purpose of the school, the salary paid to the staff and the attendance of pupils, both free and fee-paying. The masters and mistresses of these schools were often paid a substantial salary by the Trust and had free accommodation and fuel provided as well. In the absence of close supervision by the trustees, the resident masters and mistresses often enjoyed considerable personal control over the running of the school, for better or worse. As the nineteenth century went on, the demand for reform and stricter control of these endowments grew, particularly from the Catholic community whose children were precluded from attending these schools.

Similarly, the report of the Rosse commission on educational endowments (1881)[50] is a useful source for the history of an individual endowed school. The report surveyed the history and current state of endowed schools as well as taking evidence from trustees, headmasters and teachers. From these, a detailed picture of school life can be obtained. For example, women staff who were interviewed in 1881 included Mrs Eleanor Hewson, mistress of Villiers School in Limerick, Mrs Jane Armour of the Blue Coat school in Waterford, Miss Elizabeth Weir, mistress of Leamy school in Limerick and Miss Cearine Russell, matron of the Drummond institution for the orphan daughters of soldiers in Chapelizod, Dublin. Papers relating to the Rosse commission (1879–81) are available for consultation in the National Archives of Ireland. These include questionnaires returned by schools to the commission, as well as papers in the records of the commissioners of charitable bequests (CHAR 2) relating to individual endowed schools.

State supervision of endowed educational funds greatly increased following the passage of the 1885 Educational Endowments (Ireland) Act[51] under which legal

---

48 *Fortieth report of the commissioners of national education in Ireland for the year 1873* [C 965], H.C. 1874, xix, 632.   **49** *Report of her majesty's commissioners appointed to inquire into the endowments* [Kildare commission], iii, *Papers accompanying the report (tables of schools and endowments)*, H.C. 1857–8 (2336–IV), xii, pt iv, 1.   **50** *Report of the commissioners appointed by the lord lieutenant of Ireland* [Rosse commission] [C 2831], H.C. 1881, xxxv, 1.   **51** 48 & 49 Vict., c.78 (1885).   **52** See *Reports of the educational endowments (Ireland) commissioners, with proceedings, evidence and appendices*; first report (1885–6) [C 4903], H.C. 1886, xxvi, 89; final report (1894) [C 7511], H.C. 1894, xxx, pt i, 479.   **53** See, for example, Michael Quane,

schemes for the reform of schools and educational trusts were subsequently drawn up by the Educational Endowments commissioners from 1886 to 1894. These schemes were recorded in the annual reports of the commissioners, along with evidence presented by schools to the commissioners in open court. This evidence is another source of useful data on the condition of the endowed schools five years after the Rosse commission.[52] The educational endowments commissioners drew up over 200 schemes under which the endowments successfully operated; in the first year these included the Swords borough school (scheme no. 1), St Patrick's Cathedral School (scheme no. 9) and Alexandra College and school (scheme no. 10).

Other relevant material for the history of endowments can be found in the office of the commissioners of donations and charitable bequests in Dublin. A substantial number of articles on individual endowed schools, including Bishop Foy's school in Waterford, D'Israeli School in Rathvilly and Viscount Weymouth's grammar school in Carrickmacross were written by Micheal Quane of the Department of Education endowed schools branch.[53] These were published in various local historical journals and a full list may to be found in Hayes's catalogue of articles in Irish periodicals. These are a valuable starting point for researchers undertaking a study of a particular endowed school.

The following example of the history of one endowed school in Dublin highlights the main sources available to researchers working on these institutions. The Mercer's school in Castleknock, Co. Dublin was founded in 1735 in accordance with the last will and testament of a wealthy spinster named Mary Mercer who, incidentally, also endowed Mercer's hospital in Dublin. The five school trustees were the Church of Ireland archbishop of Dublin, the dean of Kildare, the dean of St Patrick's, the archdeacon of Dublin and the minister of St Bridget's church. The endowment consisted of 747 acres, 2 roods and 15 perches of land with an annual income of £531 3s. 5d. Although Miss Mercer's will did not confine the school endowment to Protestant pupils, the endowment came to be used in that way.

When the school first opened in Rathcoole in west Co. Dublin it was attended by twenty girl pupils. However, in the 1820s it relocated to an empty schoolhouse belonging to Morgan's school for boys beside the Royal canal in Castleknock.[54] The purpose of the school was 'the maintenance of as many Protestant children as the residue of the income will afford after paying £92 6s. 2d. to the sick poor of

---

'Bishop Foy's School, Waterford' in *Cork Hist. & Arch. Soc. Jn.*, 71, nos 213–14 (Jan.–Dec. 1966), pp 103–22; idem, 'The Hibernian Marine School, Dublin' in *Dublin Historical Record*, 21 (Mar. 1967), pp 76–8; idem, 'D'Israeli School, Rathvilly' in the *Jn. R.S.A.I.*, 77:1 (July 1948), pp 11–23; idem, 'Gilson Endowed School, Oldcastle, Co. Meath' in *Ríocht na Midhe*, 4:3 (1969), pp 34–54. The Quane papers are in the NLI. **54** *Report of her majesty's commissioners appointed to inquire into the endowments* [Kildare commission], iii, *Papers accompanying the report (tables of schools and endowments)*, H.C. 1857–8 (2336–IV), xii, pt iv, 16–17; Michael Quane, 'Mercer's School, Rathcoole and Castleknock Co. Dublin' in *Jn. R.S.A.I.*, 93 (1963), pp 9–35; Lesley Whiteside, *A history of the King's Hospital* (Dublin, 1975), pp 187–9. Mercer's School merged with The King's Hospital in 1966.

the parishes of St Peter, St Bridget, St Nicholas Without and St Luke'. The curriculum emphasized the practical skills of knitting and 'plain and fancy needlework' but also included general education in 'reading, writing, grammar, geography, arithmetic, English and Roman history'. In 1856 the matron who was in charge was paid a good salary of £80 by the Trust[55] and enjoyed free apartments, fuel, and a garden. The school had sufficient room for one hundred pupils including twenty boarders; in 1856 there were thirty-three girls on roll, of who four were paid an annual fee of £12.

When an assistant commissioners of the Endowed schools' commission visited the school in October 1856, he found it reasonably efficiently run but he was critical of the poor state of the building:

> The state of the instruction in the school was satisfactory. I examined the girls in reading, geography, English history and grammar, and was pleased with their proficiency in all these departments, except the last. The discipline and internal management of the institution seemed good. The defects of the building are, that it contains no bathroom or water closet; the privies are bad; there is no separate washroom for the girls, who are obliged to use the laundry for that purpose; and that the lavatory accommodation is miserably inadequate, there being only six basins for thirty-three children. All the children in the school are obliged to conform to the Established Church, although no such restriction was imposed by the will of the foundation.[56]

Dissatisfaction with endowed schools such Mercer's, whose resources were underutilized and often confined to one denomination, led to demands for stricter supervision of such school endowments which resulted in the setting up in 1881 of another educational endowments commission, this one chaired by the earl of Rosse. Mercer's school received another visit by one of the commissioners and the secretary of the trustees Revd M.W. Jellett, the agent of the trustees Mr B.W. Rooke and the matron of the school, Miss Kate Curtis were interviewed.[57] By then, the condition of the building had somewhat improved but the school still had only thirty-two pupils, of whom seven were fee-paying. The standard of the general academic education of the girls had improved and some had entered for the Trinity College examinations for women, introduced in 1869, and also for the Intermediate Education Board examinations. Miss Curtis reported that she had been headmistress/matron since 1864. She explained that the girls had two hours

---

55 The master of Castleknock boys' parochial school was paid £50 per annum; the mistress of the girls' parochial school received £25 per annum and the female national teacher in Clontarf was paid £20 per annum: see *Report of her majesty's commissioners appointed to inquire into the endowments* [Kildare commission], iii, *Papers accompanying the report (tables of schools and endowments)*, H.C. 1857–8 (2336–IV), xii, pt iv, 16–17. **56** Ibid., 40–1. **57** *Report of the commissioners appointed by the lord lieutenant of Ireland* [Rosse commission], ii, pp 230–4 [C 2831], H.C. 1881, xxxv, 230–4.

of schooling in the morning and two hours in the evening and were required to do housework and to make their own clothes. The other school staff were a housekeeper and a gardener who, according to Miss Curtis, had 'to pump the water, go to the post, and do a great many other things'.[58]

Under the Educational Endowments (Ireland) Act of 1885, the Educational endowments commissioners drew up a scheme (no. 3) to combine the Mercer's endowments with those of the nearby Morgan's school for boys.[59] However, the trustees of Mercer's school were opposed to the scheme. Revd Morgan Jellett, secretary of the trust, told the Endowments commissioners:

> There is no necessity for having Mercer's school connected with Morgan's at present. The founders never intended anything of that kind. That is proved by the fact that the school was intended to be connected with St Peter's and that the locality of the school was removed from one place to another.[60]

Among those whom the commissioners interviewed on this occasion in 1885 were the agent Mr Rooke and Miss Curtis, who had been matron in 1881. She was still the only teacher and the condition of the school had changed little in the intervening four years. In the end, the trustees of Mercer's successfully resisted the commissioners' proposed scheme, arguing that its endowments were for the benefit of one denomination and were under their exclusive control. Therefore the school continued as a small institution for Protestant girls with insufficient resources until 1966 when it was merged with the King's Hospital where the schools records are now deposited.[61]

A very useful source for the study of endowed schools is the Dr Michael Quane papers in the National Library. These contain files relating to the history of endowed school such as Midleton College, Cork (MS 17,954), Preston's schools at Navan and Ballyroan (MS 17,958), and Viscount Weymouth School, Carrickmacross (MS 17,954). For Wicklow, there are files on the Carysfort Royal School, Macreddin (MS 17,919), on Wicklow School, Dunganstown School and Glendalough School (MS 17,967).[62]

---

58 Ibid.   **59** Morgan's School, Castleknock had been founded in 1784 under the will of Richard Morgan for 'the clothing, lodging, dieting and education of children of reduced Protestant parents, and for apprenticing them to Protestant masters' see *Report of her majesty's commissioners appointed to inquire into the endowments* [Kildare commission], iii, *Papers accompanying the report (tables of schools and endowments)*, H.C. 1857–8 (2336–IV), xii, pt iv, 16–17.   **60** *First report of the educational endowments (Ireland) commissioners, with proceedings, evidence and appendices, for 1885–6* [C 4903], H.C. 1886, xxvi, 200–4.   **61** According to Whiteside, '... increasing educational demands and insufficient endowments meant that the alternatives were closure or takeover' (*The King's Hospital*, p. 189). The records of Mercer's School consist of Board minutes, 1832–1968, accounts, 1864–1901 and lists of pupils, 1865–1931.   **62** Hayes, *Sources for the history of Irish civilization, first supplement, persons* (Boston, 1979), pp 631–3.

This short account of material which is available for a county study shows the wealth of detail that can be drawn from official records to examine the growth of educational provision in a local area and the history of individual national schools. The details in these official records can be added to by local records available in the school itself, such as registers and roll-books, or in other records such as local newspapers, local histories, school photographs and oral memory.

The official records of the national school system in particular became increasingly detailed as the nineteenth century progressed, and broader educational issues such rates of attendance, curriculum development, teaching methodology, discipline codes, etc can be examined through the yearly statistics, inspectors' annual reports, subject organizers' reports in areas such as music, elementary science, woodwork, reports on the work of the national teacher training colleges, as well social issues which affect the efficacy of education such poverty, health, employment and emigration. The value of local studies in education is that they reveal the importance of the voluntary sector at both primary and secondary level in the development of the Irish education system. At primary level the national system was dependent on the response of each locality to apply for aid from the State and to agree to fulfil the conditions of that aid. The National Board's role, therefore, from the outset was largely supervisory, ensuring that public aid was being used in the required manner. The rules and regulations for national schools continued to grow throughout the century and eventually they covered most areas of the school curriculum, minimum attendance rates, building grants, teachers' salaries and pensions, but the schools themselves remained under local management, usually attached to the local parish. By 1900 there were 8,684 national schools in operation of which 8,371 offered free education. As the school curriculum expanded it became more difficult for small parish schools to provide the required range of subjects and demand for larger amalgamated schools grew in the twentieth century.

At secondary level the voluntary schools, both those under Protestant and Catholic management, also continued to control their own affairs and their relationship to the State was only through the Intermediate examination system of payment by results. Although the old endowed schools came gradually under increased State scrutiny following the two endowed schools commissions of 1857–8 and 1881 and culminating in the Educational Endowments Act of 1885, here again the schools themselves remained autonomous institutions with their own governing bodies, guarding their independence. Only in the areas of curriculum and examinations, teachers' qualifications and registration, salaries and pensions did the State exercise a degree of control in return for financial grants. In the vocational sector the local authorities operated technical schools in the towns, supported by the central body of the DATI, providing an opportunity for further education in science, apprenticeship and commercial courses. A marked feature of the education system however noticeable at local level, was the lack of contact or administrative organization between the three main sectors of education each of which worked through a different government board. The commissioners of national education operated at primary level, the Intermediate Education Board at secondary and the Department of Agriculture and Technical Education at technical level. In a local area, therefore, there was little structure or incentive to encourage planned educational development.

Conclusion

The value of local studies in the history of education is not just that they reveal the important role of education in a local community; they also serve as useful micro-studies of policy implementation. As this guide has shown, the nineteenth century brought the development of a highly centralized educational system with administrative boards in Dublin which attempted to keep in direct contact with each school in receipt of a State grant. The success of educational policy, therefore, depended on the development of a complex administrative structure and detailed record keeping. The official papers generated by these various government boards contain a wealth of data, much of which has yet to be examined and used by historians. At the same time, however, the structure of the Irish education system allowed for considerable flexibility and the educational institutions, as voluntary bodies, were able to operate with a certain degree of freedom and to adapt the system to suit local needs. The balance of power between Church and State in nineteenth-century Ireland contributed to this situation because the Church of Ireland as the Established Church was unwilling to surrender its historic role of dominance in education while the Catholic Church demanded the right to control the education of Catholic children.

Given the importance of local initiative in developing educational provision for communities throughout the whole of Ireland, local studies are especially revealing. The role of the parish in the national school system, that of the voluntary and autonomous secondary school within the Intermediate examination system, and the relationship between the locally-controlled technical school and the Department of Agriculture and Technical instruction, all indicate the balance of power and control that was so central to the development of educational provision. Towards the end of the nineteenth century efforts to create a local regional or county council basis for the administration of education failed, and technical education was the only sector to thrive on a county structure. The three sectors of education – primary, secondary and technical – developed separately, with little direct communication or co-operation between them. Yet within a specific local community, the availability of all three levels of education was crucially important and local studies can (by virtue of their narrow geographical range) shed valuable light on developments at all three levels as well as examining what relationship if any existed between them.

The government boards of education left a wealth of valuable records containing wide ranging and diverse contemporary insights into educational policies, management, controversies, decisions and issues of the day. At local level there are fewer available records as records for individual schools have tended to be much less well preserved. One important result of the increased interest in the history of educational provision at local level is that school records have become more valued and their preservation given higher priority. Only by examining the development of education at both central and local levels in Ireland will we reach a deeper understanding of the historical processes by which this came about.

Select bibliography

GUIDES

Helferty, S. & R. Refaussé (eds), *Directory of Irish archives* (Dublin, 4th ed., 2003)
Lohan, R., *Guide to the archives of the Office of Public Works* (Dublin, 1994)
Refaussé, R., *Church of Ireland records* (Dublin, 2000; 2nd ed., 2006)
Sheehy, D. & P.J. Corish, *Records of the Irish Catholic Church* (Dublin, 2001)

DOCUMENTS

Corcoran, T. (ed.), *State policy in Irish education, 1536–1816: selected texts* (Dublin, 1916)
— (ed.), *Education systems in Ireland from the close of the middle ages: selected texts* (Dublin, 1928)
Hannigan, K. (ed.), *The national school system, 1831–1924, facsimile documents* (Dublin, 1984)
Hyland, Á. & K. Milne et al. (eds), *Irish educational documents* (3 vols, Dublin, 1987–95)
Luddy, M. (ed.), *Women in Ireland, 1800–1918: a documentary history* (Cork, 1995)
Parkes, S.M., *Irish education in the British parliamentary papers in the nineteenth century and after, 1801–1920* (Cork, 1978)

SECONDARY WORKS

Akenson, D.H., *The Irish education experiment: the national system of education in the nineteenth century* (London, 1970)
—, *A mirror to Kathleen's face: education in Independent Ireland* (Dublin, 1975)
—, 'Pre-university education, 1782–1870' in W.E. Vaughan (ed.), *A new history of Ireland*; v, *Ireland under the union, part i, 1801–1870* (Oxford, 1989), pp 523–37
—, 'Pre-university education, 1870–1922' in W.E. Vaughan (ed.), *A new history of Ireland*; vi, *Ireland under the union, part ii, 1870–1921* (Oxford, 1996), pp 523–38
Barnes, J., *Irish industrial schools, 1868–1908* (Dublin, 1989)
Brenan, M., *Schools of Kildare and Leighlin, A.D. 1775–1835* (Dublin, 1935)
Brown, T., *A social and cultural history of Ireland* (London, 1981; rev. ed., 2004)
Burke, H., *The people and the Poor Law in 19th-century Ireland* (Dublin, 1987)
Connell, P., *Parson, priest and master – national education in Co. Meath, 1824–41* (Dublin, 1995)
Coolahan, J., *Irish education, history and structure* (Dublin, 1981; new ed., 2003)
—, *A history of Ireland's school inspectorate, 1831–2008* (Dublin, 2009)
—, *The ASTI and post-primary education in Ireland, 1909–1984* (Dublin, 1984)
Corish, P.J., *A history of Irish Catholicism, v: Catholic education* (Dublin, 1971)
—, *Maynooth College, 1795–1995* (Dublin, 1995)
Cullen, M. (ed.), *Girls don't do honours – Irish women in education in the nineteenth and twentieth centuries* (Dublin, 1987)

Harford, J., *The opening of university education to women in Ireland* (Dublin, 2008)

Kelly, A., *Compulsory Irish: language and education in Ireland, 1870s–1972* (Dublin, 2002)

Keogh, D., *Edmund Rice, 1762–1844* (Dublin, 1996)

—, *Edmund Rice and the first Christian Brothers* (Dublin, 2008)

Larkin, E., *A history of the Roman Catholic Church in Ireland in the nineteenth century*, vols I–VII (London & Dublin, 1975–96)

Logan, J., *Teachers' Union: the T.U.I. and its forerunners in Irish education, 1899–1994* (Dublin, 1999)

Luddy, M., *Women and philanthropy in nineteenth-century Ireland* (Cambridge, 1995)

McCartney, D., *UCD: a national idea. The history of University College Dublin* (Dublin, 1999)

McDowell, R.B. & D. Webb, *Trinity College, Dublin, 1592–1952: an academic history* (Cambridge, 1982)

McElligott, T.J., *Secondary education in Ireland, 1870–1921* (Dublin, 1981)

McGrath, T., *Politics, interdenominational relations and education in the public ministry of Bishop James Doyle of Kildare and Leighlin, 1786–1834* (Dublin, 1999)

McManus, A., *The Irish hedge school and its books, 1695–1831* (Dublin, 2002)

McMillan, N. (ed.), *Prometheus's fire – a history of scientific and technological education in Ireland* (Carlow, 2000)

MacShuibne, P., *Paul Cullen and his contemporaries, 1820–1902* (3 vols, Dublin, 1962, 1965)

Milne, K., *The Irish charter schools, 1730–1830* (Dublin, 1997)

Moody, T.J. & J.C. Beckett, *Queen's, Belfast, 1845–1949: the history of a university* (2 vols, London, 1959)

Morrissey, T.J., *Towards a national university: William Delany, S.J. (1835–1924)* (Dublin, 1983)

—, *William J. Walsh, archbishop of Dublin, 1841–1921* (Dublin, 2000)

Murphy, J.A., *The college: a history of Queen's/University College, Cork* (Cork, 1995)

Ó Buachalla, S., *Education policy in twentieth-century Ireland* (Dublin, 1988)

O'Connell, M.R. (ed.), *O'Connell, education, Church and State* (Dublin, 1992)

Parkes, S.M., 'Higher education, 1793–1908' in W.E. Vaughan (ed.), *A new history of Ireland; vi, Ireland under the union, part ii, 1870–1921* (Oxford, 1996), pp 539–70

Raftery, D. & S.M. Parkes, *Female education in Ireland: minerva or Madonna, 1700–1900* (Dublin, 2007)

Robins, J., *The lost children: a study of charity children in Ireland, 1700–1900* (Dublin, 1980)

Titley, E.B., *Church, State and the control of schooling in Ireland, 1900–44* (Dublin & Montreal, 1983)

Index